Disclaimer

The food menus in Part Three (1) and Appendix 2 of this report, though health-promoting in normal circumstances, may not be suitable for some people. Anyone who is in doubt should seek medical advice.

Acknowledgements

We would like to thank Age Concern England for their encouragement, guidance and financial support throughout this project.

We would also like to express our gratitude to the following individuals for their encouragement and advice in putting together these budgets:

Evelyn McEwen and Sally West of Age Concern

Professor Janet Askham

Ruth Hancock

Nick Hegan

Professor John Veit-Wilson

We are particularly indebted to Holly Sutherland, Director of the Microsimulation Unit, Department of Applied Economics, University of Cambridge, for using *POLIMOD* to estimate the gross incomes required by pensioner households to reach LCA level. Without these calculations, the scale of the pensioner poverty trap would not have become so apparent.

For their assistance with pricing, special thanks are due to: Age Concern Enterprises Ltd, Age Concern Insurance Services, Allied Carpets, Argos, Co-op (CWS), Empire Stores, Kwik Save, MFI, National Health Service Executive (Dental Research), Poundstretcher, Sainsbury's and Shoe City.

We would also like to acknowledge the research into budget standards carried out between 1990 and 1992 by nutritionists at King's College London, home economists at Sheffield Hallam University, and researchers in the Department of Social Policy and Social Work at the University of York. That research was coordinated by Professor Jonathan Bradshaw (University of York).

Finally, we wish to thank Susan Raven for her editorial assistance in preparing the manuscript.

Low Cost but Acceptable incomes for older people

A minimum income standard for households aged 65-74 years in the UK

January 1999 prices

Edited by Hermione Parker

Research: Michael Nelson, Nina Oldfield, Julie Dallison
Sandra Hutton, Barbara Hegan, Sophia Paterakis,
Holly Sutherland, Marilyn Thirlway

The POLICY PRESS

First published in Great Britain in February 2000 by The Policy Press

The Policy Press
University of Bristol
34 Tyndall's Park Road
Bristol BS8 1PY
UK

Tel no +44 (0)117 954 6800
Fax no +44 (0)117 973 7308
E-mail tpp@bristol.ac.uk
http://www.bristol.ac.uk/Publications/TPP

ISBN 1 86134 214 4 √
© The Policy Press 2000

Hermione Parker is Director of the Family Budget Unit, King's College London.

The Family Budget Unit (FBU) is an educational charity (No 298813) and private limited company (No 2211830), founded in 1987, with three objectives:

- to advance the education of the public in all matters relating to comparative living standards and living costs throughout the United Kingdom;

- to carry out research into the economic requirements and consumer preferences of families of different composition, for each main component of a typical family budget;

- to publish the useful results of such work.

Contact: The Family Budget Unit, Department of Nutrition and Dietetics, King's College London, 150 Stamford Street, London SE1 8WA. Tel (020) 7848 4349; Fax (020) 7848 4185.
For their work on this project, the FBU was funded by **Age Concern England**

Cover design by Qube Design Associates, Bristol
Front cover: Photograph supplied with the kind permission of Age Concern.
Printed in Great Britain by Hobbs the Printers Ltd, Southampton

Contents

List of tables and figures

Tables

Figures

Figure (i): **Weekly expenditures required to reach LCA level**
Compared with Income Support and NI retirement pensions
January 1999, £ week

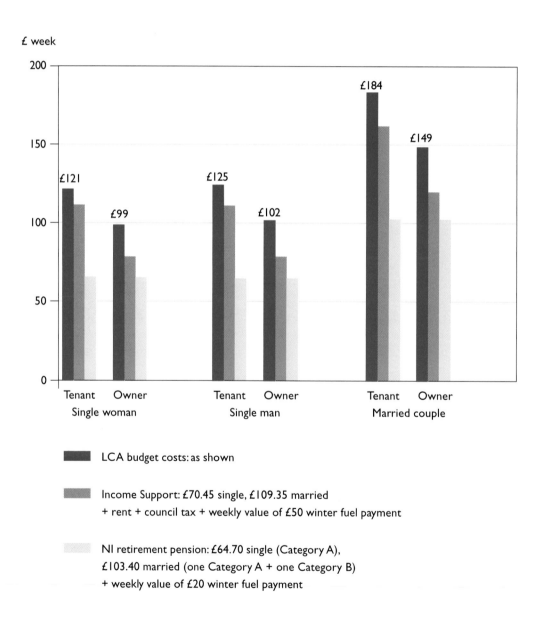

£ week

LCA budget costs: as shown

Income Support: £70.45 single, £109.35 married
+ rent + council tax + weekly value of £50 winter fuel payment

NI retirement pension: £64.70 single (Category A),
£103.40 married (one Category A + one Category B)
+ weekly value of £20 winter fuel payment

Summary

How much does it cost older people, living in the UK, to reach an acceptable living standard and avoid social exclusion? This study, the second in a series, is an up-to-date attempt to answer this question.

The aims of the report are to:

- stimulate debate about the incomes required to avoid poverty;
- inform government decision making;
- introduce readers to the method of calculating living costs called *budget standards*.

The study estimates the living costs of men and women aged 65-74 years at a living standard called *Low Cost but Acceptable* (LCA), with the latter defined as the poverty threshold. Budgets are presented for single women, single men and couples, as local authority tenants and as owner-occupiers. The date of the information is January 1999.

The report contains essential information for individuals and organisations concerned with the well-being of older people, including: central and local government; the pensions industry; employers; residential homes; social services; trade unions; voluntary organisations; and older people themselves.

Outside the UK, budget standards serve as benchmarks for social policy, personal taxation, life insurance, pensions, money advice, debt orders and many other purposes. The most widely used standard, called *Modest-But-Adequate* (MBA) or *Reasonable*, measures the level of living at which most people aim: well clear of poverty but nowhere near affluence. In 1995 and 1997, the Family Budget Unit produced pensioner budgets at MBA level and found it beyond the reach of most older people in the UK.

Though lower than MBA, LCA is sufficient to provide a healthy diet, material security, social participation and a sense of control. Accepted standards for nutrition, housing, warmth, clothing and personal care are used and the research is assisted by discussion groups composed of low-income adults from the relevant age groups. First the required expenditures for each household type are calculated, then they are compared with Income Support (IS) and National Insurance (NI) pensions.

Five findings (£ week, January 1999)

- LCA costs (including housing), up to: £121 (woman), £125 (man), £184 (couple)
- LCA costs (car owners), up to: £141 (woman), £145 (man), £200 (couple)
- IS shortfalls (no car), up to: £20 (woman), £24 (man), £28 (couple)
- NI pension shortfalls (no car), up to: £60 (woman), £66 (man), £80 (couple)
- IS required amounts, up to: £94 (single), £138 (married)
- NI pensioners particularly at risk: due to the poverty trap, tenants need gross incomes of up to £130 (single) and £184 (married) to avoid poverty

Four policy recommendations

- Swift action by government: to show the goods and services benefits will buy
- A national debate: on living costs and living standards
- Cross-party support: for scientific estimates of human need
- Living standard impact statements: alongside all policy proposals

List of abbreviations

BREDEM	Building Research Establishment Domestic Energy Model
CIPFA	Chartered Institute of Public Finance and Accountancy
COHSE	Confederation of Health Service Employees
COMA	Committee on Medical Aspects of Food Policy
CWS	Co-operative Wholesale Society /Co-op
DIY	Do It Yourself
DRV	Dietary Reference Value
DoH	Department of Health
DSS	Department of Social Security
ESRC	Economic and Social Research Council
FBU	Family Budget Unit
FES	Family Expenditure Survey
FRS	Family Resources Survey
GHS	General Household Survey
HEA	Health Education Authority
HMSO	Her Majesty' Stationery Office (replaced by The Stationery Office, 1996)
LCA	Low Cost but Acceptable
MAFF	Ministry of Agriculture, Fisheries and Food
MBA	Modest-But-Adequate
NALGO	National Association of Local Government Officers
NDNS	National Diet and Nutrition Survey
NFS	National Food Survey
NHS	National Health Service
NI	National Insurance
NIC	National Insurance Contribution
NSP	Non-Starch Polysaccharides
NUPE	National Union of Public Employees
POLIMOD	Microsimulation model of The Microsimulation Unit, Department of Applied Economics, University of Cambridge
ONS	Office for National Statistics
OPCS	Office of Population Censuses and Surveys
RNI	Reference Nutrient Intake
SAS	Statistical Analysis System
SO	Stationery Office Ltd (replaced HMSO in 1996)

Preface

Few would disagree with the government's aim of tackling poverty and social exclusion. However, missing from pensions and income policy is any attempt to address the fundamental question 'How much do older people need to avoid poverty and social exclusion?' Currently politicians and policy makers put forward proposals intended to provide a decent income in retirement or to tackle poverty but do so without an assessment of the income levels needed to achieve these goals. Older people also frequently raise this issue when they ask how can they be expected to live on the basic state pension and what the basis is for current rates.

Age Concern commissioned the Family Budget Unit to carry out this research to provide, for the first time, income standards to help establish what older people need to avoid poverty. Based on previous research by the Family Budget Unit and others, Age Concern has argued that older people need a minimum of £150 a week to achieve a modest but reasonable life-style. However, when we first proposed this figure (1997) only around a quarter of single pensioners had incomes of this level. We therefore decided to investigate what older people need as a minimum in order to avoid poverty.

A great strength of the methodology used by the Family Budget Unit is that it looks not only at what families spend, but what they need to spend, and even more importantly, it takes into account the views of older people currently having to manage on low incomes.

One important conclusion is that even with the recent increases in Income Support (Minimum Income Guarantee) older people reliant on means-tested benefits do not have sufficient income to avoid poverty. However, the implications are even more serious because official estimates indicate that between 530,000 and 870,000 pensioners entitled to Income Support are living on less. Low take-up is one of the main problems of means-tested benefits. However, as the report demonstrates, people are also caught in a poverty trap whereby those with private pensions or savings can be little better off, or in some cases have lower net incomes, than those dependent on benefit. Instead of letting the state pension continue to fall in relation to living standards it must be increased and uprating policy must ensure that it maintains its real value.

Of course avoiding poverty in retirement is not the end goal – most people will have much higher expectations for their retirement. But as so many older people are currently having to manage on low incomes, we urge the government and others to accept the need to establish minimum income standards to help determine pension and benefit rates and inform other areas of policy. We hope this research will be an important step towards that goal.

Sally Greengross
Director General, Age Concern, England

Figure (ii):   LCA logo

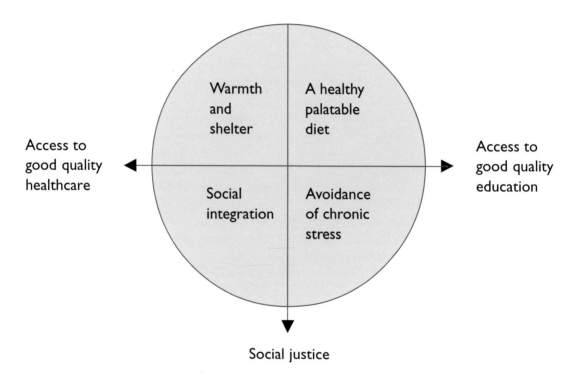

Low Cost but Acceptable

Introduction

Hermione Parker

1 Missing link in the government's pension review

On 15 December 1998, the Secretary of State for Social Security, Alistair Darling MP, presented his Department's Green Paper on Pension Reform (DSS,1998a) to the House of Commons. Major changes were proposed, without any scientifically based assessment of pensioner needs or living costs.

The purpose of this study is to help fill the resulting information gap. The date of the information is January 1999.

The following is an extract from the Secretary of State's statement:

> A pension is the most important asset that people have, more important even than buying a house. That is why we want to put pensions on a sound footing, where every individual is guaranteed a decent income in retirement and where people can rely again on secure and effective private pensions, delivering security for today's pensioners and peace of mind for tomorrow's.

> ...Today, I am announcing a radical new pensions policy. It is radical because it guarantees a decent income for all pensioners. For the first time ever a lifetime's work will not lead to dependency on means-tested benefits in retirement.

> ... In future there will be a new contract. The state will guarantee that everyone who retires in poverty will receive a minimum income guarantee well above the current level of income support – beginning at £75 a week for a single pensioner and £116 a week for a pensioner couple. (House of Commons Hansard, 15 December 1998, columns 761 and 762)

Three questions arise:

- *What constitutes a "decent income in retirement"?*
- *Is £75 a week sufficient for single pensioners to avoid poverty?*
- *Is £116 a week sufficient for pensioner couples to avoid poverty?*

2 Structure of this report

The study addresses the above questions by estimating the incomes required by men and women in the age range 65-74 years to reach a living standard called *Low Cost but Acceptable* (LCA), with the latter defined as a poverty threshold which is sustainable, health-promoting and conducive to social integration.

Table (i):	Six pensioner budgets Age range 65-74 years LCA level, January 1999
Single woman, owner-occupier	
Single woman, tenant	
Single man, owner-occupier	
Single man, tenant	
Married couple, owner-occupiers	
Married couple, tenants	

In presenting its findings the Family Budget Unit (FBU) makes no specific policy recommendations. Ideally the incomes of older people would be above LCA level; certainly they should not be below it. Our purpose here is to set out and quantify the parameters for debate. The LCA budgets are healthy and typical of spending (or would-be spending) by older households. The problem is that they are beyond the means of many.

The study was commissioned and funded by Age Concern England, as an investigation into the adequacy of benefit levels and as a tool to assist in the benchmarking of future benefit upratings. It is hoped that the information in this report will be of interest to the many individuals and organisations concerned with the well-being of older people, including central and local government, voluntary organisations, social services, trade unions, money advisers, residential homes, pensions advisers and (most important of all) older people themselves.

The structure of the report is straightforward. Part One summarises the background to the debate. Part Two explains the methods used by the FBU, in particular the distinction drawn between budget standard expenditures and variable expenditures. Part Three explains and prices the budget standard expenditures (food, clothing, personal care, household goods, household services and leisure). Part Four explains and gives illustrative costs for the variable expenditures (including housing, fuel and transport). Part Five adds the budget standard and variable costs together; compares the resulting spending totals with Income Support; and grosses them up for income tax (less any benefits to which there is entitlement) to show the gross incomes (State pension plus occupational pension, private pension or investment income) required to reach LCA level, that is, *to avoid poverty*. Part Six summarises the findings.

3   One of several approaches

To put this study in perspective, it may be helpful to explain that budget standards methodology is but one of several methods used to estimate the incomes required to avoid poverty. In his Preface to *Low Cost but Acceptable: A minimum income standard for the UK: Families with young children* (Parker, 1998), Professor John Veit-Wilson reminded readers that "the best answers to problems are those where comparable conclusions are reached whichever way you approach them" (Veit-Wilson, 1998a, pp xiii-xiv).

The household income levels required, on average, to avoid poverty can be discovered in at least four distinct ways, Veit-Wilson wrote:

- By discovering *the social indicators of deprivation* and the income levels at which severe deprivation takes place, as in the studies by Mack and Lansley (1985), and Gordon and Pantazis (1997).

- By *attitudinal research*, surveying the household incomes which the population on average considers the minimum necessary on which they can 'make ends meet', as described by Van den Bosch (1993).

- By intensive discussion of household need in *focus groups* of the ordinary population, as in the work of Middleton and her colleagues at Loughborough University (1994).

- By means of *budget standards*, bringing together "the expertise of the social sciences, statistics and the natural sciences such as nutrition and human ecology, as carried out by the Family Budget Unit" (Bradshaw, 1993).

Veit-Wilson also wrote that:

The authority and power of these various approaches lies in their roots in our society's common culture. No one can realistically dispute their findings on the grounds that they are nothing more than personal subjective opinions – even if some British politicians have tried to divert popular attention by making such mendacious assertions. But why should politicians do so? Chiefly because they fear the implicit criticism which such scientific findings contain of the levels of income maintenance which they and their officials have created and asserted to be adequate – their minimum wage rates, their income tax thresholds, their contributory pensions and other social security benefits and their means tests and assistance benefits. Yet in other democratic countries the subject is approached much more openly, and it is considered proper to set up and maintain Governmental Minimum Income Standards, reflecting political views of the common culture's reasonable minimum level of living for human dignity which all citizens should enjoy. Indeed, the European Union recommended member states to set such standards, but no UK government has yet done so. (Veit-Wilson, 1998a, p xiv)

4   *Inequalities in Health* report

The FBU findings are relevant to the report on health inequalities chaired by Sir Donald Acheson (Acheson, 1998); and the Department of Social Security's Green Paper *A new contract for welfare: Partnership in pensions* (DSS, 1998a). Since 1978, death rates have fallen across all social groups, but "the difference in rates between those at the top and bottom of the social scale has widened" (Acheson, 1998, p 11, *Mortality*). Increasing inequality is a major cause. While the top decile point of median real household disposable incomes (before housing costs) more than doubled between 1961 and 1994, the bottom decile point rose by 62% (Acheson, 1998, p 16). Indexation of pensions to prices instead of earnings in the early 1980s has produced a deterioration in the relative position of benefit recipients, including pensioners and especially those wholly dependent on the NI State Retirement Pension. For although older people on low incomes can supplement their NI pensions by claiming Income Support, many do not do so.

Regarding the 'material well being of older people', the Acheson Report made three main recommendations:

- *... policies which will further reduce income inequalities and improve the living standards of households in receipt of social security benefits* (Recommendation 3).

- *... uprating of benefits and pensions according to principles which protect and, where possible, improve the standard of living of those who depend on them and which narrow the gap between their standard of living and average living standards* (Recommendation 3.2).

- *... measures to increase the uptake of benefits among entitled groups* (Recommendation 3.3). (Acheson, 1998, p 125)

5   **Purpose and method**

The purpose of this report is threefold:

- to stimulate debate about the incomes required by older people to avoid poverty, with the poverty threshold defined as LCA level;

- to inform government decision making;

- to introduce readers to the method of calculating household needs and costs called *budget standards.*

Widely used in North America, the Netherlands, Scandinavia and Australia, but largely unknown in the UK, budget standards are specified baskets of goods and services which, when priced, can represent the incomes required by households of different composition to reach predefined living standards. LCA marks the threshold below which good health, social integration and satisfactory standards of child development are at risk. Although temporary economies in the budgets could be made, they would not be sustainable indefinitely.

To construct the LCA budgets, the FBU assumed hypothetical or 'model' families living in closely defined circumstances in York (Part Two, Section 3.2). Although the authors are confident that the budgets provide an accurate and representative picture of household budgeting on low incomes by men and women aged 65-74 years in the UK, readers are warned against generalising the detail of the findings for all older people. Our purpose was not to say 'This is how low-income people aged 65-74 years spend the money they have'; nor 'This is how they should spend the money they have'. Our purpose was threefold:

- to construct spending profiles which provide a healthy life-style; accord with the purchasing preferences of low-income households aged 65-74 years; and identify their unmet needs;

- to sum the costs of all the purchases together;

- where appropriate, to gross up the resulting budget costs for income tax (less any means-tested social security benefit entitlements), in order to show the gross incomes required to reach the LCA living standard.

It is our contention that without such estimates – and similar estimates for households across the life cycle – governments will not prevent poverty and hardship from continuing.

6 LCA sets a poverty threshold

This is the first time an LCA living standard for older people has been calculated and costed in the UK. The LCA logo (p xvi) encapsulates the LCA concept. The costs of most healthcare are excluded, on the assumption that it is freely and readily available. But the costs of access to it – mainly transport – are included, as are food purchases, housing, fuel, clothing, personal care, household goods and services, leisure and other costs which together promote healthy, socially inclusive living in the UK at the end of the second millennium.

Within the logo, LCA is defined as a living standard which takes account of psychological and social as well as physical needs. Warmth, shelter and a healthy, palatable diet are necessary but, on their own, insufficient. Social integration is also necessary (such things as being able to buy presents for children and grandchildren, have birthday and Christmas outings, go to clubs or pubs, share a drink with friends). So too is the avoidance of chronic stress.

At the bottom of the LCA logo, the words *Social justice* indicate a system where older people are not treated as second-class citizens.

7 Twelve months' unique research

The figure-work in this report is the result of twelve months' research by the FBU's team of specialists, based at the Department of Nutrition and Dietetics, King's College London. We are, however, concerned with far more than nutritional needs. As with the FBU's Modest-But-Adequate (MBA) budgets for pensioners (Parker, 1995), which were also funded by Age Concern, every detail of every budget is recorded and priced. Food menus have been prepared as a guide to the choices available within the food budgets, and all the budgets, including the menus, have been cross-checked with pensioner groups in London; urban areas of East Sussex, Tyne and Wear, Lancashire and the West Midlands; and one rural area in Somerset.

In FBU methodology, discussion groups constitute an integral part of the research process, in this case

by providing insights into the shopping patterns and priorities of older households on low incomes. Equal attention is paid, however, to accepted standards for housing, nutrition, warmth, clothing, personal care, household items and leisure. In some cases the components budgets are linked to one another. For example, the clothing budgets correlate with the assumed house temperatures, and expenditure on public transport is reduced if the household owns a car. Reference to accepted standards is necessary, because the expenditures reported in the low-income discussion groups are somtimes less than amounts required to avoid poverty.

For further information about the FBU discussion groups, see Part Two, Section 3.4 and Appendix 3.

8 Background statistics

8.1 Population figures

The age group chosen for this study, 65-74 years, accounts for over half of all retirement pensioners. Those aged 75 years or over were not included, because their needs and living costs are likely to be different.

Table (ii), based on a Parliamentary Written Answer, gives a breakdown by age and marital status of Britain's older age groups. Using rounded figures, the 65-74 years age group comprises 2.2 million men and over 3.0 million women, more than 5.0 million persons in all.

Table (ii):	Pensioner population, 000s (1996-97 estimates) By age and marital status				
Age years	**60-64**	**65-69**	**70-74**	**75-79**	**80+**
Single men	–	250	210	210	260
Single women	320	550	710	670	980
Couples	–	960	810	500	360

Note: The figures refer to Great Britain only.

Source: *Hansard* Written Answer: 18 January 1999, column 372
Pensioners' Income Series dataset, Family Resources Survey (FRS)

8.2 Indexation to prices or earnings?

The problem is poverty in the midst of plenty, at a life-stage when there is little if anything that those affected can do to remedy the situation. As more of us live into our seventies, eighties and nineties, the scale of the problem increases and will not go away until retirement pensions (private as well as public) are increased in line with average earnings instead of prices. This is because earnings (on average) increase by 1%-2% a year faster than prices.

It is inconceivable – or is it? – that a political party in the UK would win a general election on a ticket promising National Insurance (NI) retirement pensions of £27 a week. *Yet £27 a week is what the rate of Category A retirement pension would have been in January 1999 had it been uprated in line with prices since its introduction in 1948 (DSS, 1999a) – enough to purchase the LCA food baskets summarised in Table 9, plus a margin of £2 for single men and £4 for single women, to cover their other needs.*

Indexation of any social security benefit to price increases instead of earnings is a covert way of phasing it out. Table (iii) shows the effects of price indexation since 1980 on NI retirement pensions.

Each year their value relative to the earnings of the working population has diminished. If pensions had been increased in line with earnings since 1980, by April 1999 the Category A pension (for a single person) would have been £90.50 instead of £66.75 a week (an additional £23.75 a week, or £1,235 a year); and Category A + B pension (for married couples on the contributions of the husband) would have been £142.30 instead of £106.70 (an additional £35.60 a week, or £1,851 a year).

One result of price indexation is the large number of older people claiming means-tested benefits. In May 1998, out of 3.5 million households aged 65-74 years, an estimated 420,000 (12%) were receiving Income Support and a further one million (29%) were receiving one or more means-tested benefits (*Hansard*, 25 May 99, column 103). Yet, as will be shown, Income Support is well below the LCA standard calculated for this report (Table [iv]).

A further 600,000 pensioner 'benefit units' (all age groups and counting couples as one unit) were disqualified from Income Support on grounds of 'excess capital', yet their incomes were below Income Support levels (*Hansard*, 9 November 1998, column 91).

Table (iii): **National Insurance (NI) retirement pension**
Values at selected uprating dates
1980-99, £ week

Uprating date	Actual rate paid increased by RPI	Rate if increased by average earnings	Rate if increased by higher earnings/prices
Category A			
Nov 1980	27.15	27.60	27.60
Nov 1985	38.30	41.35	42.40
Apr 1990	46.90	58.70	60.25
Apr 1995	58.85	77.35	80.40
Apr 1998	64.70	86.25	90.60
Apr 1999	66.75	90.50	95.05
Category A + B			
Nov 1980	43.45	43.45	43.45
Nov 1985	61.30	63.05	66.70
Apr 1990	75.10	92.40	94.75
Apr 1995	94.10	121.65	126.30
Apr 1998	103.40	135.65	142.35
Apr 1999	106.70	142.30	149.30

Source: *Hansard*, Parliamentary Written Answers: 30 June 1999, column 206
26 July 1999, column 107

Take-up of means-tested benefits is considerably lower than take-up of universal benefits. Take-up of Income Support by pensioners is between 63% and 73% and take-up of housing benefit and council tax benefit is also low (DSS, 1999b).

9   The FBU budgets are illustrative

Although great care has been taken (through the pensioner discussion groups) to ensure that the budget contents match the preferences and spending patterns of low-income men and women aged 65-74 years, the baskets of goods and services costed here are illustrative. Nobody is trying to influence spending habits, although the food budgets were devised with healthy eating in mind. It goes without saying that few older households are likely to spend their incomes in precisely the ways shown here. Elements of the budgets can be prioritised in different ways, to suit different households, one household using its leisure money for outings, another for hobbies. Experience in countries where budget standards research is more firmly established suggests that the amounts spent tend to be similar. At this stage, the FBU's purpose is to signpost the need for *every* household to be able to make such choices. By including money for leisure, charitable giving and alcohol, the budgets provide small but necessary margins for emergencies such as debts and illness.

10   Budget standard costs and variable costs

All the budgets distinguish between 'budget standard costs' and 'variable costs'. The budget standard costs comprise food, clothing, personal care, household goods and services and leisure. The variable costs comprise housing, council tax, fuel, transport, NHS charges, insurances, debts/fines/maintenance orders, job-related costs, seeking work costs, pets, alcohol, tobacco and charitable donations. Experience in other countries, notably Sweden, shows that this distinction is particularly helpful to money advisers. During the initial interview, people seeking advice are first asked for details of their households (number and gender of adults; number, age and gender of children) on the basis of which their

probable budget standard costs are calculated by computer. They are then asked about their variable costs, the details of which are also recorded on computer. Once all the required information is on disk, the computer quickly calculates their total required spending, and the gross (before tax) income necessary to generate that level of spending. Consultations can then begin to tackle the client's debt or other problems.

11 The costs of credit

By showing the costs of credit in the present budgets as 'nil', the prices paid for durables by some low-income households are unrealistically low. Some firms target low-income households with poor credit ratings by advertising that 'no credit checks are made', but the total amounts charged can be over twice the normal cash price. In such cases the prices shown in the FBU budgets are too low. We recognise this problem; however, the costs of credit incurred by individual pensioners can be logged under Variable costs, Section 7, *Debts, fines, maintenance orders.*

12 Limitations of the report

To the criticism that some low-income households pay fuel charges or rents in excess of those shown here, the answer also lies in the variable costs format, because it allows users to specify the actual fuel costs incurred. The fuel costs estimated for this report assume well-insulated housing in York. In other areas average temperatures may be higher (or lower); moreover, fuel costs vary according to the fuel used and the quality of the insulation.

Transport is another highly variable component of household budgeting, hence the inclusion of a car owner's budget (Table 35). Also, some readers may require vegetarian or ethnic minority diets. At present the food budgets assume a typically British diet. We are aware of this limitation and will tackle it when resources permit.

Finally tobacco! Though signposted in Part Four, Section 12, no purchases of tobacco are included in the budgets, because they are intended to promote healthy living. A space for tobacco is nevertheless included under Variable costs.

13 Findings

Two main findings emerge. The first concerns the inadequacies of Income Support, the second the effects of the pensioner poverty trap on the gross incomes required by pensioners to reach LCA level:

- *INCOME SUPPORT. The government's proposed minimum income guarantees, of £75 a week for single pensioners and £116 for couples, are insufficient to prevent poverty in old age.*

Assuming local authority tenants and owner-occupiers on the outskirts of York, gas central heating, supermarkets and public transport nearby, the Income Support shortfalls in January 1999, by comparison with the LCA standard, were greater for couples than single people and for owner-occupiers than council tenants. The net additional transport costs of the car owners (by comparison with non-car owners and assuming annual car mileage of 5,000 miles per household) are £20.00 a week for single people and £16.00 for couples, who save more on their bus fares (Tables 34 and 35).

The Income Support shortfalls in Table (iv) vary between £11 a week for a single woman tenant who relies entirely on public transport and drinks no alcohol; and £44 a week for a couple (owner-occupiers), who have paid off their mortgage, run a 1992 Ford Escort and between them drink an average of 18 units of alcohol a week. Although the weekly shortfalls may look unimpressive, multiply them by 52 weeks a year and you get annual shortfalls of between £570 and £2,300 a year.

- *THE PENSIONER POVERTY TRAP. Continuing indexation of NI retirement pension to prices, alongside indexation of the Income Support allowances to earnings, is likely to trap more older people on incomes below, or only marginally above, LCA level – for the rest of their lives.*

In January 1999, NI retirement pensions were £64.70 a week for single people and £103.40 for married couples claiming on the contribution record of the husband, compared with required net incomes at LCA level of up to £125 a week for single pensioners and £184 for couples, both in local authority housing (Table 53).

Table (iv) also shows the second incomes, *in addition to NI retirement pensions*, required by single people and couples in the 65-74 years age range, to reach LCA level, in January 1999. Tenants require higher incomes than owner-occupiers (who are assumed to have paid off their mortgages), but the shortfalls vary according to the different tax and benefit regulations pertaining to the second incomes. Financially, earnings seem the best bet, but only if a suitable job is available which does not involve work expenses.

Table (iv): LCA shortfalls: Income Support and NI retirement pension
Households aged 65-74 years, January 1999, £ week

	Single woman		Single man		Married couple	
	Tenant	Owner	Tenant	Owner	Tenant	Owner
A Income Support shortfalls						
Without a car	10	20	14	24	22	28
With a car	30	40	34	44	39	44
B NI retirement pension shortfalls						
Type of additional income						
Earnings	49	30	63	35	80	40
Second pension	61	31	66	36	80	42
Investment income	61	34	66	37	80	45
Tax-free investement income	56	34	60	37	80	45

Assumptions: Alcohol included in the budgets.
None of the NI retirement pensioners have a car.

Sources: Tables 44, 45, 46, Appendix 4

14 References

Acheson, D. (1998) Report of the *Independent Inquiry into Inequalities in Health*, London: The Stationery Office.

Bradshaw, J. (ed) (1993) *Budget standards for the United Kingdom*, Aldershot: Avebury.

Department of Social Security (DSS) (1998a) *New ambitions for our country: A new contract for welfare*, Cm 3805, March, p 38.

DSS (1998b) *A new contract for welfare: Partnership in pensions*, Cm 4179, December, London: The Stationery Office.

DSS (1999a) *The abstract of statistics for social security benefits and contributions and indices of prices and earnings*, 1998 edn, Section 5, London: The Stationery Office.

DSS (1999b) *Income-related benefits, estimates of take-up in 1996/7 (revised) and 1997/98*, October, London: The Stationery Office.

Gordon, D. and Pantazis, C. (1997) *Breadline Britain in the 1990s*, Aldershot: Ashgate.

Mack, J. and Lansley, S. (1985) *Poor Britain*, London: Allen and Unwin.

Middleton, S., Ashworth, K. and Walker, R. (1994) *Family fortunes: Pressures on parents and children in the 1990s*, London: Child Poverty Action Group.

Parker, H. (ed) (1995) *Modest-but-adequate budgets for four pensioner households. October 1994 prices*, London: funded and published by Age Concern England.

Parker, H. (ed) (1998) *Low Cost but Acceptable: A minimum income standard for the UK: Families with young children*, Bristol: The Policy Press.

Van den Bosch, K. (1993) 'Poverty measures in comparative research', Chapter 1 in J. Berghman and B. Cantillon (eds) *The European face of social security*, Aldershot: Avebury.

Veit-Wilson, J. (1998a) Preface to H. Parker (ed) *Low Cost but Acceptable: A minimum income standard for the UK: Families with young children*, Bristol: The Policy Press.

Veit-Wilson, J. (1998b) *Setting adequacy standards: How governments define minimum incomes*, Bristol: The Policy Press.

Part One

How much does it cost to live?

1   Purpose and method

The purpose of this study is to estimate the needs and living costs of men and women aged 65-74 years, at a Low Cost but Acceptable (LCA) living standard, with the latter defined as *the income threshold below which older people risk poverty*. The figure-work is dated January 1999.

The method, called *budget standards*, is similar to that used for an earlier Family Budget Unit (FBU) report, which estimated the living costs at LCA level of families with young children (Parker, 1998). First, the goods and services required for healthy, socially inclusive living by each household type (single women, single men, married couples) are determined, priced and costed – the research at this stage being assisted by focus groups composed of low-income men and women from the relevant age groups. Second, the resulting budgets are compared with Income Support. Third, they are grossed up for income tax (less any means-tested benefits), to show the gross incomes (National Insurance pension + occupational pension, or personal pensions, or investment incomes) required to reach LCA level. Full take-up of all social security benefits to which there is entitlement is assumed throughout.

2   Budget standards explained

Budget standards are specified baskets of goods and services which, when priced, can represent the incomes required by households of different composition to reach predefined living standards. The methodology can be traced to the work of the German social statistician Ernst Engel in the middle of the 19th century, but more particularly to Seebohm Rowntree's survey of the population of York in 1901 (Rowntree, 1901, 2001: forthcoming).

There are nevertheless important differences between Rowntree's survey approach and the budgets produced by the FBU. For his primary poverty measure, Rowntree deliberately chose budgets irreducibly restricted to core costs (food, clothing, shelter and fuel/hygiene) with a tiny margin for other needs required for 'merely physical efficiency', in order to show that some earnings were too low for any kind of social life at all. By contrast, the FBU aims to cost typical household budgets on which a decent social life can be pursued, at a *Modest-But-Adequate* (MBA) level (Bradshaw, 1993) and at LCA level (Parker, 1998). For its LCA budgets, moreover, the FBU distinguishes between 'variable costs', like housing, fuel and transport, and 'budget standard costs', like food and clothing, which, at a given living standard, tend to be similar for similar household types.

Elsewhere in Europe, in North America and in Australia, MBA (or 'reasonable') and low-cost are the standards regarded as most useful. The term 'modest-but-adequate' was first used by the United States Bureau of Labor in 1946 to describe its City Worker's Family Budget, which aimed to "satisfy prevailing standards of what is necessary for health, efficiency, the nurture of children and participation in community activities" (Wynn, 1972, p 37). Figure 1 (borrowed from Wynn, 1972) is illustrative. Level 1 marks the poverty threshold, level 5 is at five times level 1, level 2 is at twice level 1. The FBU's LCA budgets mark a poverty threshold which, like levels 2 and 5, is intended to be sustainable over long periods. But the gap between the FBU's MBA and LCA budgets is smaller than in Figure 1, which is included here for illustrative purposes.

Figure 1:   The prosperity number scale measuring the standard of living

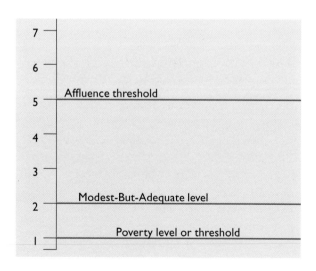

Source: Wynn (1972, p 165)

3   Budget standards outside the UK

Budget standards are used as reference points in devising or monitoring income maintenance programmes in a number of countries outside the UK, including Australia, Finland, France, Germany, the Netherlands, Norway, Sweden and the USA (Veit-Wilson, 1998). In Australia, in 1995, the Commonwealth Department of Social Security commissioned the Social Policy Research Centre at the University of New South Wales to develop a set of budget standards. The results, which were published in March 1998, are expected to inform future governments of Australia in relation to adequacy standards. The main strengths of a budget standard are said to be its focus on needs, the transparency of the approach and its flexibility. Although budget standards do not provide a complete answer to the measurement of need, they provide "an additional source of information that can support decisions about adequacy and household budgeting" (Saunders et al, 1998).

4   Why Britain needs budget standards

The introduction of budget standards in the UK would be in the interest of taxpayers as well as beneficiaries. As so often in the past, major reform of pensions is currently underway without first addressing the question:

*How much does it cost older people,
living in the United Kingdom at the turn of the millennium,
to avoid poverty and social exclusion?*

Although exact figures are hard to come by, this year roughly £200 billion (£65 a week per man, woman and child) will be spent by central and local government on income maintenance programmes of one sort and another (cash benefits and allowances, benefits in kind, income tax allowances and income tax reliefs) without any scientifically based estimates of the needs and living costs of either the taxpayers who finance them or the beneficiaries who receive them (HM Treasury, 1999).

Table 1 (on p 4) sets out the rates of National Insurance (NI) basic pension and Income Support for older people in January 1999 and April 1999. In January 1999, the reference date for this study, Category A National Insurance pensions (for fully paid up contributors) were £64.70 a week and Category B National Insurance pensions (for wives) were £38.70 a week; adding up to £103.40 a week for a married couple on the contributions of the husband. Minimum income guarantees through Income Support were somewhat higher: £70.45 for single people aged 65-74 years and £109.35 for couples (plus council tax, rent, winter fuel allowance and passport benefits). Due to the inadequacy of the NI basic pension (by comparison with living costs), in May 1998 an estimated 26% of pensioner benefit units aged 65-69 years and 31% of pensioner benefit units aged 70-74 years (counting couples as one unit) were receiving at least one means-tested benefit. An estimated 12% of benefit units in each of the above age ranges depended on income support (House of Commons *Hansard*, Written Answer: 25 May 1999, column 103). A further 230,000 were eligible but did not claim (House of Commons *Hansard*, Written Answer: 19 October 1998, columns 957-8).

In April 1999 (three months after the January 1999 reference date for this study) NI pension rates were increased by 3.2% (in line with inflation during the reference period), while Income Support rates were increased by 6.5% and will in future be uprated in line with average earnings instead of price increases. One consequence is likely to be more older people with full NI contribution records claiming Income Support and getting caught in the 'pensioner' poverty trap, as a result of which quite small shortfalls in pensioner net incomes require disproportionately large increases in gross incomes to bring them up to LCA level (Part Two, Figure 2).

5   The need for informed debate

Every FBU 'shopping basket' comprises social and psychological as well as physical necessities. The LCA amounts represent the minimum amounts below which large numbers of older people risk ill-health and social exclusion, as they juggle between physical and other necessities. Some readers may

Table 1:   NI retirement pension and Income Support compared
January 1999 and April 1999, £ week

Pensioner status and age	NI basic state pension			Income Support		
	Jan 99	Apr 99	Increase	Jan 99	Apr 99	Increase
Single						
60-64	64.70	66.75		70.45	75.00	
65-74	**64.70**	**66.75**	**3.2%**	**70.45**	**75.00**	**6.5%**
75-79	64.70	66.75		72.70	77.30	
80+	64.95	67.00		77.55	82.25	
Married man						
60-64	103.40	103.40		109.35	116.60	
65-74	**103.40**	**106.70**	**3.2%**	**109.35**	**116.60**	**6.6%**
75-79	103.40	106.70		112.55	119.85	
80+	103.90	106.95		117.90	125.30	

Notes:

(a) The amounts of basic state pension shown for couples are on the assumption that the wife's pension is based on her husband's NI record. If she has a sufficient contribution record to receive a basic state pension in her own right, the couple's combined basic state pension is equal to that for two single people, which is higher than their Income Support entitlement.

(b) Winter fuel payments (per pensioner household):
   January 1999: £20 (£50 if receiving Income Support). Winter 1999-2000: £100.

conclude that poverty in old age could be avoided by introducing minimum guaranteed pensions at the levels portrayed here, but this is not necessarily the case, owing to the variability of certain living costs, for example, housing, fuel and transport. The purpose of the FBU's work is to help inform the decision-making process, raise public awareness and encourage debate, not to make recommendations.

6   On the definition of 'necessaries'

The LCA budgets strengthen the case for a minimum income or adequacy standard with a scientific basis to it, calculated using agreed methods and open to public inspection and debate, as opposed to covert methods subject to government secrecy provisions. Such a standard could provide a reference point for the various tiers of the income maintenance system, from minimum wages, income tax allowances, maintenance and debt or fine orders through to long- and short-term social security and social assistance benefits.

The standard should be kept outside party politics. It should be fair and be seen to be fair. It should be uprated annually in line with earnings and be

regularly reconstructed, because needs, like prices, change with time – luxuries become necessities and necessities become luxuries. The standard should also be sufficiently flexible to take account of regional variations in costs and it should be set out in such a way that money advisers can take account of the particular circumstances of their clients and courts of law can exercise discretion. A key question is the definition of necessities. In most developed economies, the provision of benefits sufficient to purchase physical necessities – food, clothing, warmth and shelter – is an accepted principle of good government. However, 'social' necessities – personal care, household goods, household services and leisure – are given a lower priority, so people skimp on physical necessities, or run into debt, to buy presents for their children and grandchildren.

On the definition of 'necessaries', the 18th-century Scottish economist Adam Smith was nearer the mark than recent UK governments. Social necessities, Smith argued, are no less important than physical necessities. The difference is that they vary according to the societies in which people live:

By necessaries I understand not only the commodities
which are indispensably necessary for the support of life,

but whatever the custom of the country renders it indecent for creditable people, even of the lowest order, to be without.... A linen shirt, for example, is, strictly speaking, not a necessary of life.... But in the present times, through the greater part of Europe, a creditable day-labourer would be ashamed to appear in public without a linen shirt.... Custom, in the same manner, has rendered leather shoes a necessary of life in England. The poorest creditable person of either sex would be ashamed to appear in public without them. In Scotland, custom has rendered them a necessary of life to the lowest order of men; but not to the same order of women, who may, without any discredit, walk about barefooted. In France they are necessaries neither to men nor to women, the lowest rank of both sexes appearing there publicly, without any discredit, sometimes in wooden shoes, and sometimes barefooted.

Under necessaries, therefore, I comprehend not only those things which nature, but those things which the established rules of decency have rendered necessary to the lowest rank of people. All other things I call luxuries. (Smith, 1778)

7 Alternative approaches

In his book *Setting adequacy standards*, John Veit-Wilson asks whether social science can discover and reliably test "a boundary or threshold of income (for any given household size and composition) above which the dominant defined adequate real level of living on average is achieved, and below which it is not" (Veit-Wilson, 1998, pp 15-16). He then distinguishes three scientific approaches to such research:

* the deprivation indicator approach

* the attitudinal approach

* the budget approach

* *Deprivation indicator approach.* The public view of minimum living standards is identified by surveys of what people call necessities, both material and social, which no one should be without. Surveys reveal the proportion of the population without the socially-defined necessities, and whether this is by choice or because of lack of income. Statistical analysis then reveals the income levels below which different levels of deprivation occur. An enforced lack of several necessities at low

income levels is taken to indicate poverty. Well-known examples of this approach in the UK are the works of Mack and Lansley (1985), and Gordon and Pantazis (1997).

* *Attitudinal approach.* On the assumption that individuals are the best judges of the incomes they need in order to reach acceptable living standards, surveys reveal the minimum income levels at which households on average report they can 'only just make ends meet', and respondents' estimates of the income levels which they considered 'insufficient' or on which they could only manage 'with some difficulty'. Adjusting for variations in household size and composition, statistical methods are then used to report the average levels of incomes which the public believes are required for minimum decency and below which, in their view, poverty lies. (This research was originally developed by economists at Leyden University in the Netherlands. See Van den Bosch, 1993.)

* *Budget approach.* This approach, says Veit-Wilson, is:

... a hybrid between empirical and prescriptive methods of finding minimum income levels. Unlike wholly prescriptive budget methods using nutritional science but ignoring social science evidence of customary diets and consumption patterns, this approach ... avoids prescribing the minimum level of living. Instead, it shows the income levels at which a range of conventional life-styles could in theory be achieved, and leaves it to the user to prescribe what minimum level of living is acceptable. (Veit-Wilson, 1998, p 19)

There are two main versions of the budget approach. The first, which is the method used by the FBU, endeavours to include and cost a family's whole purchases. The second, used by Seebohm Rowntree and more recently by the US National Research Council's Panel on Poverty and Family Assistance, restricts the budgets to core items such as food, clothing and utilities, the costs of which are rounded up by a 'margin' or 'multiplier' to take account of other needs (Section 10 below).

8 The Beveridge Report

Forty years after Seebohm Rowntree's study of poverty in York, in the report which came to form the basis of Britain's post-war welfare state, Sir William Beveridge outlined benefit rates which, he said, would be enough to live on:

> *The flat rate of benefit proposed is intended in itself to be sufficient without further resources to provide the minimum income needed for subsistence in all normal cases.* (Beveridge, 1942, para 307, p 122)

In fact, as shown by John Veit-Wilson's study of the Beveridge Committee's working papers and other records (Veit-Wilson, 1992), Beveridge's proposed amounts were not based on objective study of need. Instead, what Beveridge actually did was to rationalise the rough benefit levels already decided upon by the coalition government – with current unemployment benefit rates, lesser eligibility and public expenditure costs in mind – by setting out the amounts necessary for rent, food, clothing and fuel, plus a small 'margin' for wastage.

Had Beveridge used budget standards as the basis for his recommended benefit amounts, the rates introduced in 1948 might have been higher. Instead, says Veit-Wilson, they were arguably more austere than Rowntree's 'primary poverty' standard.

9   US Panel on Poverty and Family Assistance

All measures of poverty require regular review, because needs as well as prices change with time. In the United States in 1995, a Panel on Poverty and Family Assistance published a report on the concepts, methods and information needed for a poverty measure to update the existing US measure, which, by then, was more than 30 years old (Citro and Michael, 1995). The Panel also considered issues regarding the establishment of standards for welfare payments to families with children.

In deciding upon their recommendations, the US Panel used scientific evidence of customary patterns of living wherever possible, but took the view that the determination of a particular minimum standard was ultimately a matter of careful judgement. Unlike Rowntree, they did not try to estimate the main components of a minimum level of living, adding a small margin for additional items, but instead adopted the approach of calculating the cost of core essentials (food, clothing, shelter and utilities)

and multiplying that cost by some small amount (ranging from 1.15 to 1.25) to generate a margin sufficient to allow for the costs of other necessary but incidental expenses, such as household supplies, non-work-related transport and personal care (Citro and Michael, 1995, pp 151-3).

For a reference family of two adults and two children the Panel suggested a range of between $13,700 and $15,900 a year at 1992 prices. They also recommended that the new poverty threshold be uprated annually in line with changes in consumption of the basic goods and services contained in the poverty budget.

10   Sweden's '*Konsumentverket*'

In devising its LCA budgets, the FBU was influenced by the household budgets produced by Sweden's National Board for Consumer Affairs (*Konsumentverket*), although the Swedish budgets are at a level of living called 'reasonable' (*skälig*) which is closer to the FBU's MBA budgets than to its LCA budgets.

Of particular interest in the Swedish budgets is the distinction drawn between 'budget standard' costs and 'variable' costs and the implications of this approach for money advice. Used on their own, say the Swedes, budget standards lack the flexibility necessary to take account of budget components such as housing, transport and childcare, the costs of which are particularly variable. With this distinction in mind, in 1986 *Konsumentverket* wrote a money advice computer model (*Budgetråd*), now used by 80% of Sweden's municipalities, which distinguishes between two sorts of information:

- normative judgements, based on expert opinion, concerning people's needs;

- non-standardised (or variable) costs based on actual expenditures incurred. (*Konsumentverket*, undated)

The model comprises an income section and an expenditure section. Having ascertained the composition of the client's household, the adviser enters their income from all sources into the model. Expenditures follow, in two parts. First come the budgets estimated using traditional budget standards methodology (food, clothing, recreation, hygiene, consumables, household goods, leisure, electricity and home insurance). Then come the non-standardised or 'variable' costs such as housing and transport. In cases of money advice, clients are expected to keep an account of all their variable expenses.

In Sweden the *Konsumentverket* budgets have been influential in a number of respects. Although social security benefit levels and income tax allowances are not based on them, the budgets are used as reference points. They are also used in courts of law to help assess ability to pay fines, debts and maintenance orders (Veit-Wilson, 1998, Chapter 4).

For the FBU's LCA budgets, the Swedish format has been used, with adjustments to take account of the situation in the UK.

11   References

Beveridge, Sir W. (1942) *Social insurance and allied services*, Cmd 6404, London: HMSO.

Bradshaw, J. (ed) (1993) *Budget standards for the United Kingdom*, Aldershot: Avebury.

Citro, C.C. and Michael, R.T. (eds) (1995) *Measuring poverty: A new approach*, Washington, DC: National Academy Press.

Gordon, D. and Pantazis, C. (1997), *Breadline Britain in the 1990s*, Aldershot: Avebury.

HM Treasury (1999) *Budget 99*, HC 298, March, London: The Stationery Office.

The Swedish National Board for Consumer Affairs (*Konsumentverket*) (undated) *An abstract of the Swedish budget counselling model: Budgetråd*, Stockholm: *Konsumentverket*, S-118.

Mack, J. and Lansley, S (1985) *Poor Britain*, London: Allen and Unwin.

Parker, H. (ed) (1998) *Low Cost but Acceptable: A minimum income standard for the UK: Families with young children*, Bristol: The Policy Press.

Rowntree, B.S. (1901) *Poverty: A study of town life*, London: Macmillan.

Saunders, P. et al (1998) *Development of indicative budget standards for Australia*, Research Paper No 74, Budget Standards Unit, Sydney, Australia: University of New South Wales, p ii.

Smith, A. (1778) *The wealth of nations*, Book V, Chapter 11.

Van den Bosch, K. (1993) 'Poverty measures in comparative research', Chapter 1 in J. Berghman and B. Cantillon (eds) *The European face of social security*, Aldershot: Avebury.

Veit-Wilson, J. (1992) 'Muddle or mendacity? The Beveridge Committee and the Poverty Line', *Journal of Social Policy*, vol 21, no 3.

Veit-Wilson, J. (1998) *Setting adequacy standards: How governments define minimum incomes*, Bristol: The Policy Press.

Wynn, M. (1972) *Family policy: A study of the economic costs of rearing children and their social and political consequences*, Harmondsworth: Penguin Books.

Part Two

Low Cost but Acceptable

1   A reference point

The purpose of the Low Cost but Acceptable (LCA) standard is to provide reference points showing how much it costs households of different composition, at different stages of the life cycle and in different circumstances, to maintain a living standard which, though simple, provides a healthy diet, material security, social participation and a sense of control – indefinitely. This report measures the living costs, at the LCA standard, of single people and couples in the age range 65-74 years, living either in local authority housing, or as owner-occupiers with their mortgages paid off. Budgets for this age group at the more generous, Modest-But-Adequate (MBA) standard have already been published (Bradshaw, 1993; Parker, 1995). Budgets at the LCA standard are necessary in order to provide minimum benchmarks for public provision. Future reports will estimate living costs at MBA and LCA level across the life cycle.

Underlying the research is the quest for social justice: wages, benefits, taxes, debt orders, maintenance orders and fines that are 'fair' and seen to be 'fair'. Although budget standards have their limitations, without them the risks of poverty and injustice are greatly magnified. In England and Wales people are still imprisoned for debt. In 1994, an estimated 27% of prison receptions were fine defaulters (NAPO, 1996). If magistrates were better informed regarding living costs, this situation might improve.

The budgets in this report are benchmarks. To reach the LCA standard, some households need more and others less than the amounts shown here, depending on their circumstances. At LCA level, two findings stand out. First, the narrowness of the margins for unforeseen expenditures, as a result of which older people have to exercise the utmost care to avoid running into debt, and those with higher costs than those assumed here are particularly at risk. Second, the poverty trap effects of overlaps between the tax and benefit systems, as a result of which, for example, in January 1999 a single pensioner paying £33.08 local authority rent and £6.44 council tax, was worse off if he/she had investment income of £20-£50 a week than without it (Figure 2 and Tables 47-50).

2   Why save?

The disincentive effects of the pensioner poverty trap are similar to those of the poverty trap for people of working age, except that they undermine the savings motive as well as the work ethic. The (almost) flat lines, peaks and troughs of Figure 2 are accounted for by the capital thresholds and tariff incomes applied to means-tested benefits.

The additional gross incomes necessary to bring the net incomes of NI pensioners to LCA level depend partly on the sources of those additional incomes, each source being subject to different tax and benefit regulations. For tax purposes, earnings and pension incomes are treated similarly, but investment income is treated differently. For benefit purposes, earnings are treated differently to pensions and differently again to investment income. Tax-free investment income is in a class of its own, but all investment income is taxed at a lower rate (within the basic-rate tax band) than either pensions or earnings.

The housing benefit and council tax benefit regulations disregard small amounts of earnings, but not pensions. This explains why lower levels of earnings than of second pensions are needed to reach required levels of spending power (in this case the LCA standard). Income from investments is fully disregarded by the income tests for means-tested benefits, but the capital from which the income arises is taken into account in the capital limits regulations. For example, in January 1999, the first £3,000 of capital in each case was disregarded, but on capital between the upper and lower limits a 'tariff income' was applied, in other words, savers lost part of the reward for their savings. Older people are disqualified from Income Support if they have capital in excess of £8,000, and from housing benefit and council tax benefit if they have capital in excess of £16,000. This explains why couples with investment income suddenly lose benefits and become dramatically worse off when their joint additional income reaches £18.50 a week. The intricacies of the regulations are explained elsewhere (West, 1999).

Figure 2: **THE PENSIONER POVERTY TRAP**
Additional gross incomes to reach **LCA** level,
according to the source of the additional income

Tenants aged 65-74 years receiving full **NI** retirement pensions
Alcohol included in the budgets
January 1999 prices, £ week

(a) SINGLE PEOPLE
NI category A pension: £64.70 week

(b) MARRIED COUPLES
NI category A + B pensions: £103.40 week

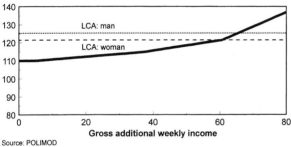

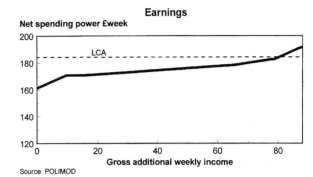

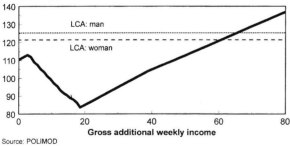

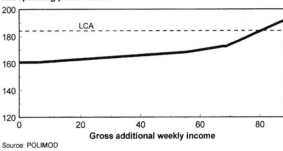

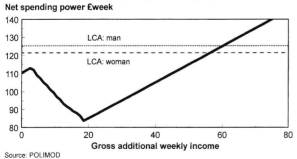

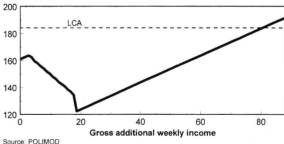

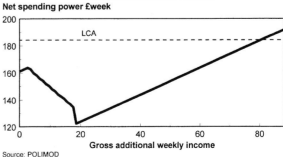

The calculations for Figure 2 assume that pensioners receive income at an interest rate of 6% a year on capital, which sounds high but is considerably less than the interest rate assumed by the Department of Social Security (DSS). For example, a pensioner with an investment income of £15 a week is assumed by the FBU to have capital of £13,000, whereas capital of more than £3,000 is assumed by the DSS to contribute a weekly income of £1 for every £250 of capital (an effective interest rate of 20.8%). This explains why couples relying on investment income to top up their National Insurance (NI) retirement pensions lose their entitlement to means-tested benefits and become dramatically worse off on incomes well below LCA level.

Once pensioners have incomes high enough to pay income tax (£104.04 in January 1999 for single people and £167.60 for couples), the type of investment income received also affects the amounts of income required to reach LCA level. If the income is tax-free, the LCA standard is reached with lower gross incomes than if tax is deducted at source. For single people, the effects of this are clearly visible in Figure 2(a), but for couples the different tax treatment is not obvious, because the tax is not payable until their combined gross incomes are higher. Figure 2 illustrates the pensioner poverty trap in January 1999, first for tenants, then for owner-occupiers.

Precise figures, including assumed housing costs, are available in Tables 46-50.

3 How the budgets are established

3.1 Model families and housing types

Detailed budgets are presented for three household types; first, as local authority tenants, then as owner-occupiers who have paid off their mortgages (Table 2). All household members are between the ages of 65 and 74 years. None is in paid employment.

Table 2: Household types and housing tenure

- *Single woman, aged 65-74 years*
(a) Local authority tenant
(b) Owner-occupier

- *Single man, aged 65-74 years*
(a) Local authority tenant
(b) Owner-occupier

- *Couple, each aged 65-74 years*
(a) Local authority tenants
(b) Owner-occupiers

3.2 Location

As with previous FBU budgets, the city of York remains the main pricing centre. York provides a social and cultural base, with a well-defined pattern of community services, leisure activities and housing provision. Housing profiles in York – local authority rented and owner-occupied – were chosen, because they are broadly representative of housing occupied by low-income older people across the UK. In a recent study, York was found to be remarkably close to the national average in many key determinants of living standards (Huby et al, 1999).

3.3 Pricing

The budgets were priced in January 1999, using national retail outlets (including mail order outlets) wherever possible. The Co-op (CWS), Kwik Save and Sainsbury's provided price databases, which were used to find economy lines and low, but not necessarily the lowest, prices for food, household goods and some leisure and personal care products. Other retailers (Allied Carpets, C&A, MFI, Poundstretcher and Shoe City) allowed researchers to visit their branches to collect prices. Argos, Daxon, Empire Stores, Index and JD Williams catalogues were also sources of prices for some leisure, clothing and durable goods. Leisure services were priced in York. Local shops, York market and local services were also used when it was difficult to obtain prices from a national pricing base, for example repair of washing machines and servicing of appliances.

- *Pricing of durables:* the weekly costs of durables are calculated by dividing each item's purchase price by its life expectancy (in years or weeks).

- *Sale goods, second-hand goods, DIY:* no sale or second-hand prices, home-produced goods or home-grown food are included in the budget standard. This is due to the difficulty of attaching prices and lifetimes to second-hand goods and of procuring them at the appropriate time.

- *'Do-it-yourself' services:* these are included at basic prices.

3.4   Inclusion criteria

At MBA level, generally, the reference point for inclusion of key items is 50% ownership for the particular household type, according to national surveys. At LCA level the reference point is 80%, but is not (and cannot be) rigidly adhered to, because family circumstances differ and ownership statistics are sometimes conflicting or unavailable. For example expenditure surveys give data on spending frequency rather than ownership rates.

Circumstances exist in which an 80% inclusion test is too high, for instance car ownership in rural areas. With careful money management, an LCA budget should be sufficient to eat healthily, take an inexpensive annual holiday and avoid major debt problems. Yet neither mortgage payments nor a car can be ruled out. Rented housing may be unavailable and a car may be a necessity. Home contents insurance, in some locations, is fast becoming a necessity.

A decision was taken to include consideration of the following at LCA level:

Holidays: After consultation with voluntary organisations, the view was taken that everybody needs a break, therefore a week's holiday in the UK is included in the LCA leisure budgets. Most people can do without a holiday for a year or two, but these budgets are designed to be sustainable indefinitely.

Alcohol: 14 units of alcohol for men, 6 units for women and 18 units for couples are included, as an option. An alternative alcohol-free budget results in higher expenditure on food. This is to take account of the food value of the alcohol foregone.

Tobacco: The difference between alcohol and tobacco is that tobacco is unambiguously damaging, whereas alcohol in moderation can be beneficial for health reasons and for socialising. Tobacco is listed, not as a recommendation, but in recognition of the principle of consumer choice. By publicising the cost of tobacco, its impact on the household budgets of low-income families becomes immediately apparent.

Gifts: The idea of gifts is a difficult one for budget standards methodology. Gifts exchanged with people outside the household are not usually included, on the assumption that the value of the gift purchased roughly equates to the value of the gift received. However, this concept of gifts was not always appreciated by the discussion groups, so a small number of items are included, which may or may not be given as a gifts, for example, cut flowers and perfume. The budget standard for older people includes gift vouchers for grandchildren, because such gifts are unlikely to be reciprocated.

3.5   Data sources

National surveys: The Family Expenditure Survey (FES), General Household Survey (GHS), Transport Survey, National Food Survey (NFS), Family Resources Survey (FRS) and the National Diet and Nutrition Survey.

Market research reports: Consumer Association, Euromonitor and Mintel.

Health and good practice standards: The Department of Health, the Health Education Authority and local authorities.

Commerce and institutions: Information was obtained on consumer behaviour from organisations including the Post Office, British Telecom, retailers in clothing and pharmaceutical goods and leisure outlets.

Low-income discussion groups: Twelve discussion groups, composed of non-related, low-income adults aged 65-74 years and living in financial and household circumstances similar to those of the FBU model families, proved a valuable source of information. An interview guide was developed with the following objectives:

- to facilitate the process of obtaining information about the shopping patterns of low-income households in the 65-74 years age group;

- to draw up a framework for the food menus and shopping lists;

- to assist in validation of the budgets, that is, assess their acceptability (see p 17);

- to learn about the realities of life on a low income.

With the help of local voluntary organisations, groups were recruited in London, four urban areas of East Sussex, Lancashire, Tyne and Wear and the West Midlands, and one from a rural area of Somerset. Group meetings were held before and after the draft budgets were drawn up. During round one, the focus was on shopping patterns, key items of expenditure and eating habits. During round two, the focus was on the acceptability of the draft budgets.

Participants were separated into three groups consisting of single women, single men and couples (one spouse only). The single women had gross weekly incomes of £95-£142. The single men had gross weekly incomes of £88-£122. The couples had gross weekly incomes of £147-£213. These gross weekly incomes fit the selected income centiles for low-income households in the 1995-96 FES, shown in Appendix 1. Each group discussion lasted about two hours and attendance costs were reimbursed. The average size of a group was six.

The quality of information gained from the discussion groups made them a valuable tool for budget standards methodology, but they were not a representative sample of older people. Instead they were drawn from established community groups, each with its own in-built membership bias. Geographically, the groups were fairly well spread across England, but no groups were recruited from Scotland or Wales. The rural discussion group consisted of eight low-income, older women, from a village with a population of 850. The purpose of the rural group was to gain an understanding of the similarities and differences between the shopping patterns of rural compared to urban dwellers. Single men were less well represented numerically than single women, but many of the couple households provided a man as spokesperson.

4   Budget formats

4.1   A new approach

Conventional budget standards, as devised by Rowntree, Beveridge and the FBU for its MBA standard (Bradshaw, 1993) take no account of variations in needs and living costs over which families have little or no control, for example housing, transport and fuel. For its LCA budgets the FBU has broken new ground by distinguishing between budget standard expenditures, which are relatively constant, and variable expenditures, which are not. A new format has been introduced which enables users to specify the variable expenditures incurred by themselves or (in the case of money advisers) their clients (Table 3).

This format will be used for all future FBU budgets, hence the inclusion of job-related and seeking work costs in the pensioner budgets. In the budgets described here no job-related costs are incurred, but some people aged 65-74 years do incur them, so they need to be included.

Table 3:   LCA budget components

Budget standard expenditures	Variable expenditures
Food	Housing
Clothing	Fuel
Personal care	Transport
Household goods	NHS charges
Household services	Insurances
Leisure	Debts/fines/maintenance orders
	Job-related costs
	Costs of seeking work
	Pet costs
	Alcohol
	Tobacco
	Charitable giving

4.2   Budget standards explained

A *budget standard* calculates the average amount of money needed by a particular type of family (or household) each week, month or year, to reach and maintain a predefined living standard. Budget standard expenditures (unlike variable expenditures) are assumed to be the same for all households of the same composition. Although different households make different choices, the evidence from Sweden suggests that the total amounts spent (at a particular living standard) are similar.

As with the MBA budgets, the LCA budget standard involves research in six stages:

- define the living standard;

- identify the goods and services to be included;

- determine the required quantities of those goods and services;

- identify their appropriate quality;

- set lifetimes for durables;

- price them.

In 1991, the MBA baskets of goods and services were described as benchmark budgets for the "prevailing standard of living" in the UK (Bradshaw, 1993). For the LCA budgets, with the exception of food, the MBA baskets serve as reference points. In selecting the goods and services for the LCA budgets, the first task was to adjust the contents of the 1991 MBA baskets, to reflect changes over the previous seven years. From then on lifetimes were set for every budget item, taking into account quality (measured by brand and price) and rate of use. The MBA lists of items were reduced and modified to bring them to LCA level, partly by reducing the number of duplicated items and partly by replacing some MBA items with appropriate alternatives.

The setting of lifetimes is particularly important, because an item's lifetime provides its weekly cost. For example, if a 125g tube of toothpaste lasts eight weeks, its weekly cost equals its unit cost divided by eight. An item's lifetime depends on a number of factors, including the number of people using it and its quality, which can often be inferred from its price and brand. In the clothing schedule in Appendix 4, specifications similar to the following are included:

> Woman's winter coat: *classic, wool/polyamide, January 1999 price £59.99, replacement rate, 10 years. Average cost £6.00 a year (£0.12 a week).*

Full details of the LCA budget standards for clothing, personal care, household goods, household services, leisure goods and leisure activities are in

Appendix 4. By way of illustration, Table 4 summarises the LCA clothing budget for women aged 65-74 years.

Table 4:	Summary clothing budget Woman aged 65-74 years LCA standard January 1999, £ week
Outerwear	2.50
Underwear and nightwear	1.57
Accessories	0.09
Shoes	0.79
Sewing repair kit	0.07
Total	**5.02**

The LCA food baskets were not derived from the MBA food baskets; they were drawn up independently. As with MBA, the starting point is the National Food Survey (NFS), but the selection of foods purchased by a particular household type is drawn from lower income bands than those used for the MBA baskets.

Using the 1995/96 Family Expenditure Survey (FES), the income bands at which the different household types spent 30% of their net incomes (after housing costs) on food were identified. The starting point for the LCA food baskets then becomes the foods purchased by single women, single men and couples aged 65-74 years (as reported in the NFS), within these defined income bands.

4.3 Variable expenditures explained

For the purposes of this report, the term *variable costs* means those costs which, though 'fixed' for individual households in the short to medium term, can be extremely variable between households. Rent, fuel and transport are key examples. Unlike the budget standard expenditures, the variable expenditures are not recommendations, they are illustrative. They are nevertheless typical of consumer expenditure at this level of living in the UK; they fit the circumstances described in the text and they provide the prescribed standard. Fuel consumption, for example, tallies with the heating standard. When using the variable expenditures format for money advice or in courts of law, however, the expenditures shown would normally be the actual expenditures incurred by clients. A space for debts and debt interest is left under variable costs for this purpose.

A key distinction is drawn between core variables and life-style variables:

- *Core variables:* These are essentials such as housing, fuel, transport, childcare and healthcare. They also include expenditures which may not have been essential in the first place, but become so once entered into, for example debts and pets.

- *Life-style variables:* Going to the pub, smoking, sharing a bottle of wine with friends, giving to charity, playing the Lottery ... none of these activities is, strictly speaking, necessary. Yet in Britain in 1999 they are facts of life which cannot be brushed aside. Not only are alcohol and tobacco hard to give up, in certain circumstances they promote social inclusion and ease stress. From a budgeting point of view they also provide a margin for fines, breakages and debt repayments. Without such margins households in financial stress have to cut back on necessities.

5 Validation

5.1 Family Expenditure Survey (FES)

Although the FES is one of many references used by the FBU, the FES and FBU figures are not strictly comparable. This is because the purpose of the FES is to provide information about spending trends, using random selected households and two-weekly spending diaries, whereas the purpose of the FBU budgets is to estimate the living costs of hypothetical (or model) families, using recognised nutritional, housing and heating standards and empirical research indicating consumer preferences (Section 3.5). The FBU figures assume rents near to the local authority national average and owner-occupiers who have paid off their mortgages, whereas the FES figures reflect the wide variety of housing costs across the UK. Expenditure on tobacco is included in the FES but not in the FBU budgets, which are intended to be health-promoting.

The classification of items in the FBU budgets nevertheless follows the FES framework (housing, fuel, food, alcohol, tobacco, clothing, household goods and services, personal care, motoring, fares and leisure).

According to the 1997/98 FES, average weekly expenditure by *retired households not mainly dependent on State pensions* was £164 (single) and £276.40 (couples) (ONS, 1998, Tables 4.3 and 4.9). Table 5 relates the LCA budgets for households aged 65-74 years to the average spending of retired single and couple households. It shows that the FBU's single tenants require about 75% of average expenditure in the UK to reach the LCA living standard. Couple tenants need 67%. Single homeowners who have paid off their mortgages require about 60% of average expenditure. Couples need 54%.

Table 5: **LCA budgets, households aged 65-74 years, January 1999 as % of average weekly spending* by retired households FES (1997-98)**

FBU tenants	% of average spending
Single woman	74
Single man	76
Couples	67
FBU owners (mortgage paid off)	
Single woman	60
Single man	62
Couples	54

* Households not mainly dependent on State pensions.

For *retired households mainly dependent on state pensions* (ONS, 1998, Tables 4.2 and 4.8) the LCA budgets are above FES average spending in both single and couple households.

5.2 Low-income discussion groups

The low-income discussion groups were reconvened to validate the budgets drawn up by the FBU for their particular household types. In addition to the urban groups, one rural group was again included in the validation process. To organise the validation, information sheets and semi-structured interview guides were drawn up for each component of a typical household budget. The information sheets contained selected items from the budgets, with details of place of purchase, quantity required and lifetime. In addition the groups were shown specimen menus and a weekly shopping list for food.

Participants were asked for comments on what level of expenditure they thought would be acceptable for a household similar to their own, bearing in mind the following:

> *With careful budgeting the model family would be*
> *expected to feel comfortable and warm, have a healthy*
> *diet and be able to participate in social activities within*
> *the communities in which they live.*

Participants were also asked to prepare themselves for the forthcoming discussion by producing their own weekly budgets.

Participants' sample budgets

These proved to be of particular interest. Clearly, for the participants of the FBU discussion groups, budgeting is nothing new. Table 6 summarises the weekly spending of a single older woman with a disposable income of £85.60 a week. In January 1999 her weekly expenditure was £87.56, resulting in a deficiency of almost £2 a week. She lived in local authority housing and received housing benefit. She made no provision for replacement clothing, holidays or insurance.

Table 6: **Weekly expenditure**
Single older woman
Tenant, living alone
January 1999, £ week

Rent (50% housing benefit)	11.56
Council tax	5.00
Water	5.00
Gas	4.00
Electricity	5.00
TV licence	2.00
Telephone	5.00
Food, cleaning materials, personal care	40.00
Bus fares and newspapers	10.00
Total weekly expenditure	**87.56**
Net weekly income	**85.60**
Weekly deficit	**1.96**

Table 7 summarises the spending of a single man with an average disposable income of £116.59. He is an owner-occupier who maintains his property to a high standard. He spends £119.90 (on average) a week, resulting in an average reduction in his savings of £3.31 a week.

Table 7: **Weekly expenditure**
Single older man
Owner-occupier, living alone
January 1999, £ week

Rent/mortgage	0.00
Council tax	2.29
Water	5.53
Gas	5.08
Electricity	6.01
TV licence	1.80
Cable TV and telephone rental	3.00
Telephone/postage	9.89
Food and drink	25.19
Meals out	13.25
Fares (bus and rail)	4.70
Entertainment	1.05
House insurance (building and contents)	4.28
House repairs, maintenance, decoration	26.09
Cleaning materials	0.99
Gardening expenses	2.82
Christmas and birthday purchases	3.85
Clothing	2.88
Newspapers	1.20
Total weekly expenditure	**119.90**
Net weekly income	**116.59**
Weekly deficit	**3.31**

Acceptability of FBU budgets

There was general acceptance of the FBU budgets, although a few sections required additional clarification and some adjustments were subsequently made. If the budgets were challenged, they tended to be considered "too mean". Only a small number of items were generally said to be "too generous".

It became evident that many older people expect good quality clothing, which they cannot afford, so they buy at charity shops or in sales. Men's and women's coats in the draft budgets were in general said to be too few and too cheap for the length of time they were expected to last. Men wanted a better quality suit included, with a longer lifetime. Women found top clothes old-fashioned and suggested more tops, skirts and trousers. Neither charity shops nor sales were visited in drawing up the LCA clothing budgets. However, clothes were priced in discount stores and market stalls to achieve acceptable quality at lower prices.

In the case of household linen, quantities of towels, tea towels and bed-sheets were said to be too low to account for realistic laundering procedures.

The cost of the weekly food basket, at about £3 per person per day, was generally considered reasonable, although the prices of some items (bread, cheese, fish and yoghurts) were said to be too low. Acceptance of the menus was high, with the exception of fruit and vegetables, which exceeded most people's intake.

Wide-ranging leisure activities were reported, but most thought the amounts allocated for leisure spending reasonable. It was confirmed that out-of-season holidays were acceptable and even preferred. The idea that gifts were reciprocated was only partially appreciated. Part of the giving was not reciprocated, especially gifts for grandchildren and godchildren.

Differences between rural and urban shopping
Shopping in rural Somerset is conducted at less frequent intervals than in the urban areas visited. The women use the village shop/post office for everyday items and newspapers. A mobile fish van calls weekly and a local hardware van also visits. Commenting on the draft budgets, the group agreed that they had little use for special occasion or sports clothing. Most of their clothing is purchased through mail order catalogues, such as Empire Stores, Littlewoods and Kays. Most are traditional vegetable growers and use home produced foods. Due to the high cost of travel, they rely more heavily than their urban counterparts on postal and telephone services.

Budget adjustments
As a result of the validation process, some budget adjustments were made. The women's clothing schedule was modernised and better quality coats, suits and special occasion clothes were included, with longer lifetimes attached. The leisure budget was redrawn, to give a more interesting (but no

more expensive) leisure profile. Each household was allocated six £5 gift vouchers, as gifts for children. The personal care budget was adjusted in small ways, for example by replacing electric razors with disposable ones, by increasing the number of boxes of tissues (which were used far more often than envisaged) and by including permanent waves (hair style) for women. The quantity of household linen items was increased and some lifetimes of items reduced. The number of telephone calls (said to be too generous) was reduced to a low-user level. Some prices in the shopping basket were adjusted in line with general comments and there was some overall balancing of the food profiles between different households. Further information about the discussion groups is in Appendix 3.

6 Methodological issues

6.1 Part normative, part empirical

Like the MBA budgets, the LCA budgets involve a combination of normative judgements concerning people's needs together with empirical data showing how consumers spend the money they have. For the normative judgements the FBU relies on recognised standards for nutrition, housing, warmth and exercise. FBU dieticians recommend less sugar than is generally consumed and the food energy value of alcohol is taken into account in the food budgets. For the empirical data, reliance is placed on consumer reports, national surveys and material provided by the discussion groups, which explored the spending patterns of low-income older people.

6.2 Benchmarks, not specifications

Although great care has been taken to ensure that the budgets reflect the preferences and choices of consumers at LCA level (while promoting a healthy life-style), the budget totals depend crucially on the variable expenditures (which, though representative, are illustrative) and on the assumptions made, for instance whether or not to include alcohol and whether or not the families need a car. The budget totals are therefore best regarded as benchmarks, not policy recommendations.

6.3 Illustrative, not actual families

Similarly, because the budgets are based on hypothetical rather than actual families, it would be wrong to generalise the required expenditure of the families shown here for people in the 65-74 year age group as a whole. The fact that a pensioner couple living in the circumstances portrayed in Table 44 requires a gross weekly income of £184 a week (including alcohol in the budget) to reach LCA level does not mean that pensioner couples living in different circumstances need precisely the same amount. The figures are indicators.

6.4 Capital costs

Household expenditure includes 'capital' items which most people regard as essential. The main 'capital' items in the LCA budgets for elderly people, along with the lifetimes attached to them, are shown in Table 8. Lifetimes were estimated on evidence from market research, underpinned by the periods of time families are likely to live in the same house, and validated by the low-income discussion groups. At the LCA standard, in many instances lifetimes were extended beyond the manufacturers' recommendations.

Table 8: LCA budgets, main durables and lifetimes (in years)

Durable	Life-time	Durable	Life-time
Beds	20	Gas cooker*	17
Bedding	9	Hairdryer	4
Curtains	10	Washing machine*	15
Carpets	13-15	Lawn mower	20
Three-piece suite	15	Television	15
Furniture and fittings	25	Vacuum cleaner*	15
Fridge freezer	17	Tools	15

* Repairs and servicing of equipment included.

The use of credit to buy durable goods is a very usual part of family budgeting, although low-income pensioners in the FBU discussion groups stressed their lack of access to credit. The majority had post office accounts for pension transactions and dealt in cash on a daily basis. In some areas Credit Unions were said to be the only place where credit is obtainable. The DSS Social Fund helps Income Support claimants to meet occasional

expenses such as clothing and footwear, furniture and household equipment, improvements, maintenance and security of the home. In January 1999 budgeting loans were highly discretionary and cash-limited, but since April 1999 a new formula has been devised, based on a series of complicated tests and other factors. The size of a budgeting loan is small, with a minimum of £30 and a maximum of £1,000. Repayment takes priority over living expenses and other debts.

The distinction between capital costs and running costs is difficult to draw and raises contentious issues. The traditional budget standards method of pricing durables (and the method used by the FBU) is to divide purchase prices by estimated lifetimes. The recent Australian budget standards report uses the same method, but includes criticism of it on the grounds that the budget standard then includes the 'notional cost' of items already owned by the household. From a social policy viewpoint, they say, there may be a case for excluding such costs in the short term (Saunders et al, 1998). In Britain, this was the logic behind the long-term additions with supplementary benefit, abolished in 1988. Yet some claimants, particularly older people, depend on Income Support for long periods and replacement of durable goods is important.

There is, moreover, a significant difference between the Australian report (financed by government, with social security benefit rates in mind) and the FBU's LCA budgets, which have not been commissioned by government and are intended to be sustainable indefinitely, by wage and salary earners as well as by social security benefit claimants. If at some time in the future a British government decides to use the FBU budgets (either MBA or LCA) as reference points for State pensions or Income Support, any shortfalls should be easily identifiable.

7 References

Bradshaw, J. (ed) (1993) *Budget standards for the United Kingdom*, Aldershot: Avebury.

Huby, M., Bradshaw, J. and Corden, A. (1999) *A study of life: Living standards in the City of York 100 years after Rowntree*, York: Joseph Rowntree Foundation, York Publishing Services.

NAPO (1996) 'Women, sentencing and custody, July 1995', quoted in R.R. Epstein, *Imprisonment for debt: A report for the Nuffield Foundation*, p 10.

ONS (Office for National Statistics) (1998) *Family spending 1997-98*, London: The Stationery Office.

Parker, H. (ed) (1995) *Modest-But-Adequate budgets for four pensioner households*, *October 1994 prices*, London: FBU, Department of Nutrition and Dietetics, King's College London.

Saunders, P., Chalmers, J., McHugh, M., Murray, C., Bittman, M. and Bradbury, B. (1998) *Development of indicative budget standards for Australia*, Research Paper Number 74, Budget Standards Unit, Sydney: Australia, University of New South Wales.

West, S. (1999) *Your rights guide: A guide to money benefits for older people, 1999-2000*, London: Age Concern England.

Part Three

Budget standards

I   Food

1.1   LCA food standard

Budget standards for food are required in order to establish the levels of expenditure necessary to reach dietary adequacy. The food budgets and menus in this report represent a Low Cost but Acceptable (LCA) and healthy diet for older people. The aim is a budget which will satisfy the recommended intakes of all nutrients, meet guidelines for healthy eating, be palatable and accord with the consumer preferences of older people living in the UK in 1999.

1.2   Purpose of the food budgets

Although average life expectancy in the UK has increased during the past one hundred years – from 45-50 years in 1900 to 75-80 years now – by the time people reach 60 years of age, it is substantially lower for those on low incomes than for the better off (Wang et al, 1997). Poor nutritional status is common in older people in Britain, especially those on low incomes (DoH, 1992a; Finch et al, 1998). Better diets in older people are associated with longer life, lower morbidity (Morley et al, 1995; Schlenker et al, 1998), better nutritional status and lower health costs.

The LCA food baskets have been adjusted to allow for healthier eating practices, in line with recommendations from the Department of Health (1991) and the Health Education Authority (1996a, 1996b and 1997). They also take into account two recently published guidelines on healthy eating for older people (MAFF, 1993; Caroline Walker Trust, 1995). These sources, together with feedback from the FBU's discussion groups (see Appendix 3), have been used to inform the choice of foods and menus presented here.

1.3   Food budget calculations

The aim is to produce food baskets which:

* represent a pattern of consumption characteristic of older households, living at LCA level in the UK;

* contain a balance of foods, which will promote short-term and long-term health in older people;

* be based on foods which are palatable and widely available at low prices.

The budget calculations presented here are based on food purchasing profiles described in the National Food Survey (NFS) for the years 1992-95 (MAFF, 1993-97), in households thought to have spending patterns typical of the LCA level (Appendix 2). These food purchasing profiles resemble the food consumption patterns of a comparable group of older people in the 1994-95 National Diet and Nutrition Survey (Finch et al, 1998). Food baskets were costed in January 1999, using unpublished price bases from the Co-op (CWS), Kwik Save and Sainsbury's. The costs of foods purchased and eaten away from home, and of alcoholic beverages, are based on Family Expenditure Survey (FES) data for 1992-96 (ONS, 1993-96). Details of the methodology are in Appendix 2.

A unique feature of the budgets is the inclusion of illustrative menus (Tables 11-13), showing how the proposed baskets of foods could be used to feed households of different composition.

1.4   LCA food budgets compared with MBA food budgets

The LCA food budgets differ from the FBU's Modest-But-Adequate (MBA) food budgets in two ways:

* they are based on the food purchasing patterns of households at a lower income level;

* they use foods that can be purchased at low prices.

The main consequence of these differences is a more restricted, cheaper diet, but one which nevertheless meets standards for healthy eating.

1.5   Discussion groups

As with the LCA budgets for families with young children (Parker, 1998), an important addition in developing the LCA price base was a series of group discussions, during which choices of items for purchase were discussed with older people from income bands believed to represent the LCA living standard.

1.6   Summary food budgets

Table 9 shows illustrative food costs for three household types. The home food components are based on adjusted NFS purchasing profiles, costed using the Co-op (CWS) Sainsbury's and Kwik Save price bases in January 1999. The alcohol component is based on Health Education Authority guidelines. Food eaten away from home is based on FES data, but only some of the meals eaten away from home are purchased – others are free, at the homes of friends or relatives.

Several aspects require clarification:

- *Men's and women's food baskets compared.* The home budget for the single man is approximately 16% greater than that for the single woman. This is because energy requirements in men (9.71 MJ) are 22% higher than in women (7.96 MJ) (DoH, 1991). Additionally, men and women both have visitors, who share food, but women are likely to have more visitors than men (10% versus 3% of meals according to the NFS). The extra food required has been included in the baskets and in the menus.

- *Economies of scale.* The sum of the costs of the weekly food budgets for a single-man household and a single-woman household (£43.09) is substantially greater than the budget for the couple household (£36.91). This is partly because single households miss out on economies of scale. Many of the larger packs available (especially those in economy line foods) do not suit the consumption patterns of single households, either because foods purchased in larger quantities would exceed their use-by dates before being eaten (unless the diets were made very monotonous), or because portions of the food would need to be frozen (for example bread), which was unacceptable to many of the discussion group participants (although freezers are widely available and are included in the LCA budgets).

- *Supermarket and local prices compared.* Shopping for food is often a daily activity, partly for positive reasons related to social contact and physical activity; and partly to avoid heavy shopping bags. Supermarket customers with large orders are sometimes able to take advantage of free home

delivery schemes, but this is an unlikely option for customers at LCA level. Local shops are the only other alternative, but their prices tend to be higher than supermarket prices (Piachaud and Webb, 1996).

The price base for costing the LCA food budgets included a small Co-op, with higher prices typical of local shops. The costs of the home food budget using Sainsbury's and a small, local Co-op were on average above the values shown in Table 9, whereas the costs using a larger Co-op and Kwik Save were on average below the values in Table 9. The differences in costs between the dearest and cheapest outlets was £4-£5 a week for the single households and around £8 a week for the couple households.

The budgets in Table 9 reflect food costs in a range of food outlets likely to be available to many older shoppers, rather than the cheapest food outlets available. If the shopping were limited to the more expensive outlets – for reasons of access or mobility – at least £2 per person per week would need to be added to the food budget totals in Table 9 to achieve LCA level.

1.7   Alcohol

Alcohol in moderation can confer physiological and social benefits on older people (Caroline Walker Trust, 1995). The food budgets have therefore been costed with and without alcohol. Where alcohol is included, small reductions in the amounts spent on food allow for the additional dietary energy obtained from alcoholic beverages.

The derivation of the alcohol budgets is shown in Table 10. Consumption is limited to not more than two thirds of the healthy drinking limits set by the Health Education Authority (1996b). These limits are 21 units a week for men and 14 units for women, where one unit equals half a pint (275 ml) of beer, a glass (125 ml) of wine, or a single (25 ml) of spirits.

Table 9:   **Summary food budgets**
             Households aged 65-74 years
             LCA standard, January 1999, £ week

Food group	Single woman	Single man	Couple
Bread, cakes, biscuits	1.85	2.01	3.18
Cereals	0.60	1.00	1.52
Carcass meat	2.88	5.46	6.17
Meat products	1.76	1.42	3.00
Fish	2.41	2.48	3.67
Fats	0.36	0.36	0.60
Milk and milk products	1.65	1.28	2.66
Cheese	0.26	0.29	0.57
Eggs	0.43	0.43	0.64
Potatoes	1.10	1.29	1.93
Vegetables	2.40	2.21	4.39
Fruit	2.25	2.41	4.72
Sugar	0.27	0.27	0.61
Beverages	0.76	0.62	1.05
Other home foods	0.59	0.95	0.65
Soft drinks	0.18	0.18	0.36
Sweets and chocolate	0.34	0.34	1.19
Total home food budget	*20.09*	*23.00*	*36.91*
+ Foods purchased and eaten away from home	2.46	2.46	4.90
Total budget (no alcohol included)	**22.55**	**25.46**	**41.81**
Adjusted total for food if alcohol is included*	21.93	24.04	40.12
Alcohol	2.22	5.64	7.31
Total budget: food plus alcohol	**24.15**	**29.68**	**47.43**

* If alcohol is included in the diet, it is necessary to reduce the energy derived from food to allow for the energy content of the alcohol. The total energy content of food plus alcohol will then be equal to the Department of Health Estimated Average Requirements for this age group (see text and Appendix 2 for further details). The cost of the food is reduced accordingly.

Table 10:   **Summary alcohol budgets**
              Households aged 65-74 years
              LCA standard, January 1999, Units of alcohol and £ week

	Units of alcohol	Cost £	Purchase quantities
Single woman			
Beer	1	0.68	6 x 440ml/8 weeks
Wine	1	0.47	1 bottle/6 weeks
Spirit	4	1.07	70cl/8 weeks
Total	**6**	**2.22**	
Single man			
Beer	4	2.25	10 x 440ml cans/4 weeks
Wine	2	0.95	1 bottle/3 weeks
Spirit	8	2.44	70cl/3½ weeks
Total	**14**	**5.64**	
Couple			
Beer	4	2.48	11 x 440ml cans/4 weeks
Wine	3	1.42	1 bottle/2 weeks
Spirit	11	3.41	2 x 70cl/5 weeks
Total	**18**	**7.31**	

The alcohol budgets also reflect levels of expenditure and proportions of expenditure on different types of drink reported in the FES (ONS, 1993-96), together with feedback from the discussion groups. The proportions of expenditure relating to different types of drink reflect the expenditures reported in the FES. The costs are based on prices of alcoholic beverages in supermarkets rather than in pubs. Single men are allocated 14 units a week (which is below the estimated 19 units based on expenditure data for men in the 65-74 year age group in the FES). Women's spending on alcohol, as reported in the FES and confirmed by the discussion groups, is proportionately smaller: £2.22 (6 units) a week, compared with £5.64 (14 units) a week for men.

1.8   Menus

The menus in Tables 11, 12 and 13 show the sort of meals which could be made from the baskets of foods in Appendix 2, Tables A2.1, A2.2 and A2.3. They were constructed in consultation with the FBU discussion groups. They conform to the nutritional guidelines for healthy eating described by the Department of Health (1991) and the Health Education Authority (1996a, 1996b, 1997). They also reflect recommendations for diets acceptable to older people (MAFF, 1993; Caroline Walker Trust, 1995). In general, the menus are composed around foods which are quick and easy to prepare and reflect gender differences in attitudes towards food preparation (for example preparation of cod fillets in white sauce, with cooked vegetables for the woman's visitor for the Friday evening meal, compared with poached eggs, bacon and tomato for the man's visitor for Tuesday lunch).

Older couples spend and report consumption well below the Health Education Authority-based limits of 24 units for couples and 10 units for women adopted for the FBU's LCA budgets for adults of working age (Parker, 1998). LCA expenditure on alcohol for single, older women becomes £2.22 a week (6 units), compared with £4.01 (10 units) for lone mothers (Parker, 1998); and £7.31 a week (18 units) for older couples compared with £8.62 (24 units) for couples with children (Parker,1998). Spirits are generally more popular among older

people than beer or wine, whereas young people drink more wine.

1.9   Data sources

The budget standards for food reported here were created using a variety of data sources, of which the main ones are: the National Food Survey (NFS), the Family Expenditure Survey (FES), Dietary Reference Values for Food Energy and Nutrients for the United Kingdom (DRVs), Health Education Authority guidelines on alcohol consumption, and January 1999 food prices (unpublished).

The initial food purchasing profiles were based on NFS purchasing data collected between 1992 and 1995 from 106 households composed of single men; 206 households composed of single women; and 187 couple households. The households were selected on the basis of incomes for older people thought to correspond to the LCA levels of expenditure (see Appendix 1 and Appendix 2, Step One).

1.10   Findings

Food consumption profiles
Tables A2.1, A2.2 and A2.3 in Appendix 2 itemise the contents of illustrative baskets of food, at LCA level, for single women, single men and couples aged 65-74 years. They also provide the basis for the menus in Tables 11, 12 and 13.

The differences in purchases between the different households reflect variations in diet reported in the NFS (MAFF, 1993-97) and the National Diet and Nutrition Survey (Finch et al, 1998). They allow for eating out, for visitors and for preferences expressed by participants in the FBU discussion groups. Amounts are based on food portion sizes, which are estimated as 'large' or 'average' according to portion size data published by the Ministry of Agriculture, Fisheries and Food (MAFF, 1998), and tailored to purchaseable quantities available from supermarkets.

Table 11: Illustrative weekly menus based on the LCA basket of foods: single woman aged 65-74 years

	Sunday	Monday	Tuesday	Wednesday	Thursday	Friday	Saturday
Breakfast	2 Weetabix 2 slices toast fruit juice	2 Weetabix 2 slices toast fruit juice	2 Weetabix 2 slices toast fruit juice	2 Weetabix 2 slices toast fruit juice	2 Weetabix 2 slices toast fruit juice	2 Weetabix 2 slices toast fruit juice	2 Weetabix 2 slices toast fruit juice
Mid-morning	banana	banana	apple	apple	apple	banana	banana
Lunch	roast chicken fillet potatoes carrots cabbage onion gravy apple and sultana crumble and ice-cream	soup salmon, lettuce and mayonnaise sandwich apple	beans on 2 slices toast yoghurt	EAT OUT	EAT OUT	soup cheese and lettuce sandwich apple	2 thin sausages grilled tomato potatoes tomato ketchup 2 slices bread apple
Mid-afternoon	bakewell slice	bakewell slice	scone and butter	roll and marmalade	roll and cheese triangle	scone and butter	bakewell slice
Supper	salmon, lettuce and mayonnaise sandwich tinned fruit salad	pork chop potatoes cabbage carrots gravy 1 slice bread yoghurt	turkey in crumb potatoes peas spinach tomato ketchup 2 slices bread	bacon (2) and ham (1) omelette (4 eggs) potatoes carrots grilled tomatoes (2) 4 slices bread (+VISITOR)	2 thin sausages potatoes peas carrots tomato ketchup 1 slice bread	cod fillet in white sauce potatoes mixed veg cauliflower 2 slices bread 2 satsumas (+VISITOR)	beef stew potatoes cabbage onion gravy 2 slices bread apple and sultana crumble

In addition, tea, coffee, milk, sugar, jam, vegetable oil, reduced fat spread, flour, biscuits, sweets, soft drinks, as per shopping list, are available for consumption throughout the week. (Bread = 1 x 800g loaf + 1 x 400g loaf = 22 + 16 slices = 38 slices total.)

Some meals have been left blank. According to the NFS, this corresponds to the average number of meals eaten away from home, for example with relatives or in a café. The NFS also shows that visitors were present for 10% of meals, and extra food has been added to account for this. (See Appendix 2, Step Two, for details of foods eaten away from home and the presence of visitors.)

Table 12: Illustrative weekly menus based on the LCA basket of foods: single man aged 65-74 years

	Sunday	Monday	Tuesday	Wednesday	Thursday	Friday	Saturday
Breakfast	2 Weetabix 2 slices toast fruit juice	2 Weetabix 2 slices toast fruit juice	2 Weetabix 2 slices toast fruit juice	2 Weetabix 2 slices toast fruit juice	2 Weetabix 2 slices toast fruit juice	2 Weetabix 2 slices toast fruit juice	2 Weetabix 2 slices toast fruit juice
Mid-morning	orange	banana	banana	banana	apple	apple	banana
Lunch	roast chicken potatoes carrots cabbage onion gravy creamed rice pudding	soup corned beef, tomato and mayonnaise sandwich tinned fruit cocktail	poached egg 2 rashers bacon ½ grilled tomato each on 2 toasts (+VISITOR)	soup cheese and pickle sandwich apple	EAT OUT	scrambled egg and beans on 2 toasts tomato ketchup banana	egg sausage 2 rashers bacon beans and potato crunchies tomato ketchup 2 slices bread apple
Mid-afternoon	EAT OUT	2 toast and marmalade	scone and butter	bakewell slice	2 toast and 2 cheese triangles	scone and butter	bakewell slice
Supper	pilchards and tomato on toast apple	stewing steak potatoes carrots cabbage onion gravy bread roll yoghurt	cod fish fingers potatoes peas sprouts tomato ketchup 2 slices bread	pork chop potatoes sprouts mixed veg tomato ketchup 2 slices bread	bangers (3) and mash peas carrots gravy bread roll ice-cream	smoked mackerel potatoes carrots peas mayonnaise 2 slices bread	shepherds pie potatoes mixed veg cabbage bread roll tinned fruit cocktail

In addition, tea, coffee, milk, sugar, jam, vegetable oil, reduced fat spread, flour, biscuits, sweets, soft drinks, as per shopping list, are available for consumption throughout the week.
(Bread = 1 x 400g loaf + 1 x 800g loaf = 16 + 22 slices = 38 slices plus bread rolls.)

Some meals have been left blank. According to the NFS, this corresponds to the average number of meals eaten away from home, for example, with relatives or in a café. The NFS also shows that visitors were present for 3% of meals, and extra food has been added to account for this. (See Appendix 2, Step Two, for details of foods eaten away from home and the presence of visitors.)

Table 13: Illustrative weekly menus based on the LCA basket of foods: couple aged 65-74 years

	Sunday	Monday	Tuesday	Wednesday	Thursday	Friday	Saturday
Breakfast	4 Weetabix 4 slices toast 2 fruit juice	4 Weetabix 4 slices toast 2 fruit juice	4 Weetabix 4 slices toast 2 fruit juice	4 Weetabix 4 slices toast 2 fruit juice	4 Weetabix 4 slices toast 2 fruit juice	4 Weetabix 4 slices toast 2 fruit juice	4 Weetabix 4 slices toast 2 fruit juice
Mid-morning	2 satsumas	2 bananas	2 apples	2 satsumas	2 bananas	2 apples	2 apples
Lunch	roast chicken potatoes cabbage swede onion gravy	2 cheese and pickle sandwiches	2 beans and 2 sausages on toast	2 soup 2 x bacon and tomato (4 slices) sandwiches	EAT OUT	2 ham (4 slices), lettuce and mayonnaise sandwich	2 eggs 2 bacon 4 thin sausages grilled tomato potato crunchies tomato ketchup
	apple and sultana crumble and ice-cream	2 rice puddings	2 yoghurts	2 bananas		2 bananas	3 slices bread
Mid-afternoon	2 satsumas	3 scones, butter and jam (+VISITOR)	2 toasts and jam	2 toast and 2 cheese triangles	EAT OUT	3 bakewell slices (+VISITOR)	2 scones and butter
Supper	2 salmon salads tomato lettuce mayonnaise	2 chicken in onion gravy potatoes cabbage cauliflower 2 slices bread	2 ham omelettes (4 eggs) potatoes peas carrots tomato ketchup	2 beef and onion pies potatoes carrots gravy 2 slices bread	2 turkey in crumb potatoes swede carrots tomato ketchup 2 bread rolls	3 cod in white sauce potatoes peas mixed veg 3 bread rolls (+VISITOR)	2 pork chops potatoes cabbage cauliflower gravy
	4 slices bread	2 apples	2 bread rolls	2 satsumas	2 oranges		tinned pears and ice-cream

In addition, tea, coffee, milk, sugar, jam, vegetable oil, reduced fat spread, flour, biscuits, sweets and soft drinks as per shopping list, are available for consumption throughout the week.
(Bread = 2 x 800g loaves +1 x 400g loaf = 22 + 22 + 16 = 60 slices.)

Some meals have been left blank. According to the NFS, this corresponds to the average number of meals eaten away from home, for example with relatives or in a café. The NFS also shows that visitors were present for 7% of meals, and extra food has been added to account for this. (See Appendix 2, Step Two, for details of foods eaten away from home and the presence of visitors.)

Visitors are assumed to be adults eating 'large' portion sizes. The amounts of butter and margarine are sufficient for spreading on the bread, scones and similar in the baskets. Items such as jam, vegetable oil, flour, biscuits and sweets are not listed in the menus, but are available for use in cooking (together with some milk and sugar) or consumption at the levels indicated by the lists of purchases. An extra Kit-Kat included for the couple household explains their extra expenditure on sweets and chocolate compared with the single-person households.

The food baskets do not include all the items that might be purchased over the course of one week, but are illustrative of the range and quantities of food likely to be purchased. The amounts suggested under one heading might well be exchanged for foods under other headings. For example bread, pasta and potatoes, all important sources of carbohydrate, might be purchased in differing amounts, according to individual preferences, but total expenditure on these items would need to remain roughly the same. Purchases of some items, especially condiments and spices, would be spread over several weeks or months. Total weekly expenditures in Table 9 are therefore illustrative, not absolute, and represent a reasonable minimum for the purchase of a healthy and acceptable diet.

Nutritional adequacy and the use of vitamin and mineral supplements

Table 14 shows the nutritional adequacy of the food baskets for each household type, as percentages of the DRVs (DoH, 1991). The food quantities were adjusted so that the total amounts of energy provided by the foods in each basket correspond to 100% of the Estimated Average Requirement (to within plus or minus 1%), after allowing for waste (10%), foods obtained and eaten outside the household food supply (approximately 5%) and the presence of visitors (3% in single-man households, 10% in single-woman households and 7% in couple households). Where alcohol is included in the diet, the amounts of food (and corresponding expenditures) have been reduced accordingly. These reductions correspond to 5.6%, 2.7% and 4.0% of the energy in the diets of the single men, single women and couples respectively.

For the majority of items, the baskets provide at least 100% of the DRVs. The exceptions are fat and saturated fatty acids (where the objective is to have intakes below 100% of the DRV); pantothenic acid and mono-unsaturated fatty acids in single woman and couple households; and copper in single woman households. The low values for pantothenic acid are due to missing values in the food composition tables and the possibility that the estimated requirement is set too high. The low value for copper is only just under 100%, moreover it is extremely unlikely that intakes at this level would lead to deficiency in healthy older people within the population. The low value for mono-unsaturated fatty acids is not of major dietary concern, although an increase (for example further substitution of oil or poly-unsaturated margarine for butter) would be desirable in relation to long-term health.

Intakes of non-starch polysaccharides (NSP or dietary fibre) are well over 100% of the DRV (17g per person per day). This contrasts with typical intakes of 13.5g per day in men and 11g per day in women in the *National Diet and Nutrition Survey: People aged 65 years and over (*Finch et al, 1998). The levels of NSP in the present baskets were achieved by including substantial quantities of fruit and vegetables, substituting wholemeal bread for some white bread and choosing a high fibre breakfast cereal (Weetabix). These levels would address problems of constipation, common in older people, and reduce risk and symptoms of diverticular disease. There is evidence that the transition from low to high fibre diets is associated with increased flatulence, which may be off-putting for some people (Webb and Copeman, 1996).

The DRV for Vitamin D has been set for this analysis at 2.5mg per day. This level is presumed to be adequate for healthy and mobile older people, who have exposure to sunlight during the summer (April-September) for an average of at least 15 minutes per day, wearing normal British dress. The baskets provide levels of Vitamin D between 137% and 223% of the DRV. For older people who are housebound and those who, for cultural reasons, cover themselves more fully, dietary Vitamin D intakes need to be of the order of 10mg per day, to prevent the development of osteomalacia and to maintain adequate levels of calcium absorption. For some subjects, therefore, use of dietary supplements may be appropriate.

The National Diet and Nutrition Survey of older people (Finch et al, 1998) reported that approximately one third of the participants living outside institutions take non-prescribed dietary supplements, the most common supplement being cod liver oil (which is an excellent source of Vitamin D – one 5ml teaspoonful contains approximately 10 μg). Typical costs of supplements containing suitable quantities of Vitamin D (as well as some other nutrients) are in the order of 30 pence to 50 pence per person per week.

Table 14:   **Adequacy of food purchases**
LCA food baskets
Households aged 65-74 years
January 1999

Nutrient	Percentages of Dietary Reference Values		
	Women	**Men**	**Couples**
Energy	100.7	100.0	100.0
Macronutrients			
Protein	152.7	165.3	152.7
Fat	86.6	97.3	92.0
Saturated fatty acids	91.3	99.5	99.8
Mono-unsaturated fatty acids	87.1	100.9	93.7
Poly-unsaturated fatty acids	101.0	112.1	101.3
Carbohydrate	110.6	101.1	106.4
Non-milk extrinsic sugars	129.6	115.3	126.8
Non-starch polysaccharides	136.1	151.9	134.7
Vitamins			
Vitamin A	211.7	183.0	156.4
Thiamin	240.1	235.7	246.4
Riboflavin	171.3	165.7	162.5
Nicotinic acid equivalents	229.3	228.5	217.1
Folate	197.8	206.8	203.6
Vitamin B_6	225.5	219.2	220.5
Vitamin B_{12}	251.0	544.4	258.1
Pantothenic acid	82.1	104.8	94.9
Vitamin C	270.8	295.9	317.8
Vitamin D	170.9	223.3	137.2
Vitamin E	364.8	340.4	325.6
Minerals			
Calcium	122.7	138.2	130.1
Iron	148.0	183.8	152.1
Sodium	198.3	279.2	210.0
Potassium	104.7	115.9	107.6
Magnesium	125.0	129.5	119.6
Copper	104.2	122.0	109.5
Zinc	131.6	121.6	108.2
Phosphorus	242.0	288.5	255.3
Fruit and vegetable portions per day	5.3	5.2	5.5

Non-milk extrinsic sugars (mainly white sugar) and sodium are present in excess of 100% of the DRV, although ideally they should be less than 100% for optimal health. In the context of the LCA baskets, however, it is very difficult to achieve these objectives without radically altering the food profiles, due mainly to the widespread presence of sugar and salt in many processed foods, particularly lower cost foods. This is a clear indication that pressure needs to be brought to bear on the food industry to reduce these substances in processed foods.

Fruit and vegetable consumption has been adjusted to achieve the Health Education Authority objective of 5 portions (at least 400g in total) per person per day (HEA, 1997).

Dental problems
Nutritional adequacy can be affected by dental problems. The menus presented in this report include a number of foods which may present problems for people with few or no natural teeth. It is possible, however, to substitute foods that are more easily chewed for items which present difficulties. For example bread could be substituted for toast at breakfast; bananas or pears for apples (bearing in mind that other fruit may cost more than apples); and cooked vegetables for salad. Difficulties may persist, however, for carcass meat and poultry, and food preparation may require the use of recipes and kitchen equipment which address these problems.

In Volume 2 of the *National Diet and Nutrition Survey: People aged 65 years and over* (Steele et al, 1998), it was reported that 41% of people aged 65-74 were edentate (that is, had none of their natural teeth) and of those who still had their own teeth 25% had them in one jaw only. Problems relating to ability to chew, and food and mouth dryness were found to be greater if the person had no teeth; energy and nutrient intakes were higher in those with more teeth and those with more occluding pairs (that is, opposite teeth in top and lower jaws). The percentages of those who eat foods "with difficulty or cannot eat at all" varied in the dentate sample from 5% for toast to 19% for raw carrots, 20% for well-done steaks, 24% for nuts and 25% for apples. Corresponding values in the edentate

sample were 13%, 41%, 33%, 42% and 50% respectively. This has important implications regarding the ability of many older people to achieve a healthy and balanced diet, even where there are no restrictions on food spending.

1.11 Acceptability of the food baskets

Draft food baskets at the LCA standard were presented to the discussion groups for comment and feedback. The initial reactions were that the content was acceptable, but that some items were priced too cheaply, which is particularly important where a branded item (for example Weetabix) is felt to be the only acceptable choice.

Participants also expressed certain preferences, some of which are taken account of in the menus:

- Light breakfasts of toast and cereal, rather than cooked breakfasts. Weetabix is a common choice, but is interchangeable with other high fibre breakfast cereals.

- One main meal and one light meal a day, with snacks in between.

- The main meal is often in the evening, but is interchangeable with lunch.

- A Sunday roast.

- Main meals consisting of meat, potatoes and two vegetables.

- Potatoes with most main meals, in preference to pasta or rice.

- Bread consumed frequently.

- Simple meals, which do not require long or intricate preparation, particularly in the single-man households.

- Little baking. Flour, eggs and margarine are included in the food baskets, in case of need, but the amounts are less for the man-only households than for the couple and woman-only households.

The acceptability of the food baskets and menus is predicated on the assumption that preferred items within the same food categories can be exchanged – for example brussels sprouts can be substituted for cabbage, lamb cutlets for pork chops – although finding equivalent foods at the same low cost may prove difficult. The avoidance of cooking by most men was confirmed in the discussion groups and is reflected in the food choices in the single man's menus, which require minimal preparation (for example oven-ready shepherd's pie rather than a home-made beef stew).

1.12 LCA food baskets compared with MBA food baskets

The LCA total home food budgets for the single woman (£20.09) and the couple (£36.91) are below the inflation-adjusted values for the corresponding MBA budgets (£20.87 and £41.41 respectively). The differences between the LCA and MBA budgets for the single woman are very small. This may be due to differences in method between the two projects. The MBA budgets were based on individual surveys conducted at a time when the National Diet and Nutrition Survey data were not available; the LCA budgets, by contrast, are based on NFS data, corroborated using nationally representative data from the National Diet Nutrition Survey and from the FBU's discussion groups. The choice of foods in the MBA budget for older women now appears more restricted than is probably appropriate for the MBA level in 1999. The MBA budgets for older people need to be revised in line with newer research practices (for example selection of appropriate NFS samples, corroboration using National Diet and Nutrition Survey data, use of discussion groups for validation). This should produce food budgets at levels that are more consistent between household types, income bands and living standards.

2 Clothing

2.1 LCA clothing standard

The LCA clothing standard for men and women in the 65-74 years age group is defined as a level which includes clothing of sufficient quantity and quality for its wearers to feel comfortable in all weathers. The wardrobe consists of everyday clothing, casual clothing, holiday clothing and a smart outfit for special occasions. Extra top clothing and thermal underwear provide additional warmth in housing which, at LCA level, is assumed to be heated to

20°C (Zone 1), compared with 21°C (Zone 1) at MBA level.

2.2 Budget schedules

Detailed clothing schedules are given in Appendix 4. These include descriptions of every item: retailers, prices in January 1999, required quantities of each item and the length of time the garments are expected to last.

2.3 Second-hand and sales clothing

In budget standard methodology, second-hand clothing and clothing bought in sales are excluded. This is due to the wide variation in the prices of second-hand goods and difficulties estimating the length of time a second-hand garment is likely to last. Although older people do buy sales goods, it cannot be assumed that the required goods are available at the required time and at the right prices.

Many group participants confirmed their use of charity shops and the habit of shopping in sales for some of their clothing. Older people described their search for style and quality, 'especially labels', in charity shops. New goods at bargain prices were sometimes obtained by making numerous trips to a particular shop, in the hope that the price of a particular garment would eventually be reduced in the sales. Occasionally, this resulted in the purchase of winter coats in summer for wear the following winter.

2.4 LCA compared with MBA

The LCA clothing budgets contain less variety than the MBA budgets developed by the FBU in 1991 (Bradshaw, 1993) and 1994 (Parker, 1995). The number and range of garments have been pared down and some of the garments are of lower quality. Where the quality is similar, clothing lifetimes at LCA level are extended. At both standards, the wardrobes contain sufficient clothing to allow for regular laundering.

2.5 Pricing

Items of clothing were priced at retail outlets suggested by the discussion groups and using market research information. Local retailers provided

**Table 15: Summary clothing budgets
Households aged 65-74 years
LCA standard, January 1999, £ week**

Clothing	Single woman	Single man	Married couple
Outerwear	2.50	2.47	4.97
Underwear/nightwear	1.57	0.66	2.23
Accessories	0.09	0.13	0.22
Footwear	0.79	0.79	1.59
Clothing repair kit	0.07	0.07	0.10
Total clothing	**5.03**	**4.12**	**9.11**

Due to rounding, there may be some discrepancies between figures shown and their totals.

information on best-selling lines and economy lines for older people. National retailers with national pricing policies were used wherever possible, for example C&A, Poundstretcher and Shoe City. Home shopping catalogues were also used (sometimes for convenience), such as Daxon, Empire Stores, Index Extra, and JD Williams. In addition some prices were collected from market stalls in York.

2.6 Types of clothes

Each household member is allocated a separate clothing list (Table 15). The clothing categories are:

- outerwear (includes coats and jackets, and main clothing)
- underwear and nightwear
- accessories
- footwear

Man's clothing
The man's wardrobe includes a classic gabardine suit for special occasions and a gabardine blazer for smart casual wear. The suit is expected to last seven years. Also included are three pairs of winter trousers, two pairs of summer trousers, four long-sleeve and two short-sleeve shirts, and a number of polo neck cotton t-shirts. Outdoor coats include a teflon jacket, a padded ¾-length winter jacket and a water-resistant cagoule. The multiples of underwear and nightwear are sufficient for once-a-week laundering. Holiday clothing includes shorts, swimwear and trainers. Footwear includes shoes suitable for town walking and smart occasions, and wellingtons for gardening activities and wet weather.

Woman's clothing
The woman's wardrobe includes a woollen winter coat with hood, a smart classic woollen coat, and a water-resistant anorak. Also included are a two-piece polyester suit and a velour winter dress for special occasions. Casual wear includes skirts, tops and trousers, sweatshirts and t-shirts, summer dresses and swimwear. Footwear includes winter and summer shoes, court shoes and town walking shoes, boots, wellingtons and slippers.

Each household has a basic clothing repair kit.

3 Personal care

3.1 LCA personal care standard

At the MBA standard, the personal care budget for men and women in the 65-74 years age group is intended to promote physical, psychological and social well-being. At the LCA standard the goal is similar, but at a lower cost. The budget categories are as follows:

- healthcare
- personal accessories
- personal hygiene
- cosmetics

3.2 Budget schedules

Detailed personal care schedules are given in Appendix 4. These include descriptions of every item: retailers, prices in January 1999, the required quantities of each item and the length of time it is expected to last.

3.3 Healthcare

The FBU budgets meet the 'normal' health needs of typical older people aged 65-74 years. According to the General Household Survey (GHS), the average person in this age group is independent, mobile and active. On average they visit the doctor six times a year, have one day restricted activity a month, and (with few exceptions) are able to go outdoors, walk down the road, get up and downstairs, bath, shower, or wash, and dress unaided (ONS, 1997a). The 1991 GHS supplement, *People aged 65 and over*, found that 83% of 65- to 69-year-olds and 81% of 70- to 74-year-olds were in 'good' or 'fairly good health'; an estimated 74% had no difficulty hearing; 86% (including those with glasses or contact lenses) had no difficulty seeing; 84% had contact with neighbours at least once a week; and 49% had contact with neighbours every day or nearly every day (ONS, 1994, Tables 12, 20, 27, 58, 59).

Although most healthcare in the UK is free of charge through the National Health Service (NHS), certain goods and services are chargeable, unless the patient has a low income or is receiving Income Support. Prescription items for all pensioners are free, regardless of income, but in January 1999 eye and dental care were not. The FBU classifies chargeable healthcare items under 'variable costs' and these are shown in Part Four, Table 37.

Basic first-aid kit and home medications box
There is no health standard for domestic first-aid kits in the UK. The LCA budget standard includes a basic first-aid kit assembled following *Which? Report* recommendations (Consumer Association, 1997a), as shown below:

- sealable tin, or plastic container
- cotton bandages, 5cm and 7.5cm
- crepe bandages, 5cm
- large gauze swabs for use as eye-pads
- gauze swabs for cleaning
- plasters

- safety pins
- strong scissors
- surgical tape
- triangular bandage
- wound dressings
- first aid information book
- thermometer
- calamine cream

Antiseptic cream is excluded, because it is said to slow down the healing process. Following consultation with health professionals and pharmacists, paracetamol, cold powders, and indigestion tablets have been added to the home medication box.

Suncreams are included in the budgets at MBA and LCA level, because of the risk of skin cancer (Consumer Association, 1996). Those most at risk are people with pale skin. Older people, although not typical sun bathers, are assumed to be out and about most days and for prolonged periods during summer day trips and holidays. The amounts of suncream included are limited but sufficient to cover the holiday period. The aim is to give a balanced view as exposure to sunlight is also recommended in moderation to provide Vitamin D. The Department of Health recommends that: "If adequate exposure to sunlight is not possible, Vitamin D supplementation should be considered, especially during the winter and early spring" (DoH, 1992a).

3.4 Personal hygiene

Standards of personal hygiene built into the baskets of goods and services are based on recommendations by the Health Education Authority and reflect the view that personal hygiene is essential to healthy living and that a regular routine is needed to keep the body clean. The standard suggests that hair should be washed with a mild shampoo once a week and teeth should be brushed with fluoride toothpaste and a medium nylon toothbrush twice a day.

Dental care

Toothbrushes, toothpaste, sterilising tablets and dental floss are included in the budgets. Toothbrushes are replaced every three months. Dentists generally agree that a compact head is better than a large head, with soft to medium, rounded nylon filaments; and many recommend the use of dental floss at least once a week (Consumer Association, 1997b). Toothpaste varies considerably in price. A standard value-for-money fluoride toothpaste tested by *Which? Report* (Consumer Association, 1997c) is included.

Partial removable dentures are worn by 48% of people with teeth, aged 65 years and older (and living outside institutions). Most common are partial 'upper' dentures (Steele et al, 1998). According to the discussion group participants, methods of cleaning dentures vary from soap, bleach and soot to sterilising tablets. Based on the assumption that most older people have some form of denture, sterilising tablets are included in the personal hygiene budget.

Hair care

According to market research (Mintel, 1996a), most shampoo users aged 65 plus are 'light users', meaning that they wash their hair once a week. Among better-off older women, the weekly shampoo and set at the hairdresser's remains popular. Just over half of all older women but very few older men, use hair conditioners. The hair care budget assumes washing and conditioning, with a mild shampoo and conditioner, once a week. Hair is trimmed six times a year for older men and three times a year for older women. Older women have a permanent wave treatment twice a year. The cost of hairdressing is based on 'pensioner day' prices.

Body care

Body care includes soap, disposable razors, nail clippers, handcream and deodorants. *Marketing Intelligence* (Mintel, 1996b) reports that the use of deodorants continues to grow for men and women. By 1996, 91% of women and 85% of men used deodorants. Usage, however, starts to decline significantly from the age of 55 years. In the 65 plus age range, 76% of women and 60% of men used a deodorant product. A small number of deodorants

are included in the basic LCA budget, less for men than for women. Disposable razors, for daily use, are included for men and a small number of razors for women. Most men in the discussion groups preferred to use disposable razors rather than electric razors or retractable blades. Usually they said that one disposable razor lasted one week.

3.5 Personal accessories

Basic items such as suitcases, wallets, handbags, umbrellas, watches and clocks are expected to last longer at LCA level than at MBA level. Apart from wedding rings, no precious jewellery is included at either standard, but a small amount of costume jewellery is included. Market research reports a growth in sales of costume jewellery (Euromonitor, 1996a). A shopping trolley is also included.

Sunglasses (UVA/UVB protection) are included, for health and safety reasons, although the number of people buying sunglasses decreases significantly with age (Euromonitor, 1996b). Personal accessories also include a hairdryer, largely on the basis of discussion group comments, although market research information indicates that ownership of hairdryers is only 46% at age 65 plus (Mintel, 1996c).

It is worth noting that Mintel market research categorises all older people together, whereas in reality there may be significant variations between the consumption patterns of younger (65-74 years) and older (74 plus years) people.

3.6 Cosmetics

Most older woman use facial skin care products sparingly, for example 75% use moisturising creams (Mintel, 1996d) and 43% use handcream or lotion (Mintel, 1996e). Make-up is used by women of all ages, but the highest use is among young women, especially teenagers. Nevertheless, most older women use some form of make-up. Lipsticks are used by 86% of women aged 55 to 64 years, declining to 77% from the age of 65 years, while face powder usage increases in the older age range. Foundation creams are used by 47% of older women (Mintel, 1996f).

The low-income discussion groups confirmed this level of use. The LCA budgets include lipstick, face powder, facial moisturiser and handcream. Purchase of a low-price perfume is included once in three years, for occasional use, or to be given as a gift. After-shave is included for men (Table 16).

Table 16: **Summary personal care budgets Households aged 65-74 years LCA standard, January 1999 £ week**

	Single woman	Single man	Married Couple
Healthcare	0.37	0.37	0.75
Personal hygiene	1.68	1.30	2.98
Personal accessories	0.39	0.22	0.61
Cosmetics	0.18	0.10	0.28
Total personal care	**2.63**	**1.99**	**4.62**

Due to rounding, there may be some discrepancies between figures shown and their totals.

4   Household goods

4.1   LCA household goods standard

The household goods budget for single people and couples aged 65-74 years sets the basic amounts of furniture, furnishing and equipment necessary to reach the LCA standard, according to dwelling dimensions and family size. The budget categories are as follows:

- furniture

- floor coverings

- household textiles and soft furnishings

- gas and electrical appliances and repairs

- kitchen equipment and hardware

- stationery and paper goods

- toilet paper, cleaning materials and products

- gardening tools, DIY tools and materials

- home security

4.2   Budget schedules

Detailed household goods schedules are to be found in Appendix 4. These include descriptions of every item: retailers, prices in January 1999, required

quantities and the length of time each item is expected to last.

4.3   How capital costs are estimated

Every family spends money on durable goods (capital expenditures) as well as consumables. Durable goods, in general, cost more than consumables in the first instance, but last longer. Some cost far more but are nonetheless necessary. The household Goods budget includes many such 'capital' items, the weekly costs of which are estimated by dividing each item's purchase price by its life expectancy in years and weeks. For example, the Household goods schedule in Appendix 4 starts with a three-piece suite, unit price £799.99, expected lifetime 15 years. This implies a yearly cost of £53.33 and an average weekly cost of £1.03. In line with budget standard methodology, no allowance is made, at this point, for the costs of credit. These are shown under Variable Costs.

4.4   Furniture

The scope for reducing the number of furniture items in the LCA older people's budgets, by comparison with their MBA equivalents, was found to be limited. Instead, lifetimes have been extended, in some cases beyond the manufacturers' recommendations. For example, manufacturers suggest replacement of beds every 17 years (Mintel, 1996g) and mattresses every 10 years, compared with LCA lifetimes of 20 years for older people's beds and 10 years for mattresses. In general, items of furniture with no fabric content have been set to last 25 years, which is three years longer than in the FBU's original MBA pensioner budgets. Following comments from the discussion groups, however, the three-piece suite and bathroom cabinet were adjusted to shorter lifetimes than previously, mainly on grounds of inferior quality. Bedside cabinets have been added to the furniture list. A one-bedroom flat includes a single bed plus a folding guest bed in the bedroom; a two-bedroom house includes a double bed in the main bedroom and a single bed in the guest room.

The LCA criteria are met by using cheaper lines (economy brands or best-buy furniture lines), while ensuring that quality is acceptable. Beds at LCA standard are basic, with headboards but without drawers. Spare beds are unsuitable for everyday use. The furniture is not self-assembly. It was priced at MFI and high-street catalogue shops, such as Argos and Index. No second-hand goods are included, although older people in the discussion groups reported having inherited second-hand pieces from family and friends and having given furniture away after moving to a smaller house. Table 17 compares the MBA and LCA furniture standards for single and couple householders, living in a two-bedroom house.

4.5 Floor coverings

All the floors are carpeted, except in the kitchen, which has a vinyl floor covering. Carpeting in the living areas is 50/50% wool/synthetic, for hard wear. Carpeting in bedrooms and bathrooms is foam-backed. Carpet lifetimes have been extended beyond the manufacturers' recommendations. For example, the living-room carpet is expected to last 13 years, compared with 11 years at MBA level.

Floor coverings were priced at Allied Carpets and include underlay and fitting.

4.6 Textiles and soft furnishings

This section includes quilts, quilt covers, pillows, pillowcases, sheets, towels, curtains, net curtains, curtain rails and lampshades. Curtains are thermal backed, blinds are included for the kitchen and bathroom windows, and a pair of net curtains is included for the downstairs window facing the street. Household linen is sufficient in quantity for weekly laundering and household size, but limited in the quantity designated for guests. At LCA level the replacement rate of household linen was adjusted in line with discussion group validation comments. Guest bed-sheets are given a life of 15 years, whereas everyday sheets are replaced after nine years. Towels last, on average, five years. A range of pricing outlets was used, including high street catalogues (Argos and Index) and others (Poundstretcher and Woolworths).

Table 17: **MBA and LCA furniture standards compared**
Households aged 65-74 years
Two-bedroom house

	MBA	Lifetime years	LCA	Lifetime years
Kitchen	fitted		fitted	
Living room	three-piece suite	17	three-piece suite	15
	tv/video unit	17	tv unit	25
	coffee tables	22	coffee tables	25
	table and four chairs	17	table and four chairs	25
	glass top display unit	22	wall unit	25
	three-drawer base unit	22	display cabinet	25
	bookcase	22	sideboard	25
	two folding chairs	17	bookcase	25
Main bedroom	single/double divan with drawers	15	double divan/headboard	20
	double tall wardrobes	17	mattress replacement	10
	double five-drawer chest	17	double tall wardrobe	25
	single three-drawer chest	17	double five-drawer chest	25
			single three-drawer chest	25
			bedside three-drawer chest	25
Spare bedroom	single divan with drawers	22	single divan/headboard	25
	combination wardrobe	22	combination wardrobe	25
	single three-drawer chest	22	double five-drawer chest	25
	short wide bookshelf	22	short wide bookshelf	25
			bedside three-drawer chest	25
			tall boy unit	25
Bathroom	cabinet	22	cabinet	20

4.7   Gas and electrical goods and repairs

All the budgets include a washing machine, fridge freezer and gas cooker. Inclusion is based partly on ownership rates and partly on public attitudes, taking account of the opinions expressed in the group discussions. The most useful surveys are the FES, the GHS and the Family Resources Survey (FRS). The FES collects details of expenditure on a small range of durable goods, by family type, across the income range, including 'one man and one woman, retired, mainly on benefits' and 'one adult, retired, mainly on benefits'. The GHS has expenditure variables for 'one adult over 60' and 'two adults over 60'. The FRS has access to durables by income level and age but not by specific age groups, for example: 'one adult over pension age', 'two adults both (or one) over pension age'. Consumer reports publish ownership rates by demographic subgroups but some report factors like class and the presence of children, which are irrelevant here. Occasionally, life-stage factors, such as 'post family/retired', or special groups such as 'families on a tight budget', provide useful indicators of consumer spending.

An 80% ownership test
In this section, the 80% ownership test was applied to washing machines, tumble dryers, microwaves, dishwashers and fridge freezers. Over 90% of older couples have access to a washing machine and fridge freezer, but for single older people the rates of access are lower, varying according to the statistical source used (63% or 70% have a washing machine and 77% have a fridge freezer). Microwaves are owned by

42% or 47% of single older people and 52% or 61% or 70% of older couples. Tumble dryers also have low access rates, which differ between surveys (ONS, 1997a, Table 3.21; ONS, 1997b, Table 9.4; DSS, 1997, Tables 2.9, 3.8).

Other appliances
All the households own a gas cooker, with the exception of the single tenants in all-electric accommodation.

Pricing
The benchmark rates at which essential appliances are replaced are based on market research and manufacturers' recommendations, where the information is available. Replacement rates at the LCA standard for pensioners, where low use is expected, are reduced below the benchmark rates; and lifetimes of some appliances are extended through the inclusion of a repair or service budget.

Appliances were priced at a range of suppliers, including Northern Electric and Gas, Yorkshire Electricity Board, Index and Argos.

Repairs and servicing
The decision to include a repair budget was taken on safety grounds and from information gathered in the discussion groups. The costs of repairs and services vary greatly. Many service engineers do not identify a call-out charge separately, but add it to the labour charge. Estimated labour costs, commonly needed spare parts and VAT are shown in Table 18.

Table 18:   **Repair and servicing of household goods**
Households aged 65-74 years
LCA standard, January 1999

Item	Lifetime years	Labour £	Parts £	Total including VAT £
Gas cooker, service	17	48.00	0.00	56.40
Washing machine service, replace drain pump	7½	45.00	15.00	70.50
Vacuum cleaner	16	9.00	14.00	27.03

4.8 Kitchen equipment and hardware

This section covers the following:

- crockery, glassware and cutlery

- kitchen equipment and utensils

- storage and cleaning hardware

- household consumables

- other hardware

At LCA standard the lists have been reduced to basic requirements and priced mainly at Argos, Index, the Co-op, Woolworths, York Market and Poundstretcher. Some economy lines were used and lifetimes adjusted to compensate for lower quality. In other cases lifetimes of good quality items were increased, or followed manufacturers' guarantees.

Crockery, glassware and cutlery
At the MBA standard, quantities and replacement rates of hardware were based largely on the Swedish budget standard. At the LCA standard the lists have been reduced to basic requirements and priced at high street catalogue stores, such as Argos and Index, hardware sections of Sainsbury's, Kwik Save, the Co-op and through home catalogue shopping. Some economy lines were used and lifetimes adjusted, where necessary, to compensate for lower quality. Other items follow the manufacturer's guarantees.

Kitchen equipment and utensils
Sufficient quantities of tableware have been included for general household use, and for special occasion family meals. Basic baking and cooking equipment, weighing scales and pots and pans are also included.

Storage and cleaning hardware
This section includes containers for food, bread, cakes, lunches and kitchen waste, plus cleaning equipment such as household brushes and dustbins. Some storage boxes are assumed to be re-usable plastic containers which originally came with food in them.

Household consumables
These include candles, cling-film, foil, paper napkins and enough batteries to run battery-powered items.

Other hardware
This section contains items such as ironing boards, clothes-airers, bathroom scales and hot-water bottles. They were priced in discount stores or catalogue stores, at lower cost than the MBA standard.

4.9 Stationery and paper goods

The number of paper goods in the MBA budgets (Christmas and birthday cards, envelopes and writing paper, note books etc) has been reduced to a basic level. But sufficient quantities remain to meet the requirements of older households.

4.10 Toilet paper, cleaning materials and products

In order to meet the LCA standard, the range and choice of MBA products have been reduced. Manufacturers' recommended amounts have been used to estimate the amounts of soap powder required and small amounts of fabric conditioner are also included. There is no allocation for laundry or launderette costs. As a standard, one roll of toilet paper per person per week is allowed for.

4.11 Gardening, DIY, tools and materials

A small set of gardening tools is included in the budget standard (Table 19). A flat without a garden is allocated a watering can and trowel/fork set for indoor plants. A house with a garden is allocated a lawn mower, hand shears, pruners, a garden broom and sufficient tools to tend a garden lawn and a small flower bed. Plants and seeds are included in the leisure budget, Section 6.

A basic DIY tool-kit and materials are also included. Examples of tools include screwdriver set, hammer, tape, stanley knife, hacksaw, paint brushes, rollers and step-stool. There is also enough paint to 'patch up' the internal decoration between professional decorators' visits. The pricing of tools and paints was mainly at Woolworths stores. The housing

Table 19:   Summary household goods budgets
Households aged 65-74 years
LCA standard, January 1999, £ week

	Single owner	Single tenant	Couple owners	Couple tenants
Furniture	2.33	1.97	2.33	2.33
Floor coverings	2.02	0.89	2.02	1.45
Textiles	1.09	0.99	1.29	1.34
Gas/electrical equipment and repairs	1.58	1.58	1.69	1.69
Kitchen equipment and hardware	1.02	1.02	1.02	1.02
Stationery and paper goods	0.44	0.44	0.44	0.44
Toilet paper, cleaning materials and products	1.49	1.49	2.26	2.26
Gardening, DIY, tools and materials	0.26	0.15	0.26	0.26
Home security	0.03	0.03	0.03	0.03
Total household goods	**10.26**	**8.55**	**11.33**	**10.81**

Due to rounding, there may be some discrepancies between figures shown and their totals.

budget standard in Part Four provides for a basic level of internal and external decoration by professionals, at low frequency rates.

4.12 Home security

A smoke alarm, window locks and door bolts are included in all the properties, for security reasons.

5   Household services

5.1   LCA household services standard

The LCA household services standard provides householders aged 65-74 years with a low-cost level of basic services including:

- postage

- telephone

- window cleaning

- shoe repairs and dry-cleaning

5.2   Budget schedules

Details of each service, description, frequency and cost can be found in Appendix 4.

5.3   Postage

The postage budget has been estimated using information on average spending provided by the Post Office, weighted to allow a realistic sum for low-income consumers. According to Royal Mail Domestic Consumer Mail Records for 1997 (Frances, 1998), UK households spent on average:

- £15.86 on first class stamps and £13.60 on second class stamps

- £1.30 on letters over 60g

- £1.95 on parcel post

- £1.35 on Christmas cards to other countries

The amounts spent by low-income households are likely to be below the average. Comments in the discussion groups ranged from almost nil to an average of two or three stamps a week. Table 20 summarises the LCA postage standard for older people.

5.4   Telephone

Surveys show that about 97% of older couples and 89% of older single people possess a telephone (ONS, 1997a, Table 3.8; ONS, 1997b, Table 3.21; DSS, 1997, Table 2.9), compared with 84% of low-income households in general (DSS, 1997, Table 3.8).

Table 20: **Summary postage budget**
Households aged 65-74 years
LCA Standard, January 1999

	Item cost	Single person		Couple	
	£	Items year	£ week	Items year	£ week
First class stamps	0.26	26	0.13	51	0.26
Second class stamps	0.20	35	0.13	70	0.27
Letter post, 200g	0.60	1	0.01	1	0.01
Parcel post, 350g	0.92	1	0.02	1	0.02
Airmail letter, zone 1, 20g	0.63	1	0.01	2	0.02
Airmail letter, Europe, 40g	0.44	1	0.01	2	0.02
Average weekly cost			**0.31**		**0.59**

Due to rounding, there may be some discrepancies between figures shown and their totals.

All the households in this report (both single men and women and couples) are assumed to own their telephones. The LCA telephone standard is calculated from statistics showing the average length of domestic calls and the average number of minutes for which households use their phone lines each day (Information obtained from British Telecom in 1998). It is assumed that the average duration of calls is the same for all users, but that low-income users make fewer calls. It is also assumed that older people do not own mobile phones, although they occasionally make calls to mobile users, such as tradesmen.

The method of estimating the 1991 MBA telephone standard used average domestic accounts, weighted for household size and composition. Since then, better information has led to a more precise method of calculating cost. For the 1999

pensioner budget the FBU stipulate the number of calls made per household per week. In addition, changes in the detail of the telephone standard now mean that past telephone budget standards are not strictly comparable with present levels. Detail changes include the costing of a purchased telephone (formerly in the leisure goods budget), the exclusion of call box charges (based on discussions with older people), and no account taken of the costs of installing a line for new users (which happens rarely). Lastly, single and couple households are given the same number of calls on the basis that the number of calls in single households equals the number in two people households.

In Table 21, the telephone budget of £45.11 a quarter is shown as a weekly cost of £3.47 for single and couple households.

Table 21: **Summary telephone budget**
Calls and £ week
Households aged 65-74 years, LCA Standard, January 1999

Calls	UK local	UK national	Fixed to mobile	Calls abroad	Cost week
A Average number of calls (middle-range UK households)	154.00	3.00	1.40	0.25	
B Average number of calls LCA, older people	12.00	2.00	0.50	0.00	
Costs	£	£	£	£	£
C Total cost £ week including VAT	0.88	0.36	0.15	0.00	1.39
D Weekly line rental + VAT					2.06
E Average weekly cost of telephone purchase every 15 years					0.02
Total weekly cost = C+D+E					**£3.47**

Table 22: Summary household services budgets
Households aged 65-74 years
LCA standard, January 1999, £ week

	Single man	Single woman	Couple
Postage	0.31	0.31	0.60
Telephone expenses (including VAT)	3.47	3.47	3.47
Window cleaning	1.50	1.50	1.50
Shoe repairs	0.05	0.06	0.11
Dry cleaning	0.08	0.07	0.15
Total household services	**5.41**	**5.41**	**5.82**

Due to rounding, there may be some discrepancies between figures shown and their totals.

5.5 Window cleaning

The discussion groups indicated that many older people use the services of a window cleaner, but only for external cleaning. They reported costs of between £3 and £5 per fortnight. The figures for window cleaning in Table 22 are based on local costs in York.

5.6 Shoe repairs and dry-cleaning

These are included at a basic level (Table 22), the discussion groups having indicated that they are not common costs. Nowadays, most shoe soles and heels are manufactured out of synthetic materials and the shoes are disposed of when in need of repair. One shoe repair every two years per person is included in the budgets. To economise, the LCA standard includes the costs of stick-on soles and heels instead of cobblers' charges.

The use of dry-cleaning services has also changed during the last decade. Clothing manufacturers increasingly produce garments that are washable rather than dry-clean only. Also, for garments that are dry-clean only, there has been a growth in the number of coin-op machines for public use. Nevertheless, many older people prefer to have their coats, jackets and suits professionally dry-cleaned at a high street shop. The LCA standard provides for one suit or coat for each person to be cleaned every two years, priced at Sketchley Cleaners.

6 Leisure

6.1 Leisure as part of health promotion

The FBU leisure standard (leisure goods plus leisure activities) aims to promote a health-promoting balance between physical activities, social activities and relaxation. According to medical experts, regular exercise promotes good health. Activities such as walking, cycling, housework and gardening all contribute to the exercise needed for healthy living. Yet most people's leisure time is mainly accounted for by sedentary activities, such as reading, watching television and listening to music.

The *Health Survey for England* (White et al, 1993) found evidence of a disturbing lack of physical well-being in older people. For example:"50% of women aged 65 to 74 years did not have sufficient strength in their thigh muscles to stand (*up*) from a chair without using their arms." One of the *Health of the Nation* targets is the development of strategies which will increase physical activities, regardless of age and ability (DoH, 1992a, 1992b). According to the report *Eating well for older people* (Caroline Walker Trust, 1995) regular exercise can have significant beneficial effects on muscle tone and appetite. Prompt resumption of an active life-style after bouts of illness is also important. "Older people should be encouraged to undertake regular physical activity, such as walking, as this strengthens and builds up muscle and bone and increases calorie requirements, which increases appetite" (Caroline Walker Trust, 1995).

6.2 LCA leisure standard

The LCA leisure standard for men and women aged 65-74 years covers the following broad range of leisure goods and leisure activities:

Leisure goods

- television, audio, video and repairs
- books, newspapers, magazines
- household games
- hobbies
- seasonal items
- garden plants, houseplants, and cut flowers

Leisure activities

- sports and other activities
- arts, entertainment, outings
- holiday expenses

6.3 Budget schedules

Detailed leisure goods and leisure activities schedules are given in Appendix 4. These include descriptions of every item (retailers' prices in January 1999, required quantity and the length of time they are expected to last) plus leisure activities schedules (description, frequency and costs).

6.4 Television, audio, video and repairs

The inclusion of durables in the LCA budget standard is based on the 80% ownership test for key durables already referred to, wherever the necessary information is available. As before, if 80% or more of households in a particular age range own a durable, that durable is included in the LCA budget for that age range and household type. So a television is included in the budget standard of all pensioner households in the age range 65-74 years, whereas video recorders are restricted to couples.

Television (including licence)
Given that older people watch television for 35 hours (on average) each week (ONS, 1997c), it is hardly surprising that televisions are found in about 98% of single older person households, and about 100% of couple households (ONS, 1997a, Table 3.21; DSS, 1997, Table 2.9). In general, neither socio-economic status nor low income appears to cause any significant reduction in ownership rates (DSS, 1997, Table 3.8). Market research trends (Mintel, 1996h) indicate that television viewing is a growing leisure activity. Viewing outside conventional viewing times has also increased, due to ownership of videos, with the result that pre-recording materials have become a vast industry. The budget includes the purchase of a TV colour licence, which in January 1999 cost £97.50 for one year.

Video recorders
In line with evidence from the GHS (1996), video recorders are included for couples but not for single older people (Table 23). The inclusion of video recorders in the LCA standard for older people is contentious, because the survey data is inconsistent. Single older people have a low ownership rate – as low as 33% – but ownership by couples is between 58% and 80%. Ownership level, however, can be expected to increase in the future. The GHS (1996) figures show rises in ownership levels for older people over the previous year of 4% for couples and 7% for single people. The overall statistical trend towards higher ownership rates was borne out by the presence of video owners in the FBU group discussions. Ownership rates in the groups indicated that single people aged 65-74 years rarely have videos, but couples overwhelmingly do have them. In general, however, there is a low statistical rate of access to video recorders in low-income families (60% according to the FRS).

Table 23: **Percentages of older people with access to a video recorder**

Source	Single %	Couples %
FES (1996-97, Table 9.4)	32.9	57.3
GHS (1996, Table 3.21)	42.0	80.0
FRS (1995-96, Table 2.9)	35.0	68.0
FRS (1995-96, Table 3.8	60.0	

Source: ONS (1997a, 1997b); DSS (1997)

Audio equipment

Other audio equipment included in the budgets includes a portable radio/cassette player and a mini hi-fi. After watching television, listening to the radio remains the nation's most popular home-based leisure activity. In 1993-94, according to the GHS, an estimated 91% of men and 88% of woman listened to the radio for an average of 16 hours each week (ONS, 1997c, Table 13.5). CD players, however, are not usual in older people households, although more older couples (34%) than single people (13%) own them (ONS, 1997a, Table 3.21).

Repairs

No repair costs are included for the TV, audio or video equipment. The television is given a lifetime of 15 years and the hi-fi is expected to last 12 years before replacement.

6.5 Sports goods

No sports goods are included in the LCA budgets for older people. This is because the sports activities in which they are involved require a minimum outlay on special items of clothing and equipment.

6.6 Books, newspapers and magazines

During the last 15 years, there has been a decline in the number of people who read a national daily newspaper. Nevertheless, the National Readership Survey for 1995 reported that 62% of men and 54% of women aged 16 years or over read a national daily newspaper. The same survey also suggests that reading habits differ between men and women. Men are more likely to read a daily newspaper and women are more likely to borrow books from public libraries and read magazines: an estimated one third of women aged 65-74 years borrow books from public libraries at least once a month (ONS, 1997c, Tables 13.10, 13.11, 13.12). In the group discussions, there was also much evidence of borrowing from public libraries, swapping and 'passing-on' of magazines and newspapers.

The LCA budgets provide for the purchase of newspapers, magazines and books at a low level, for example one magazine a month, a Saturday newspaper (including weekly guide to television programmes) and a small number of paperbacks.

This section also includes six £5 gift vouchers per household per year. The concept of exchanging gifts is a difficult one for budget standard methodology, as previously discussed. The gift vouchers represent small gifts similarly reciprocated 'in-kind' or, in some cases, not at all. This type of transaction may include, for example, gifts to grandchildren and godchildren or maybe a token gift of appreciation.

6.7 Household games and hobbies

The LCA budget includes a basic standard of games such as jigsaws, playing cards and dominoes, and provision for hobbies. Hobbies include knitting and photography, but the latter is infrequent except on holidays and special occasions.

6.8 Seasonal items

A basic Christmas decoration pack, consisting of an artificial tree with lights, decorations and tinsel is included.

6.9 Plants, flowers and garden products

Consumer research reports that 86% of adults over the age of 65 years have a garden. The products most commonly purchased by gardeners are bedding plants, fertiliser, seeds, growing media, bulbs and roses or shrubs (Mintel, 1996i). The LCA budget includes all these purchases, in small quantities, for households with a garden. For households without a garden, a greater number of cut flowers and houseplants are included. In addition, flowers delivered through a local florist for special occasions, such as a birthday or funeral, are included for all households.

6.10 Sports and activities

At LCA level it is debatable whether low-income households are able to take up leisure activities which involve payment of a charge or fee, although the discussion groups did indicate that they occasionally pay for a leisure activity. Most of the active, older people said they walk a great deal, although mainly as part of their daily shopping and visiting routine. A few belong to rambling clubs. Other activities are varied. According to the GHS, the most usual physical activities for older men are walking, snooker/pool or billiards and swimming, while for older women they are walking, keep-fit, swimming and cycling (ONS, 1997a, Table 13.8).

The LCA activity budget includes walking, carpet bowls (including a social club), line dancing and swimming. This equates to about one activity each week, an additional activity during holiday periods, and everyday walking.

6.11 Arts, entertainment and outings

At LCA standard, older people have an annual excursion to the cinema, theatre and local museum, in addition to a day trip by coach to a regional shopping centre twice a year. Other trips and visits are assumed to be free of charge, for example visiting churches, gardens, parks and exhibitions. The discussion group participants reported that they occasionally take a pub or café lunch and are involved in their own extended-family visiting and entertainment.

6.12 Holiday expenses

Holidays are considered important, for refreshment and social interaction. Consumer research reports that 85% of the population take a holiday of some description. Older people have a strong bias towards UK destinations. Just under half of the older people who take holidays take all their holidays in the UK, over 25% go abroad, the remainder take their main holiday abroad plus shorter breaks in this country (Mintel, 1996j). The main reason why older people take their holidays in Britain is for convenience in terms of travel, to see their own country and to save money.

At LCA level, an annual holiday is included for each household. The cost of the holiday, which is purchased from a local bus tour company, includes a seven-night stay in a hotel in Newquay during May. Travel is by private coach from York city centre to the hotel. The level of acceptability in the discussion groups was high for a seven-day, out-of-season holiday. As with other prices in the budget, the cost was economy level, although many in the discussion groups reported that they go on holidays subsidised by their local community centres, while others take more expensive holidays. Some people

reported that they take a week in the lowest season, in order to benefit from even lower prices.

The summary table for single and couple households differentiates between those households with and without a garden (Table 24).

Table 24:   **Summary leisure budgets**
Households aged 65-74 years
LCA standard, January 1999, £ week

	Single woman		Single man		Couple
	Owner garden	Tenant flat	Owner garden	Tenant flat	Owners/ tenants garden
Leisure goods					
TV, video, audio equipment	0.96	0.96	0.96	0.96	1.42
TV licence	1.88	1.88	1.88	1.88	1.88
Sports goods	0.00	0.00	0.00	0.00	0.00
Newspapers, magazines, books	1.24	1.23	1.34	1.32	2.09
Household games	0.02	0.02	0.02	0.02	0.04
Hobbies	0.38	0.38	0.19	0.19	0.38
Seasonal items	0.04	0.04	0.04	0.04	0.06
Garden, houseplants, etc	0.42	0.55	0.42	0.55	0.46
Total leisure goods	**4.94**	**5.06**	**4.84**	**4.96**	**6.33**
Leisure activities					
Sports activities	2.36	2.36	2.36	2.36	4.73
Arts, entertainment, outings	0.53	0.53	0.53	0.53	1.07
Holiday expenses	3.75	3.75	3.75	3.75	7.50
Total leisure activities	**6.65**	**6.65**	**6.65**	**6.65**	**13.30**
Total leisure	**11.59**	**11.71**	**11.49**	**11.61**	**19.63**

Due to rounding, there may be some discrepancies between figures shown and their totals.

7   References

Bradshaw, J. (ed) (1993) *Budget Standards for the United Kingdom*, Aldershot: Avebury.

Caroline Walker Trust (1995) *Eating well for older people: Report of an Expert Working Group*, London: Caroline Walker Trust.

Consumer Association (1996) 'Safe in the sun', *Which? Report*, June.

Consumer Association (1997a) 'First-aid kits under the microscope', *Which? Report*, June.

Consumer Association (1997b) 'Toothbrushes on test', *Which? Report*, August.

Consumer Association (1997c) 'Toothpaste on test', *Which? Report*, August.

DoH (Department of Health) (1991) *Dietary Reference Values for food energy and nutrients for the United Kingdom*, Report on Health and Social Subjects No 41, London: The Stationery Office.

DoH (1992a) *Health of the Nation: A strategy for health in England*, London: HMSO.

DoH (1992b) *The nutrition of elderly people*, Report on Health and Social Subjects No 43, London: HMSO.

DSS (Department of Social Security) (1997) *Family Resources Survey Great Britain 1995-96*, London: The Stationery Office.

Euromonitor (1996a) 'Special report on jewellery', *Market Research in Great Britain*, December.

Euromonitor (1996b) 'Sunglasses', *Market Research in Great Britain*, February.

Finch, S., Doyle, W., Lowe, C., Bates, C.J., Prentice, A., Smithers, G. and Clarke, P.C. (1998) *National Diet and Nutrition Survey: People aged 65 years and over*, Volume 1: Report of the Diet and nutrition Survey, London: The Stationery Office.

Frances, N. (1998) Memo, Post Office Research Department, Portsmouth.

HEA (Health Education Authority) (1996a) *Enjoy healthy eating*, London: HEA.

HEA (1996b) *Think about drink*, London: HEA.

HEA (1997) *Enjoy fruit and veg (with recipes)*, London: HEA.

MAFF (Ministry of Agriculture, Fisheries and Food) (1993) *Healthy eating for older people*, London: MAFF.

MAFF (1993-97) *Household food consumption and expenditure 1992-1996*, London: HMSO and The Stationery Office.

MAFF (1998) *Food portion sizes*, 2nd edn, London: HMSO.

Mintel (1996a) 'Shampoos and conditioners', *Market Intelligence*, July.

Mintel (1996b) 'Deodorants and bodysprays', *Market Intelligence*, December.

Mintel (1996c) 'Electrical haircare appliances', *Market Intelligence*, October.

Mintel (1996d) 'Facial skincare', *Market Intelligence*, December.

Mintel (1996e) 'Women's bodycare products', *Market Intelligence*, February.

Mintel (1996f) 'Make-up', *Market Intelligence*, September.

Mintel (1996g) 'Beds and bedroom furniture', *Market Intelligence*, June.

Mintel (1996h) 'VCRs/video cassette recorders', *Market Intelligence*, October.

Mintel (1996i) 'Gardening review', *Market Intelligence*, January.

Mintel (1996j) 'British on holiday at home', *Leisure Intelligence*, February.

Morley, J.E., Glick, Z. and Rubenstein, L.Z. (1995) *Geriatric nutrition: A comprehensive review*, New York, NY: Raven Press.

ONS (Office for National Statistics) (1993-96) *Family spending 1992-1996*, London: The Stationery Office.

ONS (1994) *1991 General Household Survey, people aged 65 and over*, GHS Series 22, Supplement A, London: HMSO.

ONS (1997a) *Living in Britain: Results from the 1996 General Household Survey*, London: The Stationery Office.

ONS (1997b) *Family Spending: A report on the 1996-97 Family Expenditure Survey*, London: The Stationery Office.

ONS (1997c) *Social Trends 27*, London: The Stationery Office.

Parker, H. (ed) (1995) *Modest-But-Adequate budgets for four pensioner households, October 1994 prices*, London: Age Concern England.

Parker, H. (ed) (1998) *Low Cost but Acceptable: A minimum income standard for the UK: Families with young children*, Bristol: The Policy Press.

Piachaud, D. and Webb, J. (1996) *The price of food: Missing out on mass consumption*, London: STICERD, London School of Economics.

Schlenker, et al (1998) *Nutrition in aging*, 3rd edn, New York, NY: McGraw Hill.

Steele, J.G., Shiham, A., Marcenes, W. and Walls, A.W.G. (1998) *National Diet and Nutrition Survey: People aged 65 years and over*, Volume 2: Report of the Oral Health Survey, London: The Stationery Office.

Wang, J., Jamison, D.T., Bos, E. and Vu, M.T. (1997) 'Poverty and mortality among the elderly: measurement of performance in 33 countries 1960-92', *Tropical Medicine & International Health*, vol 2, no 10, pp 1001-10.

Webb, G.P. and Copeman, J. (1996) *Nutrition of older adults*, London: Arnold.

White, A., Nicolaas, G., Foster, K., Browne, F. and Carey, S. (1993) *Health Survey for England 1991*, London: HMSO.

Part Four

Variable costs

1 Housing (including council tax)

1.1 Housing tenure

Housing is one of the costs which varies most, moreover the differences depend partly on whether the occupants are owner-occupiers or tenants. Although most older people now live in owner-occupied housing, over 75% of those in the lowest fifth and 60% of those in the next fifth of the income distribution live in rented accommodation (Hancock et al, 1999). Single older people, predominantly women, are more likely than couples to be social sector tenants, and more likely than couples to live in flats, maisonettes or rooms. Couples are more likely to live in houses (ONS, 1998, Tables 3.6, 3.7).

Low-income owner-occupiers with no mortgages to pay, on homes owned outright, may find their gross housing costs considerably less than the gross rents paid by tenants. However, the differences in net housing costs can be much smaller, according to Hancock et al (1999), due to the high maintenance and repair costs incurred by owner-occupiers and their exclusion from the housing benefit system. Between regions there are large variations in private sector rents and to a lesser extent in local authority and housing association rents. Unsurprisingly, rents and housing wealth are highest in London and the South East and lowest in Scotland and Wales.

For this report York remains as the location for housing costs, because of its central location and its nearness of fit to average local authority rents in the UK.

1.2 FBU housing standard

For illustrative purposes, the budget schedules in Part Five of this report use housing costs based on three housing types: a local authority one-bedroom flat, a local authority two-bedroom terraced house, and a two-bedroom terraced house, owned outright. Similar properties were used for the Family Budget Unit's (FBU's) Modest-But-Adequate (MBA) housing budget in 1991 (Bradshaw, 1993). By using local authority housing as a reference point (or standard), it is possible to

avoid the large national variations in rents (and standards) found in the private rented sector. All are hypothetical, not actual, households.

The FBU housing standard combines normative judgements about the housing needs of older people with other information, for example:

- knowledge about York locations and typical houses for each household type;

- information from national housing surveys;

- compliance with established housing standards, for example the General Household Survey (GHS) 'bedroom standard', and the 'fitness standard' set in the 1989 Local Government and Housing Act:

A separate bedroom is allocated to each married couple, any other person aged 21 or over, each pair of adolescents aged 10-20 of the same sex, and each pair of children under 10. Any unpaired person aged 10-20 is paired if possible with a child under 10 of the same sex, or, if that is not possible, is given a separate bedroom, as is any unpaired child under 10. (OPCS, 1991)

The GHS provides evidence that local authority housing, in general, is more likely to match the GHS bedroom standard than owner-occupied housing, which is more likely to be underoccupied. Almost half of all local authority dwellings and almost two thirds of Housing Association dwellings, compared with 19% of owner-occupied dwellings meet the GHS bedroom standard (ONS, 1998, Table 3.10).

Descriptions of the selected LCA houses are given in Table 25. The houses are situated in different areas of York, within a short bus ride of the main shopping centre, or within walking distance. Local corner shops and supermarkets (for example the Co-op and Kwik Save) are nearby. Sainsbury's is approximately two miles away.

To help justify this accommodation for low-income older people, an analysis of the FES over the three years 1993-96 was carried out, taking account of 'income before housing'; age of occupiers (65-74 years age range); number of bedrooms; and single or couple households living independently (R. Hancock, memo dated 25 November, 1998). Although care must be taken when interpreting the

Table 25: FBU illustrative housing in York
Households aged 65-74 years
LCA standard, January 1999

Single man or woman
Local authority 1960s one-bedroom, first-floor flat, mid-terrace property. Double-brick cavity and timber windows. Rateable Value 102. Council tax banding 'A'. Four rooms, hall, brick shed and no garden. Situated on a large estate, one mile from the city centre.
Owner-occupied 1850s two-bedroom, mid-terrace house, part-modernised. Brick built and timber windows. Rateable Value 114. Council tax banding 'B'. Six rooms, hall, brick shed and rear garden. Situated ¼ mile from city centre.

Couple
Local authority 1890s two-bedroom, modernised mid-terrace house. Brick built, no cavity walling and timber windows. Rateable Value 110. Council tax banding 'B'. Six rooms, hall, brick outside store, with small yard/garden. Situated ¼ mile from city centre.
Owner-occupied 1850s two-bedroom, mid-terrace house, part-modernised. Brick built and timber windows. Rateable Value 114. Council tax banding 'B'. Six rooms, hall, brick shed and rear garden. Situated ¼ mile from city centre.

data, due to the small number of households in some cells, it seems that most single, local authority tenants live in one-bedroom properties, whereas most couples live in two-bedroom properties. Owners, as expected, show a propensity towards underoccupation (Table 26).

Length of residency is a factor in attaching lifetimes to some household fittings, curtains and floor coverings. The length of time householders remain in the same house differs according to tenure and age of occupants. According to McCafferty (1994, Table 4.12), owners aged 65-74 years are more likely than local authority tenants to remain in the same house. A national and regional survey of elderly

Table 26: Percentages of low-income households aged 65-74 years
Living in one-, two- or three-bedroom dwellings
By income level and tenure, UK 1993-96

	Local authority/ housing association rented %	Owner-occupied %	Other %	Income bands £ week
Single man				£72-£96*
one-bedroom	42	3	33	
two-bedroom	39	48	50	
three-bedroom	18	48	17	
Single woman				£76-£112**
one-bedroom	38	5	45	
two-bedroom	36	46	36	
three-bedroom	25	49	18	
Couple				£124-£163***
one-bedroom	15	4	17	
two-bedroom	48	45	33	
three-bedroom	37	51	50	

* 30th to 50th percentile FES.
** 50th to 70th percentile FES.
*** 20th to 40th percentile FES.
Source: R. Hancock, memo dated 25 November 1998

people found that 56% of owners had lived in their present house for more than 20 years, compared with 38% of local authority tenants. Not surprisingly, McCafferty (1994, p 96) found evidence that most householders (92%) "are very or fairly satisfied" with their present home and few (9%) wish to move to smaller accommodation.

1.3   Mortgages

In general, most people aged 60 or over who live in owner-occupied housing own their properties outright (80% of the couples, 91% of the single householders) (ONS, 1998, Table 3.6b). Mortgage payments are therefore not included in the illustrative budget standard.

1.4   Rents

These are taken from local authority rent returns and represent average local authority rents, between April 1998 and April 1999, in the York Unitary Authority, for a one-bedroom flat or maisonette and a two-bedroom house or bungalow (CIPFA, 1998). Properties of this type account for 29% and 20% respectively of local authority housing stock in the York area. In January 1999, average, weekly, net unrebated rents in York (excluding water and sewerage) were £33.08 for a one-bedroom flat and £41.37 for a two-bedroom house.

Most tenants receiving Income Support, or mainly dependent on state pensions, are entitled to housing benefit equal to their full rent; however, a full rent does not bring their incomes up to LCA standard. For tenants receiving National Insurance (NI) retirement pension, plus a second income from earnings, or a second pension, or investment income, housing benefit depends on the type of second income they have, as well as their total income. For example, if their second incomes were to come from occupational or personal pensions or investment income, as shown in Table 27, then none of the households would receive housing benefit. If, however, the second incomes were from part-time earnings, the single woman would receive housing benefit of over £9 a week and the single man would receive almost £2 a week. For further details, see Tables 47-50, Sections C and D.

Table 27:   **Housing benefit at LCA level NI retirement pension plus occupational or personal pension Tenants aged 65-74 years LCA standard, January 1999, £ week**

	Rent	Housing benefit 100%	Housing benefit LCA*
Single woman	33.08	33.08	0.00
Single man	33.08	33.08	0.00
Couple	41.37	41.37	0.00

* calculated using POLIMOD.
Alcohol included in the budget.
Source: Tables 47-50

1.5   Water and sewerage charges

Water and sewerage charges for the York area are billed by York Waterworks Plc and Yorkshire Water respectively and are calculated on the basis of each property's rateable value (RV). (See Table 25.)

In January 1999 the charges were £0.451 per RV for water and £0.758 per RV for sewerage services, plus annual standing charges of £21.80 for water and £22.00 for sewerage. No VAT is applied to water or sewerage bills. There are no rebates in water or sewerage charges for low-income households.

1.6   Council tax

The amounts payable depend on the assessed value of the property, entitlement to discounts (single occupiers only), and entitlement to council tax benefit. Every home is placed in one of eight charging bands (A-H), according to a valuation officer's assessment of the value of the property in April 1991. If the householder is the only adult occupant, a 25% discount applies, regardless of income. Households receiving Income Support normally receive 100% council tax benefit. Households with net incomes above the Income Support applicable amounts have their council tax benefit reduced by 20 pence for each additional £1 of net income.

Table 28: Council tax and council tax benefit entitlements at LCA level
Households aged 65-74 years
LCA standard, January 1999, £ week

	Council tax band	Council tax	Council tax benefit	
			Income Support recipients	NI pensioners at LCA level*
		£ week	£ week	£ week
Single man				
Owner	B	7.51	7.51	0.00
Local authority tenant	A	6.44	6.44	1.39
Single women				
Owner	B	7.51	7.51	2.35
Local authority tenant	A	6.44	6.44	0.00
Couple				
Owners	B	10.01	10.01	2.70
Tenants	B	10.01	10.01	0.00

* calculated using POLIMOD.
Alcohol included in the budgets.

The council tax bands relating to the FBU's illustrative dwellings and the council tax liabilities of each LCA household in January 1999 are shown in Table 28. For further details, see Tables 47-50, Sections C and D.

1.7 Maintenance

External redecoration
Local authorities are responsible for the outside maintenance of their properties. The City of York Council redecorates its properties externally approximately every four to five years. Owners, however, are responsible for their own maintenance and low-income owners probably redecorate less frequently than better-off owners. The costs of external redecoration in the budgets are based on the costs of redecorating a two-bedroom terraced property, where there is considerably more work to be done at the back than at the front, for example more windows, gates, shed doors and drainpipes. The paint in the budget is standard white gloss. Other paints, such as National Trust products, can cost twice as much. The local costs are very varied. A low, but not the lowest, estimate (£246.75 including VAT) is used and the frequency rate is set at five years.

Internal redecoration
Older people are less able than younger people to carry out internal redecoration themselves, including those who are fit and active for their age. The discussion groups reported that extended families sometimes help out with redecoration and other small jobs, but this should not be taken for granted. Only small amounts of paint and DIY decorating products are therefore included in the household goods budget. Also included are the costs of hiring a professional decorator, to redecorate one average-sized room every five years. Redecorating entails stripping-off the old paper, re-papering, and painting the woodwork. The average room is estimated to require nine rolls of wall-paper, priced at under £7 a roll plus four days labour. Priced in York, a modest estimate for one room works out at £317 including VAT.

General house maintenance
For tenants, most general house maintenance is the responsibility of the landlord. For insured homeowners, structural and content insurance covers some of the risks, such as loss of metered water, damage to interior decoration, collapse of aerials, flooding and so on.

Table 29: **York housing budgets**
Households aged 65-74 years
LCA standard, January 1999, £ week

	Single households		Couple households	
	Owners	Local authority tenants	Owners	Local authority tenants
Rent	0.00	33.08	0.00	41.37
Mortgage	0.00	0.00	0.00	0.00
Service charge	0.00	0.00	0.00	0.00
Water and sewerage	3.49	3.21	3.49	3.40
Maintenance	2.72	1.36	2.72	1.36
Total housing	**6.21**	**37.65**	**6.21**	**46.13**
Council tax – York	**7.51**	**6.44**	**10.01**	**10.01**

Uninsured costs for homeowners include a range of regular but infrequent repairs, such as electrical repair of light-fittings, plumbing repair of leaking taps, or clearance of sewerage and top-water drainage pipes. The City of York Council charges £55 plus VAT to clear a blocked sewer on private property. A similar amount would be required if a householder were to call out a plumber, or electrician, to carry out a basic repair.

The budget standard for homeowners therefore includes a sum for general maintenance equivalent to the cost of clearing a blocked drain, at a frequency rate of once in three years.

1.8 Summary housing costs

The costs in Table 29 are specific to York, which limits their application. National average rents in England and Wales, for non-metropolitan areas, are £3.74 a week *higher* than in York for a one-bedroomed flat and £1.60 *lower* than in York for a two-bedroomed house or bungalow. York, however, is nearer the national average for local authority rents than the regional average (Yorkshire and Humberside). Yorkshire and Humberside is the lowest average rent region in England and Wales (CIPFA, 1998, Table 1).

2 Fuel

2.1 LCA fuel standard

For the FBU's original budgets, which were at the MBA standard, it was decided that the fuel standard should reflect the need for people to be comfortable in terms of warmth in their homes. The right temperature is only one aspect of feeling comfortable. A high level of draughts, even at a satisfactory temperature, is uncomfortable (Bradshaw, 1993). At LCA level the same standard of comfort has been applied, although a saving in fuel has been achieved by adding an extra pullover to the clothing budget.

2.2 Housing type and house dimensions

The fuel budgets are based on housing type and house dimensions, plus the life-styles at LCA level of men and women in the 65-74 years age group. The housing specifications are summarised in Table 25.

2.3 Heating zones

To help estimate the fuel budget, each property is divided into two 'zones', of which zone 1 is the warmer. In the MBA budgets for older people, zone 1 is the whole of the downstairs and zone 2 the whole of the upstairs. In the LCA budgets for people aged 65-74 years, there is a similar division. Zone 1 is the living room for people living in flats and the whole of the downstairs for people living in houses. All the rest is zone 2 (Table 30).

**Table 30:   Heating zones and volumes
                Households aged 65-74 years
                LCA standard, January 1999**

	Local authority tenant		Owner-occupier	
	Zone 1	**Zone 2**	**Zone 1**	**Zone 2**
a) Single				
Wall m^2	11.7	12.6	27.1	28.4
Window	2.9	2.0	6.9	5.6
Roof	19.9	19.9	–	35.4
Floor	–	–	35.4	–
Volume (m^3)	52.0	53.0	103.0	101.0
b) Couple				
Wall m^2	30.9	21.9	27.1	28.4
Window	5.1	3.6	6.9	5.6
Roof	5.5	30.1	–	35.4
Floor	35.6	–	35.4	–
Volume (m^3)	92.7	82.3	103.0	101.0

2.4   Demand temperature

The option of restricting zone 1 to the living room in houses as well as flats was considered but rejected on the grounds that it would make it more difficult to maintain an acceptable temperature throughout the home. As these budgets concern elderly people, temperatures are particularly important and should not be so low as to put good health at risk.

The recommended temperatures in the FBU's MBA budget for a single woman aged 72 were 21°C in the sitting room (zone 1), 18°C in the kitchen, hall and stairway (zone 2) and a minimum at any time of 16°C (Bradshaw, 1993). In local authority accommodation (a flat) the demand temperature was set at 21°C throughout. In her low-cost budget, however, Yu (1992) noted that wearing an additional jumper can compensate for a 1°C drop in ambient temperature. The clothing budgets have therefore been set to allow for an extra jumper and the demand temperature has been lowered accordingly.

We propose a demand temperature of 20°C in zone 1 and 18°C in the rest of the house (zone 2). The demand temperature in each area is an average and allows for higher temperatures in some areas of each zone. Overall the temperature should not fall below 16° C. If the thermostat were set lower in zone 2, at 17°C, for example, it would be difficult to maintain this minimum on cold nights. Elderly people often

do not sleep well and are out of bed during the night so the dwelling should not be cold.

2.5   Heating system

For the FBU's MBA standard budget, a balanced flue gas central heating system was assumed to heat the owner-occupiers' terraced houses, while a modern, electric central heating system was assumed to heat the pensioner's local authority flat. For the LCA budgets, the owner-occupiers' terraced houses still have full gas central heating, but this time it is provided by a gas fire with a back boiler. Controls are a simple room thermostat and time switch. Hot water is supplied via a lagged hot water cylinder, with uninsulated primary pipe work. The local authority flat has the same all electric system as before.

2.6   Heating periods

The usual arrangement for households with full central heating is to heat the house for two periods (morning and evening) during the week and all day at the weekend. For householders aged 65-74 years, the daytime heating requirements are likely to be higher, although the house may be empty for some periods during the day. In the MBA budgets for pensioner households (Parker, 1995), the heating period was specified as 16 hours a day, seven days a week. A 16-hour heating period assumes that the heating is on from (say) 6am to 10pm. If the older households are relatively active, this may be more than is strictly required. But it is necessary if the night temperature is to be maintained at not less than 16°C. The LCA heating period is therefore set at 16 hours a day for seven days a week.

2.7   Heating season

The number of days in the year for which heating is required is determined within the BREDEM model using the standard degree day calculations (Andersen, 1985). These compare the outside temperature with a baseline temperature (15.5°C, for example) and on days when the outside temperature falls below the baseline it is deemed necessary to use the heating system to raise the internal temperature to the demand temperature (Table 31).

Table 31:   Fuel consumption (kWh): results of **BREDEM** estimation
Households aged 65-74 years, LCA standard, January 1999

		Space heating	Water heating	Cooking	Total gas	Electricity**	Total
Single	Local authority	5,410*	2,656	1,111*	9,177*	742	991
	Owner-occupier	1,6948	5,503	666	24,117	946	250
Couple	Local authority	12,061	6,448	1,666	20,175	1,344	215
	Owner-occupier	15,688	6,448	1,666	23,842	1,411	252

* Single pensioner in local authority flat has all-electric central heating.
** Lights and appliances.

2.8 Insulation

Yu's low-cost budget set the following insulation measures:

- 100mm loft insulation

- hot water tank jacket 75mm thick

- 60% of rooms draught-proofed

Many local authority houses in York have had cavity wall insulation fitted, but this is not widely available in the UK and is therefore not included in the LCA budgets.

In effect, although the above insulation levels are recommended, they are not used in the BREDEM estimation of fuel consumption, because BREDEM uses the number of air changes per hour as a comprehensive measure of the quality of insulation.

2.9 Ventilation rate

BREDEM uses the ventilation rate as the basis for the calculation of fuel costs and the setting of a ventilation rate over-rides specific insulation standards. Ventilation rates vary from 0.5 to 1.5 air changes per hour/ach. For the MBA standard, 1 ach is used. For her low-cost standard, Yu uses 1.5 ach. This is in order to reflect the likelihood of less good insulation in houses occupied by low-income households. However, a ventilation rate of 1.5 ach is very high and very few houses would have a ventilation rate as high as this. It can also be said that the ventilation rates in low-income households are not necessarily worse than in high-income households, because the former have had the benefit of draught-proofing offered within the Home

Energy Efficiency Scheme. For these budgets the ventilation rate is set at 1 ach.

2.10 Water heating, cooking, lighting and the cost of running appliances

All these are determined by the BREDEM model, according to the number of occupants of the dwelling.

2.11 Fuel consumption

Table 31 shows the annual fuel consumption in kilowatt hours, as estimated by BREDEM and according to the assumptions set out above.

2.12 Annual and weekly fuel costs

Table 32 summarises the annual fuel costs, based on quarterly credit accounts for gas and electricity of the FBU couples and owner-occupiers aged 65-74 years. The cost for single tenants in all-electric accommodation is based on the white meter electricity tariff for space heating and water heating.

The cost of a service charge for a gas boiler is based on the cost of British Gas One Star service, which consists of an annual boiler check, but no further call-out charges. British Gas remains the main supplier of gas in Britain, although this is changing as the gas market opens to competition. The regional electricity companies are still the main suppliers of electricity. Competition in electricity supply started in 1998.

Table 32: Annual fuel costs: based on quarterly credit accounts
Households aged 65-74 years, LCA standard, January 1999

		Single householders		Couples	
		Owner	**Local authority***	**Owner**	**Local authority**
Space heating		239.48	224.57	221.67	170.42
Water heating		77.76	0.00	91.11	91.11
Cooking		23.54	8.23	23.54	23.54
Lights and appliances		61.80	53.58	88.30	84.49
Standing charge	Gas	48.87	0.00	48.87	48.87
	Electricity	43.72	54.64	43.72	43.72
Total		**495.17**	**341.02**	**517.21**	**462.15**
Total plus VAT @ 5%		519.93	358.07	543.07	485.26
Boiler service		55.00	0.00	55.00	Included in rent
TOTAL		**574.93**	**358.07**	**598.07**	**485.26**

Due to rounding, there may be some discrepancies between figures shown and their totals.
* 90% of space and water heating charged at night rate and 10% at day rate of white meter tariff.
Cooking and lighting and appliances charged at the day rate.

The estimated annual costs of fuel (including VAT at 5%) in the specified housing are:

- £358.07 for the single person in an all-electric local authority flat;

- £574.93 for the single owner-occupier of a terraced house;

- £485.26 for the couple in a two-bedroom local authority house;

- £598.07 for the couple owner-occupiers of a two-bedroom house.

If gas were bought through an electricity company 'dual fuel' deal, the single owner-occupier would save £78.12 a year, the couple in local authority housing would save £68.48, and the couple owner-occupiers would save £77.45. The single tenant cannot reduce her costs in this way, because her flat is all-electric.

In January 1999, the Department of Social Security (DSS) gave a one-off winter fuel payment of £20 to all State retirement pensioners and £50 to those in receipt of Income Support (and certain other benefits) to help towards their fuel costs.

Table 33 shows the LCA standard weekly fuel costs for single and couple householders aged 65-74 years.

Table 33: Weekly fuel costs: based on quarterly credit accounts
Households aged 65-74 years, LCA standard, January 1999

		Single householders		Couples	
		Owner	**Local authority***	**Owner**	**Local authority**
Space heating		4.60	4.32	4.26	3.29
Water heating		1.50	0.00	1.75	1.75
Cooking		0.45	0.16	0.45	0.45
Lights and appliances		1.19	1.03	1.70	1.62
Standing charge	Gas	0.94	0.00	0.94	0.94
	Electricity	0.84	1.05	0.84	0.84
Total		**9.52**	**6.56**	**9.94**	**8.89**
Total plus VAT @ 5%		10.00	6.89	10.44	9.33
Boiler service		1.06	0.00	1.06	Included in rent
TOTAL		**11.06**	**6.89**	**11.50**	**9.33**

Due to rounding, there may be some discrepancies between figures shown and their totals.
* 90% of space and water heating charged at night rate and 10% at day rate of white meter tariff.
Cooking and lighting and appliances charged at the day rate.

3   Transport

3.1   Big variations in costs

Transport that is accessible, affordable, reliable and safe is of key importance to older people, yet it is one of the most uncertain and variable budget components. Transport costs differ according to place of residence, travel mode, travel patterns and travel frequency. Other key factors include proximity to friends, family, shops, public transport – and car ownership. As a result of economic and social change, car ownership has become a necessity for many older people.

Two illustrative transport budgets have been calculated for this report, both based on the needs of older people living within two miles of York city centre. An illustrative, car owner's transport schedule is included in Appendix 4.

3.2   Transport summary without a car

It is assumed that the family does not own a car. The shops are either local or within two miles of home. The household members travel on foot, by local bus, and the occasional taxi. Holiday travel is not included in the transport budget, because the journey by coach to the holiday destination is included in the cost of the package holiday, details of which are in the leisure budget.

The 'no-car' transport budget in Table 34 includes travel by local bus in York, at 'pensioner prices' with an annual 'bus pass'. All older people living in York are eligible for an annual bus pass at the subsidised price of £6.00 (instead of £30.00).

A single bus fare for pass-holders costs £0.35, to any part of the city at any time of day, and there are no restrictions on the number of journeys they can make in any one day.

The LCA standard includes a bus pass, 12 single bus journeys a week, one short train journey a year and two taxi rides a year. Fares to work are assumed to be nil.

Table 34:   Transport summary: without a car
Households aged 65-74 years
LCA standard, January 1999, £ week

	Single person	Couple
Motoring	0.00	0.00
Bus pass	0.12	0.23
Bus fares	4.04	8.08
Train fares	0.13	0.26
Taxi fares	0.23	0.35
Bicycles	0.00	0.00
Other	0.00	0.00
Total (rounded)	**4.52**	**8.92**

Due to rounding, there may be some discrepancies between figures shown and their totals.

3.3   Transport budget with a car

The transport summary in Table 35 includes the costs of motoring and a reduced public transport budget. Either through preference or from necessity, an estimated 9% of single older people and 48% of couples, described as "retired and mainly dependent on state pensions", own a car (ONS, 1997a, Table 9.5).

For some families car ownership is a necessity. They may live in rural areas with inadequate public transport, there may be someone in the family with a disability, or the places where they live may involve long or awkward journeys. None of these situations applies to the York families assumed for this research. The car budgets in Table 35 are based on the following assumptions:

*   households aged 65-74 years, living in a York suburb, two miles from the city centre, with an adequate local bus service and local amenities nearby;

*   by using a car, the need for other transport services is reduced;

*   the number of car miles has been set to produce low but regular engine use;

*   maintenance costs have been set to keep the car at a standard described as 'good condition';

*   none of the households has a garage; when not in use the car stands on the public highway;

*   the number of car-miles travelled is sufficient to cover most transport requirements.

3.4 Annual car miles

Car-owning households enjoy greater mobility and have a tendency to travel greater distances than those without cars. According to the National Travel Survey, the average distance travelled by car drivers is about 10,000 miles a year (DoT, 1998). The LCA motoring budget for people aged 65-74 years assumes 50% of this average.

3.5 Motoring expenses

Assuming a 1992 Ford Escort, expenses fall into five main categories:

- depreciation
- interest on loan
- insurance
- road tax
- running costs (including parking costs)

Depreciation

This is the amount of money a family needs to set aside each year in order to replace their car with one of similar standard at any given time. The Ford Escort is described in *Parker's New and Used Car Price Guide* (May 1999) as giving "lots of choice and tolerably reliable with affordable running costs". The cost of a standard 1992 model, engine size 1,300cc, five-door hatchback, in 'good condition' and regularly serviced, is shown below:

1992 (J registration) – New price £8,537 –
January 1999 price £2,135

First-year depreciation is counted as a loss of one third of the new price, after which a straight-line depreciation rate is applied, based on an assumed lifetime of 15 years.

Interest on loan

As with other capital costs in the LCA budgets, no account is taken of the cost of servicing loans. However, money advisers can take account of debt and debt interest liabilities by referring to Section 7 (Debts, fines, maintenance orders).

Insurance

The comprehensive vehicle insurance policy used here assumes a man or woman aged 60 plus years, living in a low-risk area, with maximum no-claims deduction of 67%. The Ford Escort falls into insurance group 6. The average annual cost is £69.30 per year for a single older person with a 10% loading for a two-driver policy.

Road tax

In January 1999, road tax was £150 a year.

Running costs (including parking costs)

Running costs include 4-Star unleaded petrol at £3.27 a gallon (£0.72 a litre), motor oil, a full garage service every two years, four new tyres over a period of eight years, an annual MOT and an additional £100 a year on miscellaneous repairs and services. Once a month car parking, in a short-stay car park in York, costs £1.30 for a three-hour stay.

3.6 Transport summary with a car

Table 35 summarises two LCA transport budgets, for car-owning households living in York, adjusted for lower public transport journeys and in the assumed circumstances. The single person is assumed to have the same car mileage as the couple.

Table 35: Transport summary: with a car
Households aged 65-74 years
LCA standard, January 1999,
£ week

Item	Single person	Couple (two drivers)
Bus	0.28	0.55
Train	0.13	0.26
Coach	0.00	0.00
Taxi	0.00	0.00
Bicycle	0.00	0.00
Motoring: 1992 Ford Escort		
Depreciation	7.83	7.83
Insurance	1.33	1.47
Road tax	2.88	2.88
Running costs:		
petrol	7.86	7.86
oil	0.31	0.31
new tyre	0.36	0.36
service	0.72	0.72
MOT	0.59	0.59
general repairs	1.92	1.92
car parking	0.33	0.33
Total motoring	24.13	24.27
Total	**24.54**	**25.08**

Due to rounding, there may be some discrepancies between figures shown and their totals.

4   National Health Service (NHS) charges

4.1   Healthcare is not entirely free

Although most healthcare in the UK is provided free of charge by the NHS, certain specified goods and services are charged for unless the patient is in receipt of specified social security benefits, or has a specified, chronic condition. It is for this reason that the FBU classifies NHS charges as variable costs.

4.2   Prescription charges

Adults aged 60 and over are not charged for prescription items, regardless of their income level or severity of their conditions.

4.3   Dental charges

For this report the illustrative standard for each individual covers the cost during each 15-month NHS registration period of:

- one dental examination

- one scale and polish

- one simple filling

- one synthetic resin half-denture (upper or lower jaw) including pre-treatment denture work every 10 years.

Retirement pensioners (except those living in institutions) are charged for dental examinations and treatment unless they are in receipt of Income Support or are classified, in welfare terms, as low-income households. Free treatment, in most instances, includes check-ups, treatments and appliances such as dentures and bridges.

Other adults registered with an NHS dentist pay 80% of the cost of treatment. The rest is funded by the NHS. Private dentists charge patients the full fee. The NHS dental charges used in the illustrative budget standard are shown in Table 36.

Table 36:   NHS dental charges January 1999, £ week

Treatment	100% cost	80% cost
Dental check up	5.80	4.74
Scale and polish	9.15	7.32
Filling, simple	6.20	4.96
Half denture and pre-treatment	91.35	73.08

4.4   Ophthalmic charges

The importance of eye care has long been recognised, especially as a sight test can help diagnose other health problems. The GHS (1994) reports that 97% of those aged 65 and over wear glasses or contact lenses (OPCS, 1996, Table 3.35). Yet in January 1999, only children, the chronically sick and those claiming means-tested welfare benefits or on low incomes were eligible for a free eye test. Based on prices in York £17.50 is a typical charge for an eye test. To qualify for a free NHS eye test an older person has to meet one or more of the following criteria:

- blindness, partial sight or other serious eye problems, or illnesses such as diabetes or glaucoma, or glaucoma in the family

- complex lenses

- eye-hospital patient

Since April 1999, all older people are eligible for a free eye-test, but this change post-dates the January 1999 budgets in this report.

The FBU's illustrative LCA standard for eye care (Table 37) includes the cost of one test every two years and one pair of UniVision spectacles every four years. Prescription lenses are dispensed and fitted by a high-street chemist retail shop in York. Older people receiving Income Support are eligible for DSS Optical Vouchers which cover the cost of lenses. The value of the Optical Vouchers starts at £48.20 for bifocal lenses to £125.00 for complex lenses. Where clinically necessary, supplements cover the cost of prism or tinted lenses, and special frames.

Table 37: **Summary of NHS charges Households aged 65-74 years LCA standard, January 1999, £ week**

Treatment	Single person	Couple
Prescription items	0.00	0.00
Dental check	0.07	0.14
Dental scale and polish	0.11	0.23
Dental filling, simple	0.08	0.15
Half denture + pre-treatment	0.14	0.28
Sight test, Boots	0.17	0.34
Spectacles (bifocal)	0.31	0.62
Total	**0.88**	**1.76**

5   Insurance

5.1   Everyone needs insurance

Covering risk by insurance, though costly, provides peace of mind and protects low-income families against risks that they are less able to withstand than better-off families. Recent research found evidence that uninsured households are much more likely than insured households to have low incomes and few savings, and to be in financial difficulties (Whyley et al, 1998). Half of those without contents insurance had let a policy lapse, while the other half were on the margins of financial services generally. Some intermediary schemes have been set up to close this gap. The largest reported is an 'insure with rent' scheme run by some local authorities. Some housing associations, Credit Unions and charities operate similar schemes. For further information and analysis, see also a study by Elaine Kempson and Claire Whyley, which analyses and quantifies the scale of exclusion from financial services in Britain, including older people (Kempson and Whyley, 1999).

5.2   Type of insurance cover

The insurance policies in this section have been tailored to meet the needs of older people, many of whom feel particularly vulnerable concerning their safety and security. The main risks covered are house contents and buildings. The Age Concern Insurance Service has a policy whereby the policyholder has to pay the first part (£25) of each claim for loss or damage (£1,000 excess for

subsidence, ground heave or landslip under the Buildings section). The policy insures house contents and buildings from perils outside the control of the householder, such as fire, flood, collision by vehicles, riots, escape of water or oil, theft, falling trees, subsidence and so on.

House contents insurance
This provides £10,000 cover for the one-bedroom, local authority flat; and £13,000 cover for two-bedroom (owner-occupied and local authority) houses. The cost of the policy is based on the sum insured, housing location (by post code), and area factors such as the local crime rate, the level of deprivation, and the likelihood of subsidence and so on. York premiums are on the low side by comparison with national figures. Generally, inner-city areas have much higher premiums.

The contents insurance is an indexed-linked, 'new for old' cover for domestic property kept in the home, garden or outbuildings. The basic policy covers loss of money up to £250, interior decoration damage, deeds and documents up to £1,500, and loss of metered domestic water. Extra benefits include:

- accidental breakage of mirrors, glass in furniture and ceramic hobs

- replacement of external locks if keys are lost or stolen

- cost of alternative accommodation and loss of rent

- basic accidental damage (for example damage to TV and videos)

- freezer contents

- tenants' liability for damage to the buildings.

Building insurance
This is included in the budget standard for the owner-occupiers in York. The house is a two-bedroom 1850s terrace house (Table 25). Cover extends to £61,750 rebuilding costs, including fittings and outbuildings, the cost of demolition and professional fees. Extra benefits include cover for accidental breakage of glass doors, windows, sanitary ware and ceramic hobs, damage to pipes and cables and so on.

5.3 Prearranged funeral plan

The illustrative budget standard includes the cost of a prearranged funeral plan. *Marketing Intelligence* reports that the average cost of a funeral in 1997 was £1,284, which represents a 57% rise over the last decade. The Age Concern Funeral Service was launched in 1997, when the escalating cost of a funeral was causing high levels of anxiety. Purchase of a funeral plan guarantees a future funeral at today's prices.

The plan is comprehensive, with a choice of standards (Regular, Select or Regency) and a choice of payment periods (one single payment or instalments of 12 or 120 monthly payments). There is no upper age limit to taking out an arrangement to pay for the plan over a 10-year period, but if the contributor dies before the payments are complete the fund would need to be topped up. There is no reduction if a couple take out a joint plan.

At the LCA standard, it is assumed that payments are made over 10 years at £2.88 per week for a basic funeral (Regular Plan). The DSS Social Fund has funeral grants available for eligible persons (partners, parents, close relatives of the deceased) who qualify for a means-tested welfare benefit (Income Support, housing benefit, council tax benefit) and meet the capital criteria of less than £1,000.

Table 38 includes the illustrative insurance costs of a Regular Plan for single and couple older people households. Annual premiums include Insurance Premium Tax.

Table 38: **Summary of insurance costs Households aged 65-74 years LCA standard, January 1999, £ week**

	Single person	Couple
Owner-occupiers		
Home contents	0.61	0.61
Structural insurance	1.67	1.67
Prearranged funeral	2.88	5.76
Total	**5.16**	**8.04**
Local authority tenant		
Home contents	0.47	0.61
Prearranged funeral	2.88	5.76
Total	**3.35**	**6.37**

6 Private pension contributions

Although itemised in the budget schedules, the LCA budgets for people aged 65-74 years do not show any private or personal pension costs. At this age they are more likely to be drawing out than accumulating savings.

7 Debts, fines, maintenance orders

Although itemised in the budget schedules, no costs are shown because they are so variable. This budget item is nonetheless important. Charges under this heading are likely to include debt interest (for example in connection with car purchase) as well as debt repayments.

8 Job-related costs

In the UK, retirement from paid work is not mandatory at any age. Many older people continue in paid work until well past the conventional retirement ages of 60 for women and 65 for men. Some draw their pensions at the same time. But they are in a minority. For these budgets, job-related costs are therefore excluded.

9 Costs of seeking work

Job-seeking costs (postage, stationery, telephone, travel and clothing) are seldom incurred by people aged 65-74 years.

10 Pet costs

10.1 A cat is included

In 1995 an estimated 50% of UK households owned a pet (ONS, 1997b, p 131). Therefore at the MBA standard the FBU budgets for older people include the costs of a pet (either cat or dog). At the LCA standard, for which the ownership criteria is 80% of households, the costs of a cat are shown under 'variable costs' rather than as a budget standard.

There are strong arguments for including a pet in the budget standard for older people. A.R. Jarvis, founder and director of Cinnamon Trust, has pointed out that:

... stroking a dog or cat lowers blood pressure, eases stress; pet owners recover quicker, more fully and for longer following stroke or heart attack; pet owners are generally fitter, less depressed, more able to cope with life's traumas. (Jarvis, 1998)

The Pet Food Manufacturing Association annual pet survey (Euromonitor, 1996) shows that the long-term trend in pet ownership has been rising and since 1993 cats have become more popular than dogs.

10.2 Cat food and accessories

Food and accessories were priced at Argos, the Co-op, Kwik Save and Sainsbury's, using economy lines. The amounts of food costed are based on manufacturers' recommendations. One 400g tin of cat food per day is recommended for a large adult cat. The budget, however, includes 1½ tins for a two-day supply of soft food plus a snack supplement of 50g of dried biscuits per day.

10.3 Vets' bills

Information obtained from a local veterinary surgeon (H. Robertson, MsRCVS) indicates that on average cats and dogs visit the veterinary surgery once or twice a year. Recommended annual treatments include a booster injection against flu and enteritis, at a cost of £19.75. Worming is considered necessary every three to six months and flea powder should be used regularly. Pet insurance for cats is excluded from the LCA budget on grounds of cost. The Petplan standard policy for cats ranges from £56-£86 a year, Pride Pet Protect costs £73.95, Petsure £81, and Paws Pet Basic £75 in 1998.

For low-income pet-owning households, animal charities such as the RSPCA, Cat Protection and Blue Cross hold weekly clinics in return for donations by the owners. In York the cost of surgery would have to be met by the owners, unless they are insured. For the LCA budget, the costs of treatment through a veterinary surgery are at local prices. Cat toys, treats and collars are not included. Fleas and worming preparations are purchased in the supermarket.

10.4 Weekly cost

The cat in these budgets is a rescued animal, obtained from the Cat's Protection League. The budget standard for upkeep of a cat costs £3.32 a week. Details are given in Table 39.

Table 39:   Cat expenses
             Households aged 65-74 years
             LCA standard, January 1999, £ week

Item	Cost/ unit £	Qty	Brand/ retailer	Life years	Total price	Cost/ year	Cost/ week
Cat food, 400g	0.42	242	Kwik Save	1	101.64	101.64	1.95
Cat biscuits, 375g	0.75	26	Go Cat, Co-op	1	19.50	19.50	0.38
Cat comb	1.99	1	Co-op	5	1.99	0.40	0.01
Cat basket	9.20	1	Index	7	9.20	1.31	0.03
Feeding bowl	1.49	2	Co-op	5	2.98	0.60	0.01
Cat flap	9.99	1	Staywell, Argos	14	9.99	0.71	0.01
Carrying basket	12.75	1	Cityhoppa, Argos	14	12.75	0.91	0.02
Flea powder, 113g	2.55	1	Co-op	2	2.55	1.28	0.02
Worming tablets, 24	2.49	1	Co-op	2	2.49	1.25	0.02
Cat tray	3.19	1	Co-op	5	3.19	0.64	0.01
Cat litter, 3kg	1.95	12	Co-op	1	23.40	23.40	0.45
Cat purchase	0.00	1	Rescued cat	14	0.00	0.00	0.00
Immunisation booster	19.75	1	Local	1	19.75	19.75	0.38
Cat neuter, voucher	15.05	1	Local £12	14	15.05	1.08	0.02
Total						**172.47**	**3.32**

11 Alcohol

The reasons for including alcohol in the LCA budget, its food value and its costs are set out in Part Three, as part of the food budget.

12 Tobacco

Given that the LCA budgets are intended to promote good health, tobacco cannot sensibly be included as a budget standard, but it is included as a variable. Less than 30% of men and women smoke and it is a *Health of the Nation* target to reduce that figure to 20% by the year 2000 (OPCS, 1996, p 81). Men and women in the lower socio-economic groups are twice as likely to smoke as those in professional households (OPCS, 1996, p 87). In the 65-74 years age band, 19% of men smoke, compared to 17% of women. These figures are lower than the comparable percentages for the 35-44 years age bands, but they are nevertheless significant (ONS, 1998, Tables 10.32, 10.33). The problem is that although most smokers say they would like to give the habit up, many find it difficult to do so.

Table 40 shows the cost of cigarettes, based on consumption as reported in the GHS (OPCS, 1996). The costs are based on the price of 20 Silk Cut cigarettes, at £3.48 a packet, or 17.4 pence per cigarette.

Table 40: Illustrative costs of smoking January 1999, £ week

	Cigarettes smoked	Cost
Light smoker (5 per day)	35	6.09
Average smoker (15 per day)	105	18.27
Heavy smoker (20 per day)	140	24.36

13 Charitable giving

Donations by individuals to the top 500 charities in Britain top £1.1 billion every year (Hems, 1997). This excludes money given to church collections, small charities and informal donations, for example giving to the homeless. Charitable donations are not, however, an expense that all households incur,

since a large majority of households give nothing at all.

On average, Banks and Tanner (Hems, 1997) found that, based on FES data over 20 years, less than one third of households gave to charity during a two-week period, implying a weekly participation rate of about 16% of households. The average donation by 'households who give' is £4.11 (the median is £1.27). However, the FES definition excludes giving which yields something in return, such as raffles, buying in charity shops and charitable events.

The amount of giving is significantly affected by the age of the giver and factors of social class. In addition, the presence of children and a higher proportion of women in the household raise the probability of giving. Analysis of the 1995-96 FES (ONS, 1997b, p 112) indicates average weekly giving by all households in the UK of £1.20. Households headed by a 'retired or unoccupied' person gave an average of £0.90 per week. Mintel research in 1995, however, found evidence of a greater proportion of givers of £1.15 or more per week (61%) among adults aged 65 years or over than among adults of other ages (Mintel, 1996).

The National Lottery, introduced in 1994, redirects 5.6% of its 'takings' to charity, through its charity board. It seems, however, that households who play the lottery are not necessarily the same households who are likely to give directly to charities.

The FBU takes the view that families should not be excluded from voluntary giving through lack of resources. Many participants of the FBU group discussions give regularly to charitable organisations, especially the church, and their giving is in the order of £1 a week. The illustrative figure of £0.90, per household, per week, is based on the FES estimate for voluntary giving in households during 1995-96.

14 References

Anderson, B.R., Clark, A.J., Baldwin, R. and Milbank, N.O. (1985) *Building Research Establishment Domestic Energy Model: Background, philosophy and description*, Building Research Establishment Publications.

Banks, J. and Tanner, S. (1997) *The state of donation: Household gifts to charity, 1974-96*, London: Institute for Fiscal Studies.

Bradshaw, J. (1993) *Budget standards for the United Kingdom*, Aldershot: Avebury.

CIPFA (Chartered Institute of Public Finance and Accountancy) Statistical Information Service (1998) *Housing rents statistics at April 1998*, Cumbria: Reeds.

DoT (Department of Transport) (1998) *National Travel Survey*, London: The Stationery Office.

Euromonitor (1996) 'Special report: pet foods and accessories', November.

Hancock, R., Askham, J., Nelson, H. and Tinker, A. (1999) *Home-ownership in later life: Financial benefit or burden?*, York: Joseph Rowntree Foundation, York Publishing Services.

Hems, L. (1997) 'The dimensions of the voluntary sector in the UK', in J. Banks and S. Tanner, *Dimensions of the voluntary sector*, Tonbridge: Charities Aid Foundation.

Jarvis, A.R. (1998) 'Who helps them all?', *Eagle: Exchange On Ageing, Law & Ethics*, vol 7, Issue 1, August/September.

Kempson, E. and Whyley, C. (1999) *Kept out or opted out? Understanding and combating financial exclusion*, Bristol: The Policy Press.

McCafferty, P. (1994) *Living independently: A study of the housing needs of elderly and disabled people*, London: HMSO.

Mintel (1996) 'Charities', *Market Intelligence*, March.

ONS (Office for National Statistics) (1997a) *Family spending, A report on the 1996-97 Family Expenditure Survey*, London: The Stationery Office.

ONS (1997b) *Social trends 27*, London: The Stationery Office.

ONS (1998) *Living in Britain, Results from the 1996 General Household Survey*, London: The Stationery Office.

OPCS (Office of Population Censuses and Surveys) (1991) *General Household Survey 1989*, London: HMSO.

OPCS (1996) *Living in Britain, Results from the 1994 General Household Survey*, London: The Stationery Office.

Parker, H. (ed) (1995) *Modest-But-Adequate budgets for four pensioner households, October 1994 prices*, London: FBU, Department of Nutrition and Dietetics, King's College London.

Whyley, C., McCormick, J. and Kempson, E. (1998) *Paying for peace of mind: Access to home contents insurance for low income households*, London: Policy Studies Institute.

Yu, A.C.S. (1992) *Low cost budget standards for three household types*, FBU Working Paper No 17, York: FBU.

Part Five

Budget totals

1 Budget standard expenditures plus variable expenditures plus income tax less social security benefits

1.1 All the details are recorded

At this point the budget standard expenditures in Part Three and the variable expenditures in Part Four are added together to give total spending at LCA level for each household type, in the defined circumstances.

Budgets at different levels of detail are shown. For maximum detail, readers may wish to consult the budget schedules in Appendix 4. These specify brand, retailer, price and estimated lifespan of most items in each budget. They also include a transport budget for car owners. It is attention to detail which makes budget standards methodology different from other methods of estimating living costs. In Britain, disregard for detail is one reason why social security benefit rates and income tax allowances bear insufficient relation to need. By evading the detail it is easier for governments (and society) to avoid the problem.

1.2 Frugal, but with a margin

Though frugal, the intention is that the Family Budget Unit (FBU) budgets should include sufficient 'extras' to provide an acceptable living standard during retirement, including small but necessary margins for times of unexpected need. Some readers may reckon that the budgets are too generous, others that they are too meagre – the priority, at this stage, is to signpost their importance. The households portrayed here live either in local authority rented housing or in their own homes, the mortgages for which have been paid off. All have partial central heating. No household members smoke, although spaces are left for tobacco in the variable costs format. In the main tables no household owns a car, but the estimated costs of car ownership, assuming a 1992 Ford Escort, are included in Part Four and Appendix 4. Budgets with and without alcohol have also been calculated. Debts, fines and maintenance orders are signposted

but assumed to be nil, an omission which some readers may find unduly optimistic.

1.3 Budget standard expenditures

Unsurprisingly, most of the budget standard costs are similar for tenants and owner-occupiers, although men spend more than women on food, women spend more than men on clothing and personal care, and owner-occupiers spend more than tenants on household goods (furniture, floor coverings, textiles). Differences between the food budgets with and without alcohol come about because the food value of the alcohol is taken into account for the food budgets, which are therefore lower for the households who drink alcohol. Men non-drinkers are reckoned to spend £3 a week more on food than women non-drinkers.

1.4 Variable expenditures

By far the biggest disparity in living costs is between owner-occupiers and local authority tenants. This is partly because the owner-occupiers depicted here are assumed to have paid off their mortgages, while the single tenants have rents to pay of £33 a week (rounded) for the single people in one-bedroom flats, and £41 a week (rounded) for the couples in two-bedroom terrace houses. Some of the tenants qualify for housing benefit, but none qualify for council tax benefit. The owner-occupiers pay higher council tax than the tenants, more for their fuel and house maintenance, and more for insurance. Those with part-time earnings or a second pension qualify for council tax benefit, but those with investment income do not (although their budget costs may be identical).

1.5 Taxes and benefits

In the figure-work for this chapter, liability for the taxes and entitlement to the social security benefits in Table 41 are taken into account. Full take-up of all benefits to which there is entitlement is assumed and VAT is included in the purchase prices.

Older people receiving Income Support stand to make substantial savings on healthcare (Table 42), especially those with dental or eye-sight problems. In January 1999 every pensioner household was entitled to an annual payment of £20 against their

Table 41:   Social security benefits and taxes included in the budgets

Taxes	*Social security benefits*
• Income tax	• NI retirement pension (Categories A and B)
• Council tax	• Income Support
• VAT and duty on alcohol, tobacco, petrol etc	• Passport benefits
	• Housing benefit
	• Council tax benefit

fuel costs, the weekly value of which (£0.38) is shown in Tables 47-50. Households receiving Income Support were entitled to £50. These amounts will be increased to £100 per household in winter 1999-2000.

Table 42:   Passport benefits
Households aged 65-74 years
January 1999

Benefit	Households not receiving Income Support	Households receiving Income Support
Free prescriptions	✓	✓
Help towards dental care	sometimes*	✓
Free sight tests	sometimes*	✓
Vouchers for spectacles	sometimes*	✓
Winter fuel payments	£20	£50

* Restricted to people with no more than £8,000 capital and those who qualify under the NHS low income scheme.
Notes: Free sight tests reintroduced with effect from April 1999.
Winter fuel payments increased to £100 per household, winter 1999-2000.
Source: Age Concern England

2   LCA compared with Income Support

Table 43 (dreived from Tables 44 and 45) summarises the Income Support shortfalls, by comparison with LCA level, of the households for this report. The indications are that low-income older people receiving Income Support are likely to

be less short of money if they are local authority tenants than if they are owner-occupiers, including those owner-occupiers who have paid off their mortgages. This is due to the extra house maintenance, insurance and other costs incurred by owner-occupiers. Although the gross housing costs of the tenants are higher than the gross housing costs of the owner-occupiers, their net costs (on Income Support) are lower, because rents are paid in full with Income Support.

In April 1999, Income Support rates for people aged 65-74 years were increased by twice the rate of inflation, but the extra £4.55 for single people and £7.25 for couples (Table 1) do not fill the gap.

Table 43:   Income Support shortfalls by comparison with LCA standard
Households aged 65-74 years
January 1999, £ week

	Including alcohol	Excluding alcohol
Local authority tenants		
Single woman	10.49	8.89
Single man	14.37	10.15
Couple	22.45	16.83
Owner-occupiers		
Single woman	19.67	18.07
Single man	23.56	19.34
Couple	28.26	22.64

Source: Tables 44 and 45

Table 44: **LCA standard compared with Income Support**
Local authority tenants aged 65-74 years
January 1999, £ week

	Single woman	Single man	Couple
A **Budget standard costs**			
Food (with alcohol)	21.93	24.04	40.12
Food (without alcohol)	22.55	25.46	41.81
Clothing	5.03	4.12	9.11
Personal care	2.63	1.99	4.62
Household goods	8.55	8.55	10.81
Household services	5.41	5.41	5.82
Leisure	11.71	11.61	19.63
Budget standard costs with alcohol	55.26	55.72	90.09
Budget standard costs without alcohol	55.88	57.14	91.78
+ B **Variable costs**			
Housing (of which rent £33.08 single, £41.37 couple)	37.65	37.65	46.13
Council tax	6.44	6.44	10.01
Fuel	6.89	6.89	9.33
Transport (no car)*	4.52	4.52	8.92
NHS charges	0.88	0.88	1.76
Insurances	3.35	3.35	6.37
Debts/fines/maintenance orders	0.00	0.00	0.00
Job-related costs	0.00	0.00	0.00
Seeking work costs	0.00	0.00	0.00
Pets	3.32	3.32	3.32
Alcohol: woman 6 units, man 14 units, couple 18 units	2.22	5.64	7.31
units none	0.00	0.00	0.00
Tobacco	0.00	0.00	0.00
Charitable donations	0.90	0.90	0.90
Variable costs with alcohol	66.16	69.58	94.05
Variable costs without alcohol	63.94	63.94	86.73
= C **LCA total costs including alcohol**	**121.42**	**125.30**	**184.14**
= D **LCA total costs excluding alcohol**	**119.82**	**121.08**	**178.52**
INCOME SUPPORT			
Guaranteed amounts	70.45	70.45	109.35
+ Rent	33.08	33.08	41.37
+ Council tax	6.44	6.44	10.01
+ Winter fuel payments (£50 averaged over 52 weeks)	0.96	0.96	0.96
= E **INCOME SUPPORT TOTALS**	**110.93**	**110.93**	**161.69**
INCOME SUPPORT SHORTFALLS, TENANTS			
C-E Including alcohol in the budget	10.49	14.37	22.48
D-E Excluding alcohol	8.89	10.15	16.82

Due to rounding, there may be some discrepancies between the figures shown and their totals.

* Transport car owner 24.54 24.54 25.08

Source: Table 51

Table 45: LCA standard compared with Income Support
Owner-occupiers aged 65-74 years
January 1999, £ week

		Single woman	Single man	Couple
A	**Budget standard costs**			
	Food (with alcohol)	21.93	24.04	40.12
	Food (without alcohol)	22.55	25.46	41.81
	Clothing	5.03	4.12	9.11
	Personal care	2.63	1.99	4.62
	Household goods	10.24	10.24	11.33
	Household services	5.41	5.41	5.82
	Leisure	11.59	11.49	19.63
	Budget standard costs with alcohol	56.82	57.28	90.61
	Budget standard costs without alcohol	57.44	58.70	92.30
+ B	**Variable costs**			
	Housing	6.21	6.21	6.21
	Council tax	7.51	7.51	10.01
	Fuel	11.06	11.06	11.50
	Transport (no car)*	4.52	4.52	8.92
	NHS charges	0.88	0.88	1.76
	Insurances	5.16	5.16	8.04
	Debts/fines/maintenance orders	0.00	0.00	0.00
	Job-related costs	0.00	0.00	0.00
	Seeking work costs	0.00	0.00	0.00
	Pets	3.32	3.32	3.32
	Alcohol: woman 6 units, man 14 units, couple 18 units	2.22	5.64	7.31
	units none	0.00	0.00	0.00
	Tobacco	0.00	0.00	0.00
	Charitable donations	0.90	0.90	0.90
	Variable costs with alcohol	41.77	45.19	57.96
	Variable costs without alcohol	39.55	39.55	50.65
= C	**LCA total costs with alcohol**	98.59	102.48	148.58
= D	**LCA total costs without alcohol**	96.99	98.26	142.96
	INCOME SUPPORT			
	Guaranteed amounts	70.45	70.45	109.35
+	Council tax	7.51	7.51	10.01
+	Winter fuel payments (£50 averaged over 52 weeks)	0.96	0.96	0.96
= E	**INCOME SUPPORT TOTALS**	**78.92**	**78.92**	**120.32**

INCOME SUPPORT SHORTFALLS, OWNER-OCCUPIERS

C-E	Including alcohol in the budget	19.67	23.56	28.26
D-E	Excluding alcohol	18.07	19.34	22.64

Due to rounding, there may be some discrepancies between the figures shown and their totals.

*Transport with a car		24.54	24.54	25.08

Source: Table 52

3 LCA compared with NI retirement pensions

3.1 The pensioner poverty trap

In 1948, when National Insurance (NI) retirement pensions were introduced, they were intended to become a base on which contributors would be able to build through voluntary savings (Beveridge, 1948). Fifty years on, we are edging back to the pre-Beveridge era. Due to the uprating of NI retirement pensions with prices instead of earnings and the high level of dependence by low-income NI pensioners on means-tested benefits, many older people, including those with small second pensions or investment incomes, find themselves little or no better off – sometimes worse off – than their neighbours across the road, who did not save and now rely on Income Support.

3.2 Gross additional incomes required: detailed figures

Table 46 summarises the findings in Tables 47-50. These show the gross incomes, *in addition to NI retirement pensions*, required by people aged 65-74 years to reach LCA level (assuming they are either local authority tenants or owner-occupiers with their mortgages paid off). The required additional incomes vary between £28 a week (rounded) for single women owner-occupiers (non-drinkers, whose mortgages are paid off) and £80 a week for married couples (drinkers) in rented housing.

Each table contains four main sections:

- Part A tabulates each household's budget standard expenditures.
- Part B tabulates each household's variable expenditures.
- Parts A + B calculate the total budget costs of each household, with and without alcohol.
- Parts C and D tabulate the gross additional incomes required to reach LCA level, *with and without alcohol included in the budget* and differentiating between four sources of additional income, because different types of income attract different tax and benefit regulations:
  - earned income
  - occupational and/or personal pensions
  - investment income
  - tax-free investment income

The effects of the tax and benefit systems on these additional incomes are significant. To avoid poverty a single woman in local authority housing in York needs to top up her NI Category A pension with £49 a week earned income, £61 a week second pension or investment income, or £56 a week tax-free investment income.

Table 46: Gross additional incomes required to reach LCA level
Summary figures
Households aged 65-74 years receiving NI retirement pension
January 1999, £ week

Type of additional income required	Single woman		Single man		Married couple	
	Tenant	Owner	Tenant	Owner	Tenant	Owner
Alcohol included						
Earnings	49.28	29.91	63.12	34.76	80.36	39.60
Second pension	60.69	31.16	65.54	36.01	80.36	42.10
Investment income	60.69	33.51	65.54	37.40	80.36	44.80
Tax-free investment income	56.34	33.51	60.22	37.40	80.37	44.80
Alcohol excluded						
Earnings	43.57	27.91	48.07	29.50	66.43	32.57
Second pension	55.18	29.16	60.26	30.75	74.74	35.07
Investment income	58.69	31.91	60.26	33.18	74.74	39.18
Tax-free investment income	54.74	31.91	56.00	33.18	74.74	39.18

Note: See also Figure 2, p 11.
The discrepancies in net incomes from different categories of gross income are due to the complexity of the tax and benefit systems and the high degree of dependence on means-tested benefits, especially Housing Benefit.
Source: POLIMOD and Tables 47-50

Table 47: Gross incomes required to reach LCA level
NI RETIREMENT PENSION + EARNINGS
Households aged 65-74 years
January 1999 prices, £ week

	Single woman		Single man		Couple	
	Tenant	Owner	Tenant	Owner	Tenant	Owner
A Budget standard costs						
Food (with alcohol)	21.93		24.04		40.12	
Food (without alcohol)	22.55		25.46		41.81	
Clothing	5.03		4.12		9.11	
Personal care	2.63		1.99		4.62	
Household goods	8.55	10.24	8.55	10.24	10.81	11.33
Household services	5.41		5.41		5.82	
Leisure	11.71	11.59	11.61	11.49		19.63
BUDGET STANDARD costs + alcohol	55.26	56.82	55.72	57.28	90.09	90.61
BUDGET STANDARD costs no alcohol	55.88	57.44	57.14	58.70	91.78	92.30
B Variable costs						
Housing	37.65	6.21	37.65	6.21	46.13	6.21
Council tax	6.44	7.51	6.44	7.51	10.01	10.01
Fuel	6.89	11.06	6.89	11.06	9.33	11.50
Transport (no car)	4.52		4.52		8.92	
NHS charges	0.88		0.88		1.76	
Insurances	3.35	5.16	3.35	5.16	6.37	8.04
Debts/fines/maintenance orders	0.00		0.00		0.00	
Job-related costs	0.00		0.00		0.00	
Seeking work costs	0.00		0.00		0.00	
Pets	3.32		3.32		3.32	
Alcohol	2.22		5.64		7.31	
Tobacco	0.00		0.00		0.00	
Charitable donations	0.90		0.90		0.90	
VARIABLE COSTS + alcohol	66.16	41.78	69.58	45.20	94.05	57.98
VARIABLE COSTS no alcohol	63.94	39.55	63.94	39.56	86.73	50.66
A + B Total budget costs						
With alcohol	121.42	98.59	125.30	102.48	184.14	148.58
Without alcohol	119.82	96.99	121.08	98.26	178.52	142.96

		Single woman		Single man		Couple	
		Tenant	Owner	Tenant	Owner	Tenant	Owner
C	**With alcohol**						
	Total budget costs	121.42	98.59	125.30	102.48	184.14	148.58
-	Winter fuel allowance	0.38	0.38	0.38	0.38	0.38	0.38
+	Income tax	2.07	0.00	4.83	0.00	0.00	0.00
-	Housing benefit	9.13	0.00	1.93	0.00	0.00	0.00
-	Council tax benefit	0.00	3.60	0.00	2.64	0.00	5.20
-	NI pension	64.70	64.70	64.70	64.70	103.40	103.40
=	**Gross earnings required**	49.28	29.91	63.12	34.76	80.36	39.60
D	**Without alcohol**						
	Budget costs	119.82	96.99	121.08	98.26	178.51	142.96
-	Winter fuel allowance	0.38	0.38	0.38	0.38	0.38	0.38
+	Income tax	0.92	0.00	1.82	0.00	0.00	0.00
-	Housing benefit	12.09	0.00	9.75	0.00	8.31	0.00
-	Council tax benefit	0.00	4.00	0.00	3.68	0.00	6.61
-	NI pension	64.70	64.70	64.70	64.70	103.40	103.40
=	**Gross earnings required**	43.57	27.91	48.07	29.50	66.43	32.57

Due to rounding, there may be some discrepancies between the figures shown and their totals.
Source: Parts C and D calculated using POLIMOD

Table 48: **Gross incomes required to reach LCA level**
NI RETIREMENT PENSION + SECOND PENSION
Households aged 65-74 years
January 1999 prices, £ week

	Single woman		Single man		Couple	
	Tenant	Owner	Tenant	Owner	Tenant	Owner
A Budget standard costs						
Food (with alcohol)	21.93		24.04		40.12	
Food (without alcohol)	22.55		25.46		41.81	
Clothing	5.03		4.12		9.11	
Personal care	2.63		1.99		4.62	
Household goods	8.55	10.24	8.55	10.24	10.81	11.33
Household services	5.41		5.41		5.82	
Leisure	11.71	11.59	11.61	11.49	19.63	
BUDGET STANDARD costs + alcohol	55.26	56.82	55.72	57.28	90.11	90.61
BUDGET STANDARD costs - alcohol	55.88	57.44	57.14	58.70	91.78	92.30
B Variable costs						
Housing	37.65	6.21	37.65	6.21	46.13	6.21
Council tax	6.44	7.51	6.44	7.51	10.01	10.01
Fuel	6.89	11.06	6.89	11.06	9.33	11.50
Transport (no car)	4.52		4.52		8.92	
NHS charges	0.88		0.88		1.76	
Insurances	3.35	5.16	3.35	5.16	6.37	8.04
Debts/fines/maintenance orders	0.00		0.00		0.00	
Job-related costs	0.00		0.00		0.00	
Seeking work costs	0.00		0.00		0.00	
Pets	3.32		3.32		3.32	
Alcohol	2.22		5.64		7.31	
Tobacco	0.00		0.00		0.00	
Charitable donations	0.90		0.90		0.90	
VARIABLE COSTS with alcohol	66.16	41.78	69.58	45.20	94.04	57.98
VARIABLE COSTS without alcohol	63.94	39.56	63.94	39.66	86.73	50.66
A + B Total budget costs						
With alcohol	121.42	98.59	125.30	102.48	184.14	148.58
Without alcohol	119.82	96.99	121.08	98.26	178.52	142.96
C With alcohol						
Total budget costs	121.42	98.59	125.30	102.48	184.14	148.58
- Winter fuel allowance	0.38	0.38	0.38	0.38	0.38	0.38
+ Income tax	4.35	0.00	5.32	0.00	0.00	0.00
- Housing benefit	0.00	0.00	0.00	0.00	0.00	0.00
- Council tax benefit	0.00	2.35	0.00	1.39	0.00	2.70
- NI pension	64.70	64.70	64.70	64.70	103.40	103.40
= **Gross second pension required**	60.69	31.16	65.54	36.01	80.36	42.10
D Without alcohol						
Budget costs	119.82	96.99	121.08	98.26	178.52	142.96
- Winter fuel allowance	0.38	0.38	0.38	0.38	0.38	0.38
+ Income tax	3.25	0.00	4.26	0.00	0.00	0.00
- Housing benefit	2.81	0.00	0.00	0.00	0.00	0.00
- Council tax benefit	0.00	2.75	0.00	2.43	0.00	4.11
- NI pension	64.70	64.70	64.70	64.70	103.40	103.40
= **Gross second pension required**	55.18	29.16	60.26	30.75	74.74	35.07

Due to rounding, there may be some discrepancies between the figures shown and their totals.
Source: Parts C and D calculated using POLIMOD

Table 49: Gross incomes required to reach LCA level
NI RETIREMENT PENSION + INVESTMENT INCOME
Households aged 65-74 years
January 1999 prices, £ week

	Single woman		Single man		Couple	
	Tenant	Owner	Tenant	Owner	Tenant	Owner
A Budget standard costs						
Food (with alcohol)	21.93		24.04		40.12	
Food (without alcohol)	22.55		25.46		41.81	
Clothing	5.03		4.12		9.11	
Personal care	2.63		1.99		4.62	
Household goods	8.55	10.24	8.55	10.24	10.81	11.33
Household services	5.41		5.41		5.82	
Leisure	11.71	11.59	11.61	11.49	19.63	
BUDGET STANDARD costs + alcohol	55.26	56.82	55.72	57.28	90.11	90.61
BUDGET STANDARD costs - alcohol	55.88	57.44	57.14	58.70	91.78	92.30
B Variable costs						
Housing	37.65	6.21	37.65	6.21	46.13	6.21
Council tax	6.44	7.51	6.44	7.51	10.01	10.01
Fuel	6.89	11.06	6.89	11.06	9.33	11.50
Transport (no car)	4.52		4.52		8.92	
NHS charges	0.88		0.88		1.76	
Insurances	3.35	5.16	3.35	5.16	6.37	8.04
Debts/fines/maintenance orders	0.00		0.00		0.00	
Job-related costs	0.00		0.00		0.00	
Seeking work costs	0.00		0.00		0.00	
Pets	3.32		3.32		3.32	
Alcohol	2.22		5.64		7.31	
Tobacco	0.00		0.00		0.00	
Charitable donations	0.90		0.90		0.90	
VARIABLE COSTS with alcohol	66.16	41.78	69.58	45.20	94.04	57.98
VARIABLE COSTS without alcohol	63.94	39.56	63.94	39.56	86.73	50.66
A + B Total budget costs						
With alcohol	121.42	98.59	125.30	102.48	184.14	148.58
Without alcohol	119.82	96.99	121.08	98.26	178.51	142.96
C With alcohol						
Total budget costs	121.42	98.59	125.30	102.48	184.14	148.58
- Winter fuel allowance	0.38	0.38	0.38	0.38	0.38	0.38
+ Income tax	4.35	0.00	5.32	0.00	0.00	0.00
- Housing benefit	0.00	0.00	0.00	0.00	0.00	0.00
- Council tax benefit	0.00	0.00	0.00	0.00	0.00	0.00
- NI pension	64.70	64.70	64.70	64.70	103.40	103.40
= **Gross taxable investment income required**	60.69	33.51	65.54	37.40	80.36	44.80
D Without alcohol						
Budget costs	119.82	96.99	121.08	98.26	178.51	142.96
- Winter fuel allowance	0.38	0.38	0.38	0.38	0.38	0.38
+ Income tax	3.95	0.00	4.26	0.00	0.00	0.00
- Housing benefit	0.00	0.00	0.00	0.00	0.00	0.00
- Council tax benefit	0.00	0.00	0.00	0.00	0.00	0.00
- NI pension	64.70	64.70	64.70	64.70	103.40	103.40
= **Gross taxable investment income required**	58.69	31.91	60.26	33.18	74.74	39.18

Due to rounding, there may be some discrepancies between the figures shown and their totals.
Source: Parts C and D calculated using POLIMOD

Table 50: Gross incomes required to reach LCA level
NI RETIREMENT PENSION + TAX-FREE INVESTMENT INCOME
Households aged 65-74 years
January 1999 prices, £ week

	Single woman		Single man		Couple	
	Tenant	Owner	Tenant	Owner	Tenant	Owner
A Budget standard costs						
Food (with alcohol)	21.93		24.04		40.12	
Food (without alcohol)	22.55		25.46		41.81	
Clothing	5.03		4.12		9.11	
Personal care	2.63		1.99		4.62	
Household goods	8.55	10.24	8.55	10.24	10.81	11.33
Household services	5.41		5.41		5.82	
Leisure	11.71	11.59	11.61	11.49	19.63	
BUDGET STANDARD costs + alcohol	55.26	56.82	55.72	57.28	90.09	90.61
BUDGET STANDARD costs - alcohol	55.88	57.44	57.14	58.70	91.78	92.30
B Variable costs						
Housing	37.65	6.21	37.65	6.21	46.13	6.21
Council tax	6.44	7.51	6.44	7.51	10.01	10.01
Fuel	6.89	11.06	6.89	11.06	9.33	11.50
Transport (no car)	4.52		4.52		8.92	
NHS charges	0.88		0.88		1.76	
Insurances	3.35	5.16	3.35	5.16	6.37	8.04
Debts/fines/maintenance orders	0.00		0.00		0.00	
Job-related costs	0.00		0.00		0.00	
Seeking work costs	0.00		0.00		0.00	
Pets	3.32		3.32		3.32	
Alcohol	2.22		5.64		7.31	
Tobacco	0.00		0.00		0.00	
Charitable donations	0.90		0.90		0.90	
VARIABLE COSTS with alcohol	66.16	41.78	69.58	45.20	94.04	57.98
VARIABLE COSTS without alcohol	63.94	39.56	63.94	39.56	86.73	50.66
A + B Total budget costs						
With alcohol	121.42	98.59	125.30	102.48	184.15	148.58
Without alcohol	119.82	96.99	121.08	98.26	178.52	142.96
C With alcohol						
Total budget costs	121.42	98.59	125.30	102.48	184.15	148.58
- Winter fuel allowance	0.38	0.38	0.38	0.38	0.38	0.38
+ Income tax	0.00	0.00	0.00	0.00	0.00	0.00
- Housing benefit	0.00	0.00	0.00	0.00	0.00	0.00
- Council tax benefit	0.00	0.00	0.00	0.00	0.00	0.00
- NI pension	64.70	64.70	64.70	64.70	103.40	103.40
= **Gross tax-free investment income required**	56.34	33.51	60.22	37.40	80.37	44.80
D Without alcohol						
Budget costs	119.82	96.99	121.08	98.26	178.52	142.96
- Winter fuel allowance	0.38	0.38	0.38	0.38	0.38	0.38
+ Income tax	0.00	0.00	0.00	0.00	0.00	0.00
- Housing benefit	0.00	0.00	0.00	0.00	0.00	0.00
- Council tax benefit	0.00	0.00	0.00	0.00	0.00	0.00
- NI pension	64.70	64.70	64.70	64.70	103.40	103.40
= **Gross tax-free investment income required**	54.74	31.91	56.00	33.18	74.74	39.18

Due to rounding, there may be some discrepancies between the figures shown and their totals.
Source: Parts C and D calculated using POLIMOD

4 Detailed budgets

4.1 Six budgets

Tables 51 and 52 provide greater detail of the weekly shopping lists in the six budgets (three for local authority tenants, three for owner-occupiers) produced for this report. The costs shown here are, of course, average figures spread over an item's lifetime. Each budget is in three sections:

- Section A lists and prices the budget standard components explained in Part Three.

- Section B lists and prices the variable costs components explained in Part Four.

- Section C consolidates the expenditures in Sections A and B and also shows the gross incomes required by NI pensioners aged 65-74 years, who are not receiving Income Support, to reach LCA level.

4.2 Findings

Differences in the net incomes of owner-occupiers and local authority tenants are of particular interest. The explanation lies partly in the assumption made by the FBU for this study, that the owner-occupiers have paid off their mortgages. It is also due to the complexities of the tax and benefit systems, especially the housing benefit regulations and the lack of correlation between tax liability and any predefined living standard. Owner-occupation pays dividends if you have paid off your mortgage and your retirement income takes you above the entitlement level for housing benefit. If, on the other hand, your retirement income is low enough to entitle you to housing benefit, renting may be a less costly option.

4.3 Budget schedules

For further details, including the unit prices and estimated life expectancy of all durables in the budgets, readers are recommended to turn to the budget schedules in Appendix 4.

5 References

Beveridge, Lord (1948) *Voluntary action: A report om methods of social advance*, London: George Allen and Unwin.

Table 51 (1): DETAILED BUDGETS, LOCAL AUTHORITY TENANTS
Low Cost but Acceptable living standard
January 1999 prices, £ week, with and without alcohol
MEN AND WOMEN AGED 65-74 YEARS

		Single woman	Single man	Couple
A	**BUDGET STANDARD COSTS**			
1	**FOOD**			
	Bread, cakes, biscuits	1.85	2.01	3.18
	Cereals	0.60	1.00	1.52
	Carcass meat	2.88	5.46	6.17
	Meat products	1.76	1.42	3.00
	Fish	2.41	2.48	3.67
	Fats	0.36	0.36	0.60
	Milk and milk products	1.65	1.28	2.66
	Cheese	0.26	0.29	0.57
	Eggs	0.43	0.43	0.64
	Potatoes	1.10	1.29	1.93
	Vegetables	2.40	2.21	4.39
	Fruit	2.25	2.41	4.72
	Sugar	0.27	0.27	0.61
	Beverages	0.76	0.62	1.05
	Other foods	0.59	0.95	0.65
	Sweets and chocolate	0.34	0.34	1.19
	Soft drinks	0.18	0.18	0.36
	Food away from home	2.46	2.46	4.90
	Total food			
	(a) With alcohol (see also B11)	**21.93**	**24.04**	**40.12**
	(b) Without alcohol	**22.55**	**25.46**	**41.81**
2	**CLOTHING**			
	Outerwear	2.50	2.47	4.97
	Underwear/nightwear	1.57	0.66	2.23
	Accessories	0.09	0.13	0.22
	Footwear	0.79	0.79	1.59
	Clothing repair kit	0.07	0.07	0.10
	Total clothing	**5.03**	**4.12**	**9.11**
3	**PERSONAL CARE**			
	Healthcare	0.37	0.37	0.75
	Personal hygiene	1.68	1.30	2.98
	Personal accessories	0.39	0.22	0.61
	Cosmetics	0.18	0.10	0.28
	Total personal care	**2.63**	**1.99**	**4.62**
4	**HOUSEHOLD GOODS**			
	Furniture	1.97	1.97	2.33
	Floor coverings	0.89	0.89	1.45
	Textiles	0.99	0.99	1.34
	Gas/electrical equipment and repairs	1.58	1.58	1.69
	Kitchen and hardware	1.02	1.02	1.02
	Stationery and paper goods	0.44	0.44	0.44
	Toilet paper, cleaning materials and products	1.49	1.49	2.26
	Gardening, DIY, tools and materials	0.15	0.15	0.26
	Home security	0.03	0.03	0.03
	Total household goods	**8.55**	**8.55**	**10.81**

Due to rounding, there may be some discrepancies between the figures shown and their totals.

Table 51 (2):   **DETAILED BUDGETS, LOCAL AUTHORITY TENANTS**
Low Cost but Acceptable living standard
January 1999 prices, £ week, with and without alcohol
MEN AND WOMEN AGED 65-74 YEARS

		Single woman	Single man	Couple
A	**BUDGET STANDARD COSTS (cont)**			
5	**HOUSEHOLD SERVICES**			
	Postage	0.31	0.31	0.60
	Telephone	3.47	3.47	3.47
	Window cleaning	1.50	1.50	1.50
	Shoe repairs	0.06	0.05	0.11
	Dry-cleaning	0.07	0.08	0.15
	Total household services	**5.41**	**5.41**	**5.82**
6	**LEISURE**			
	Television, video, audio equipment	0.96	0.96	1.42
	TV license (colour)	1.88	1.88	1.88
	Sports goods	0.00	0.00	0.00
	Newspapers, magazines, books	1.23	1.32	2.09
	Household games	0.02	0.02	0.04
	Hobbies, including photography	0.38	0.19	0.38
	Seasonal items	0.04	0.04	0.06
	Plants, flowers and products	0.55	0.55	0.46
	Sports activities	2.36	2.36	4.73
	Arts, entertainments, outings	0.53	0.53	1.07
	Holiday expenses	3.75	3.75	7.50
	Total leisure	**11.71**	**11.61**	**19.63**
	TOTAL BUDGET STANDARD COSTS			
	(a) With alcohol	**55.26**	**55.72**	**90.09**
	(b) Without alcohol	**55.88**	**57.14**	**91.78**
B	**VARIABLE COSTS**			
1	**HOUSING**			
	Rent	33.08	33.08	41.37
	Mortgage	–	–	–
	Service charge	0.00	0.00	0.00
	Water and sewerage rates	3.21	3.21	3.40
	Maintenance	1.36	1.36	1.36
	Total housing	**37.65**	**37.65**	**46.13**
2	**COUNCIL TAX**	**6.44**	**6.44**	**10.01**
3	**FUEL**			
	Heating and cooking	4.48	4.48	5.49
	Lights and appliances	1.03	1.03	1.62
	Standing charges for gas and electricity	1.05	1.05	1.78
	VAT @ 5%	0.33	0.33	0.44
	Boiler service	0.00	0.00	0.00
	Total fuel	**6.89**	**6.89**	**9.33**

Due to rounding, there may be some discrepancies between the figures shown and their totals.

Table 51 (3): **DETAILED BUDGETS, LOCAL AUTHORITY TENANTS**
Low Cost but Acceptable living standard
January 1999 prices, £ week, with and without alcohol
MEN AND WOMEN AGED 65-74 YEARS

		Single woman	Single man	Couple
	VARIABLE COSTS (cont)			
4	**TRANSPORT (no car)**			
	Motoring	0.00	0.00	0.00
	Bus pass	0.12	0.12	0.23
	Bus fares	4.04	4.04	8.08
	Train	0.13	0.13	0.26
	Taxi	0.23	0.23	0.35
	Bicycles including maintenance	0.00	0.00	0.00
	Other	–	–	–
	Total transport (no car)	**4.52**	**4.52**	**8.92**
	Total transport (car owners)*	*(24.54)*	*(24.54)*	*(25.08)*
5	**NHS CHARGES**			
	Prescriptions	0.00	0.00	0.00
	Eye test	0.17	0.17	0.34
	Spectacles	0.31	0.31	0.62
	Dental	0.40	0.40	0.80
	Other	–	–	–
	Total NHS charges	**0.88**	**0.88**	**1.76**
6	**INSURANCES/PENSIONS**			
	Home contents insurance	0.47	0.47	0.61
	House structural insurance	0.00	0.00	0.00
	Mortgage insurance	0.00	0.00	0.00
	Life insurance	–	–	–
	Private pension contribution	–	–	–
	Company pension contribution	–	–	–
	Other: prearranged funeral plan	2.88	2.88	5.76
	Total insurances/pensions	**3.35**	**3.35**	**6.37**
7	**DEBTS, FINES, MAINTENANCE ORDERS**			
	Debt interest	–	–	–
	Loan repayments, including Social Fund	–	–	–
	Breakages	–	–	–
	Fines	–	–	–
	Maintenance orders	–	–	–
	Other	–	–	–
	Total debts, fines, maintenance	**–**	**–**	**–**
8	**JOB-RELATED COSTS**			
	Travel	–	–	–
	Childcare	–	–	–
	Union fees	–	–	–
	Special work clothing	–	–	–
	Other	–	–	–
	Total job-related costs	**–**	**–**	**–**
9	**SEEKING WORK COSTS**	**–**	**–**	**–**

* See Appendix 4.

Due to rounding, there may be some discrepancies between the figures shown and their totals.

Table 51 (4):   **DETAILED BUDGETS, LOCAL AUTHORITY TENANTS**
Low Cost but Acceptable living standard
January 1999 prices, £ week, with and without alcohol
MEN AND WOMEN AGED 65-74 YEARS

		Single woman	Single man	Couple
B	**VARIABLE COSTS (cont)**			
10	**PETS**	**3.32**	**3.32**	**3.32**
11	**ALCOHOL**			
	Budgets with alcohol	2.22	5.64	7.31
	Budgets without alcohol	0.00	0.00	0.00
12	**TOBACCO**	**0.00**	**0.00**	**0.00**
13	**CHARITABLE DONATIONS**	**0.90**	**0.90**	**0.90**
	TOTAL VARIABLE COSTS			
	(a) With alcohol	66.16	69.58	94.04
	(b) Without alcohol	63.94	63.94	86.73
C	**TOTAL BUDGET COSTS (A + B)**			
1	**Budget standard costs**			
	With alcohol	55.26	55.72	90.09
	Without alcohol	55.88	57.14	91.78
2	**Variable costs**			
	With alcohol	66.16	69.58	94.04
	Without alcohol	63.94	63.94	86.73
3	**TOTAL COSTS (no car)**			
	With alcohol	121.42	125.30	184.14
	Without alcohol	119.82	121.08	178.52
4	**TOTAL COSTS (car owners)**			
	With alcohol	141.44	145.32	200.30
	Without alcohol	139.84	141.10	194.67

D GROSS WEEKLY INCOMES (£ ROUNDED) REQUIRED TO REACH LCA LEVEL
TENANTS AGED 65-74 YEARS (no car)

	Single woman	Single man	Couple
NI retirement pension + earnings			
With alcohol	114.00	128.00	184.00
Without alcohol	108.00	113.00	170.00
NI retirement pension + second pension			
With alcohol	125.00	130.00	184.00
Without alcohol	120.00	125.00	178.00
NI retirement pension + investment income			
With alcohol	125.00	130.00	184.00
Without alcohol	123.00	125.00	178.00
NI retirement pension + tax-free investment income			
With alcohol	121.00	125.00	184.00
Without alcohol	119.00	121.00	178.00

Note (1), Section D:
(a) For explanation of section D, see Part Five, Section 3.2, p 70.
(b) The grossing up calculations for Section D were carried out using POLIMOD.
(c) All the figures have been rounded to the nearest penny.
(d) Section D applies to non-car owners only. The total costs of car owners have not been grossed up for income tax and are not included in Section D.
Note (2): Due to rounding, there may be some discrepancies between the figures shown and their totals.

Table 52 (1): DETAILED BUDGETS, OWNER-OCCUPIERS
Low Cost but Acceptable living standard
January 1999 prices, £ week, with and without alcohol
MEN AND WOMEN AGED 65-74 YEARS

		Single woman	Single man	Couple
A	**BUDGET STANDARD COSTS**			
I	**FOOD**			
	Bread, cakes, biscuits	1.85	2.01	3.18
	Cereals	0.60	1.00	1.52
	Carcass meat	2.88	5.46	6.17
	Meat products	1.76	1.42	3.00
	Fish	2.41	2.48	3.67
	Fats	0.36	0.36	0.60
	Milk and milk products	1.65	1.28	2.66
	Cheese	0.26	0.29	0.57
	Eggs	0.43	0.43	0.64
	Potatoes	1.10	1.29	1.93
	Vegetables	2.40	2.21	4.39
	Fruit	2.25	2.41	4.72
	Sugar	0.27	0.27	0.61
	Beverages	0.76	0.62	1.05
	Other foods	0.59	0.95	0.65
	Sweets and chocolate	0.34	0.34	1.19
	Soft drinks	0.18	0.18	0.36
	Food away from home	2.46	2.46	4.90
	Total food			
	(a) With alcohol (see also B11)	**21.93**	**24.04**	**40.12**
	(b) Without alcohol	**22.55**	**25.46**	**41.81**
2	**CLOTHING**			
	Main clothing	2.50	2.47	4.97
	Underwear	1.57	0.66	2.23
	Accessories	0.09	0.13	0.22
	Footwear	0.79	0.79	1.59
	Sewing repair kit	0.07	0.07	0.10
	Total clothing	**5.03**	**4.12**	**9.11**
3	**PERSONAL CARE**			
	Healthcare	0.37	0.37	0.75
	Personal hygiene	1.68	1.30	2.98
	Personal accessories	0.39	0.22	0.61
	Cosmetics	0.18	0.10	0.28
	Total personal care	**2.63**	**1.99**	**4.62**
4	**HOUSEHOLD GOODS**			
	Furniture	2.33	2.33	2.33
	Floor coverings	2.02	2.02	2.02
	Textiles	1.09	1.09	1.29
	Gas/electrical equipment and repairs	1.58	1.58	1.69
	Kitchen and hardware	1.02	1.02	1.02
	Stationery and paper goods	0.44	0.44	0.44
	Toilet paper, cleaning materials and products	1.49	1.49	2.26
	Gardening, DIY, tools and materials	0.26	0.26	0.26
	Home security	0.03	0.03	0.03
	Total household goods	**10.24**	**10.24**	**11.33**

Due to rounding, there may be some discrepancies between the figures shown and their totals.

Table 52 (2): **DETAILED BUDGETS, OWNER-OCCUPIERS**
Low Cost but Acceptable living standard
January 1999 prices, £ week, with and without alcohol
MEN AND WOMEN AGED 65-74 YEARS

		Single woman	Single man	Couple
A	**BUDGET STANDARD COSTS (cont)**			
5	**HOUSEHOLD SERVICES**			
	Postage	0.31	0.31	0.59
	Telephone	3.47	3.47	3.47
	Window cleaning	1.50	1.50	1.50
	Shoe repairs and dry-cleaning	0.13	0.13	0.25
	Total household services	**5.41**	**5.41**	**5.82**
6	**LEISURE**			
	Television, video, audio equipment	0.96	0.96	1.42
	TV license (colour)	1.88	1.88	1.88
	Sports goods	0.00	0.00	0.00
	Newspapers, magazines, books	1.24	1.34	2.09
	Household games	0.02	0.02	0.04
	Hobbies, including photography	0.38	0.19	0.38
	Seasonal items	0.04	0.04	0.06
	Plants, flowers and products	0.42	0.42	0.46
	Sports activities	2.36	2.36	4.73
	Arts, entertainments, outings	0.53	0.53	1.07
	Holiday expenses	3.75	3.75	7.50
	Total leisure	**11.59**	**11.49**	**19.63**
	TOTAL BUDGET STANDARD COSTS			
	(a) With alcohol	**56.82**	**57.28**	**90.61**
	(b) Without alcohol	**57.44**	**58.70**	**92.30**
B	**VARIABLE COSTS**			
1	**HOUSING**			
	Rent	–	–	–
	Mortgage	0.00	0.00	0.00
	Service charge	0.00	0.00	0.00
	Water and sewerage rates	3.49	3.49	3.49
	Maintenance	2.72	2.72	2.72
	Total housing	**6.21**	**6.21**	**6.21**
2	**COUNCIL TAX**	**7.51**	**7.51**	**10.01**
3	**FUEL**			
	Heating and cooking	6.55	6.55	6.46
	Lights and appliances	1.19	1.19	1.70
	Standing charges for gas and electricity	1.78	1.78	1.78
	VAT @ 5%	0.48	0.48	0.50
	Boiler service	1.06	1.06	1.06
	Total fuel	**11.06**	**11.06**	**11.50**

Due to rounding, there may be some discrepancies between the figures shown and their totals.

Table 52 (3):   DETAILED BUDGETS, OWNER-OCCUPIERS
Low Cost but Acceptable living standard
January 1999 prices, £ week, with and without alcohol
MEN AND WOMEN AGED 65-74 YEARS

		Single woman	Single man	Couple
B	**VARIABLE COSTS (cont)**			
4	**TRANSPORT (no car)**			
	Motoring	0.00	0.00	0.00
	Bus pass	0.12	0.12	0.23
	Bus fares	4.04	4.04	8.08
	Train	0.13	0.13	0.26
	Taxi	0.23	0.23	0.35
	Bicycles including maintenance	0.00	0.00	0.00
	Other	–	–	–
	Total transport (no car)	**4.52**	**4.52**	**8.92**
	*Total transport (car owners)**	*(24.54)*	*(24.54)*	*(25.08)*
5	**NHS charges**			
	Prescriptions	0.00	0.00	0.00
	Eye test	0.17	0.17	0.34
	Spectacles	0.31	0.31	0.62
	Dental	0.40	0.40	0.80
	Other	–	–	–
	Total NHS charges	**0.88**	**0.88**	**1.76**
6	**INSURANCES/PENSIONS**			
	House contents insurance	0.61	0.61	0.61
	House structural insurance	1.67	1.67	1.67
	Mortgage insurance	–	–	–
	Life insurance	–	–	–
	Personal pension contribution	–	–	–
	Company pension contribution	–	–	–
	Other: funeral prepayment plan	2.88	2.88	5.76
	Total insurances/pensions	**5.16**	**5.16**	**8.04**
7	**DEBTS, FINES, MAINTENANCE ORDERS**			
	Debt interest	–	–	–
	Loan repayments, including Social Fund	–	–	–
	Breakages	–	–	–
	Fines	–	–	–
	Maintenance orders	–	–	–
	Other	–	–	–
	Total debts, fines, maintenance	**–**	**–**	**–**
8	**JOB-RELATED COSTS**			
	Travel	–	–	–
	Childcare	–	–	–
	Union fees	–	–	–
	Special work clothing	–	–	–
	Other	–	–	–
	Total job-related costs			
9	**SEEKING WORK COSTS**	**–**	**–**	**–**

* see Appendix 4.

Due to rounding, there may be some discrepancies between the figures shown and their totals.

Table 52 (4): **DETAILED BUDGETS, OWNER-OCCUPIERS**
Low Cost but Acceptable living standard
January 1999 prices, £ week, with and without alcohol
MEN AND WOMEN AGED 65-74 YEARS

		Single woman	Single man	Couple
B	**VARIABLE COSTS (cont)**			
10	**PETS**	**3.32**	**3.32**	**3.32**
11	**ALCOHOL**			
	Budgets with alcohol	2.22	5.64	7.31
	Budgets without alcohol	0.00	0.00	0.00
12	**TOBACCO**	**0.00**	**0.00**	**0.00**
13	**CHARITABLE DONATIONS**	**0.90**	**0.90**	**0.90**
	TOTAL VARIABLE COSTS			
	(a) With alcohol	**41.78**	**45.20**	**57.98**
	(b) Without alcohol	**39.56**	**39.56**	**50.66**
C	**TOTAL BUDGET COSTS (A + B)**			
1	**Budget standard costs**			
	With alcohol	56.82	57.28	90.61
	Without alcohol	57.44	58.70	92.30
2	**Variable costs**			
	With alcohol	41.78	45.20	57.98
	Without alcohol	39.56	39.56	50.66
3	**TOTAL COSTS (no car)**			
	With alcohol	98.59	102.48	148.58
	Without alcohol	96.99	98.26	142.96
4	**TOTAL COSTS (car owners)**			
	With alcohol	118.61	122.50	164.74
	Without alcohol	117.01	118.28	159.12
D	**GROSS WEEKLY INCOMES (£ ROUNDED) REQUIRED TO REACH LCA LEVEL OWNER-OCCUPIERS AGED 65-74 YEARS (NO CAR)**			
	NI retirement pension + earnings			
	With alcohol	95.00	99.00	143.00
	Without alcohol	93.00	94.00	136.00
	NI retirement pension + second pension			
	With alcohol	96.00	101.00	146.00
	Without alcohol	94.00	95.00	138.00
	NI retirement pension + investment income			
	With alcohol	98.00	102.00	148.00
	Without alcohol	97.00	98.00	143.00
	NI retirement pension + tax-free investment income			
	With alcohol	98.00	102.00	148.00
	Without alcohol	97.00	98.00	143.00

Note (1), Section D:

(a) For explanation of section D, see Part Five, Section 3.2, p 70.

(b) The grossing up calculations for Section D were carried out using POLIMOD.

(c) All the figures have been rounded to the nearest penny.

(d) Section D applies to non-car owners only. The total cost of car owners have not been grossed up for income tax and are not included in Section D.

Note (2): Due to rounding, there may be some discrepancies between the figures shown and their totals.

Part Six

Findings

1   Five main findings

All the households in this study are assumed to be 65-74 years of age and are hypothetical, not actual, households. Five main findings emerge.

1.1   First finding: LCA budget costs

To reach LCA level – and live healthily – the required incomes vary according to age, gender, household composition, heating system, availability of public transport and other variables. All the households in this study are assumed to live on the outskirts of York, with easy access to public transport. UK prices are used wherever possible.

Table 53 shows required net incomes (without a car). These vary mainly according to household composition and housing tenure (local authority rented or owner-occupied with the mortgage paid off). To avoid poverty, single, older women require net weekly incomes of between £97 and £121; single, older men require net weekly incomes of between £98 and £125; older couples require net weekly incomes of between £143 and £184. In each case the higher figures refer to local authority tenants and the lower figures to owner-occupiers, who are assumed to have paid off their mortgages. For householders with mortgages to pay the budget totals would be higher, but such households are in a minority.

Table 53:   Summary of LCA budget costs
Households aged 65-74 years
January 1999, £ week
Rounded figures
NO CAR

	With alcohol	*Without alcohol*
Tenants		
Single woman	121	120
Single man	125	121
Couple	184	179
Owner-occupiers		
Single woman	99	97
Single man	102	98
Couple	149	143

Source: Tables 51 and 52

1.2   Second finding: LCA shortfalls NI retirement pensions

In January 1999, the NI retirement pension was £64.70 a week for single people and £103.40 for couples (on the NI contributions of the husband). These low rates result in shortfalls in gross income of between £30 and £61 a week for single women; £35 and £66 for single men; and £40 and £80 for married couples (Table 54), depending mainly on housing tenure (owner-occupiers or tenants). The shortfalls are large – over £4,000 a year for couples in rented housing – yet all the households are assumed to be fully paid-up contributors to the National Insurance system introduced in 1948, in return for which they were promised retirement pensions sufficient to prevent poverty, without the dreaded means test.

Table 54:   LCA shortfalls
NI retirement pensioners to
LCA level
Age 65-74 years
January 1999, £ week
Rounded figures
NO CAR

	Earnings	Second pension	Investment income	Tax-free investment income
Tenants				
Single woman	49	61	61	56
Single man	63	66	66	60
Married couple	80	80	80	80
Owner occupiers				
Single woman	30	31	34	34
Single man	35	36	37	37
Married couple	40	42	45	45

Source: Table 46 (POLIMOD)

To reach LCA level, single women (tenants) need to top up their NI pension with earnings of £49 a week, or a second pension/taxable investment income of £61 a week; or tax-free investment income of £56 a week. Single men (tenants) need an extra £60 – £66 a week, depending on the source of their incomes. Couples (tenants) need an extra £80 a week. For owner-occupiers who have paid off their mortgages, the income shortfalls are smaller.

1.3 Third finding: LCA shortfalls Income Support

Low-income NI pensioners who submit to a means test and meet its capital and other requirements, can top up their NI pensions with Income Support. But Income Support too is below LCA level. In January 1999 the shortfalls were up to £24 a week (single) and £28 (married) – without a car (Table 55). In this case, owner-occupiers do even worse than tenants, who get their rent and council tax paid in full.

In April 1999, the Income Support rates for older people were increased by more than twice the rate of inflation, but it still falls short of LCA level, as well as adding to the pensioner poverty trap.

Table 55: **LCA shortfalls**
Income Support recipients
Age 65-74 years
January 1999, £ week
Rounded figures
NO CAR

	With alcohol	Without alcohol
Tenants		
Single woman	10	9
Single man	14	10
Married couple	22	17
Owner-occupiers		
Single woman	20	18
Single man	24	19
Couple	28	23

Source: Tables 44-45

1.4 Fourth finding: LCA shortfalls with a car

For increasing numbers of older people, car ownership is becoming a necessity. Without a car they can no longer shop, socialise, or do the 101 other things which have become part of mainstream living. That is why the Family Budget Unit prepared a car owner's budget (Table 35). Assuming a second-hand, 1992 Ford Escort, an annual car mileage of 5,000 miles and some savings on public transport, car ownership increases expenditures at LCA level by £20 a week (single householders) and £16 a week (couples), who are assumed to save more than single people on their bus fares.

Table 56 summarises the weekly shortfalls in Income Support, by comparison with LCA level, for car owners aged 65-74 years. Annual shortfalls (rounded) vary between £1,500 for a single woman (tenant) who drinks no alcohol, and £2,300 for a couple (owner-occupiers), who have paid off their mortgage and drink an average of 18 units of alcohol per week between them. For NI pensioners (not shown here) the situation is more complicated, because car ownership requires incomes which take some of them into income tax, in which case the gross incomes required to run a car exceed the net incomes.

Table 56: **LCA shortfalls**
Income Support recipients
Age 65-74 years
January 1999, £ week
Rounded figures
CAR OWNERS

	With alcohol	Without alcohol
Tenants		
Single woman	31	29
Single man	34	30
Married couple	39	33
Owner-occupiers		
Single woman	40	38
Single man	44	39
Married couple	44	39

Sources: Tables 34, 35, 44, 45

1.5 Fifth finding: NI retirement pensioners are particularly at risk

The situation of NI retirement pensioners is a cause for particular concern, especially tenants and the minority of owner-occupiers who have not paid off their mortgages. The local authority tenants in this study require net incomes of up to £130 a week (single) and £184 a week (married) to reach LCA level, compared with NI retirement pensions in January 1999 of £65 a week (single) and £103 (couples). The owner-occupiers require net incomes of up to £102 a week (single) and up to £148 a week (couples). Car owners, whether tenants or owners, require a further £20 a week (plus income tax) if they are single; and £16 a week (plus income tax) if they are married. For NI pensioners little has changed since January 1999.

2 Four policy recommendations

2.1 Swift action by government

In April 1999, NI retirement pensions were increased in line with inflation, while Income Support was increased by over twice the rate of inflation. The effects of this policy on the living standards of low-income, NI pensioners need further thinking through. The challenge now is for government to show the range of goods and services social security benefits will buy; how much its officials think can be deducted in income tax and council tax without exacerbating poverty in old age; and how much can rightfully be removed from older people on low incomes for debt arrears, fines and prosecutions, without damaging their health, trespassing on decency or causing social exclusion.

2.2 A national debate on living costs and living standards

Two-and-a-half years after New Labour took office, continuing ignorance – at all levels of society – about living costs and living standards remains a cause for concern. Just as shoppers need to know the prices and quality of the goods on offer, so voters need to know whether New Labour's New Deal will result in all households on low incomes reaching a sustainable – and socially acceptable – living standard. For older people, sustainability is imperative. Most of us could manage on Income Support, even at its current rates, for a few weeks or even months. Older people are expected to be able to manage for the rest of their lives.

This is not to say that government should accept the LCA budgets presented here without question. Some readers may think that certain costs are too high, others that they are too low. Thanks to computers, neither reaction presents the technical problems experienced by earlier budget makers. With the details of every item recorded on disk, alterations are relatively easy to make. It is politics that stands in the way. What is needed is a national debate on living costs and living standards.

2.3 Cross-party support for scientifically assessed estimates of human need

If in time the Family Budget Unit's LCA budgets (including those yet to be completed) come to be accepted as reference points for UK social security benefit levels, it will be up to the government of the day to encourage debate about the goods and services claimants can do without, and any new ones which need to be included. Such decisions should not, however, be made by reference to expenditure data alone, because *households on low incomes cannot spend money they do not have*. Nor should the case for using budget standards as reference points for public policy be allowed to become a party political matter. Ideally all the political parties would support policy reviews based on scientifically assessed estimates of human need.

2.4 Living standard impact statements

All policy proposals which affect living standards at the bottom of the income distribution should be subject to rigorous investigation – using budget standards methodology – before they are put to Parliament and again during their passage through Parliament.

Unless this happens, the injustices identified in this report will continue.

Average, minimum and maximum gross weekly incomes
Single women, single men and couples aged 65-74 years
Income centiles, Family Expenditure Survey (1995-96)

Table A1.1: Income centiles, Family Expenditure Survey (1995/96), single women aged 65-74 years

Income centile	N	Mean	Minimum	Maximum
0-5	15	57.09	27.25	62.82
5-10	12	63.99	63.02	65.28
10-15	17	65.29	65.29	65.32
15-20	15	65.86	65.39	66.60
20-25	15	68.40	67.06	70.28
25-30	15	71.41	70.31	72.60
30-35	14	75.26	72.71	77.67
35-40	15	82.81	78.88	85.58
40-45	15	89.39	87.20	90.54
45-50	15	93.04	90.61	95.25
50-55	15	100.85	95.43	104.49
55-60	15	113.02	105.12	118.24
60-65	15	122.12	118.56	127.04
65-70	14	131.12	127.11	135.17
70-75	15	140.57	135.69	146.54
75-80	15	156.08	148.61	163.65
80-85	15	173.61	166.44	183.61
85-90	15	197.72	185.93	210.26
90-95	15	238.98	210.99	268.18
95-100	14	361.25	271.74	651.56

LCA	
MBA	

Table A1.2:   Income centiles, Family Expenditure Survey (1995/96), single men aged 65-74 years

Income centile	N	Mean	Minimum	Maximum
0-5	6	65.20	60.85	68.70
5-10	6	70.18	68.97	71.80
10-15	6	75.24	72.57	78.48
15-20	6	84.85	79.79	89.14
20-25	6	91.41	89.34	93.29
25-30	6	96.90	93.37	100.37
30-35	6	105.27	100.54	111.17
35-40	6	113.84	111.68	118.33
40-45	6	120.12	118.36	122.19
45-50	6	125.32	122.29	128.21
50-55	7	133.01	130.05	135.54
55-60	6	146.37	141.11	151.87
60-65	6	156.07	152.24	158.56
65-70	6	167.76	160.31	177.46
70-75	6	188.28	177.74	200.73
75-80	6	224.57	208.16	242.02
80-85	6	262.47	248.71	274.51
85-90	6	315.13	298.72	331.14
90-95	6	366.78	341.77	375.88
95-100	6	663.74	395.89	926.01

LCA

MBA

Table A1.3: Income centiles, Family Expenditure Survey (1995/96), couples aged 65-74 years

Income centile	N	Mean	Minimum	Maximum
0-5	14	94.65	0.38	114.13
5-10	14	118.64	114.22	123.07
10-15	15	126.28	123.29	130.34
15-20	14	137.81	130.66	145.08
20-25	15	151.06	146.96	156.49
25-30	14	161.93	158.40	165.07
30-35	15	169.13	165.21	173.65
35-40	14	177.76	173.70	182.38
40-45	15	189.37	182.95	196.42
45-50	14	204.14	197.60	210.71
50-55	15	217.64	211.03	225.77
55-60	14	234.74	226.00	245.78
60-65	15	255.83	246.76	268.40
65-70	14	279.18	271.83	288.84
70-75	15	304.24	290.43	319.32
75-80	14	337.86	319.65	357.40
80-85	15	375.92	357.99	392.90
85-90	14	423.81	392.92	458.16
90-95	15	511.57	467.93	573.12
95-100	14	964.20	603.11	1870.29

LCA

MBA

Appendix 2

Food methodology

LCA food budgets, households aged 65-74 years

Each budget was constructed using a combination of normative (expert) judgements and behavioural data concerning patterns of food purchasing and food consumption in the UK. The process involved seven main steps, plus an eighth step to adjust for the inclusion of alcohol.

Step One: *Define the current home food purchasing patterns of households believed to represent LCA level, using National Food Survey (NFS) data.*

The NFS was used as a database to provide information on usual consumption patterns at a level regarded as LCA. NFS data for 1992-95 (MAFF, 1993-97) were obtained from the Economic and Social Research Council (ESRC) Data Archive at Essex University and analysed using the Statistical Analysis System (SAS Institute Inc, 1998). Data were amalgamated over the four years to produce lists of purchases, based on the 263 NFS food codes for each household type at an appropriate level of income.

In order to select an appropriate group of households from the NFS to define the initial food baskets, it was necessary to decide from which income bands the households should be taken. In composing her poverty measure in 1965, Orshansky used the average US household food share of one third of net income in 1955 as multiplier for the cost of a 'thrifty' (short-term) diet (Orshansky, 1965, pp 3-29). As rising standards over four decades have in the meantime reduced the average proportion of net incomes spent on food to around, or even below, one fifth, food share expenditures above a third of already low net incomes suggest a very low relative level of living.

For the purposes of the LCA project, the decision was therefore taken to adopt 30% of net income after housing costs as the cut-off value (Citro and Michael, 1995, pp 108-16). Using FES data, the income band corresponding to this level of expenditure was found to lie between centiles 30 and 50 of the income distribution for the single men, between centiles 50 and 70 for the single women, and between centiles 20 and 40 for the couple households (Appendix 1). The difference in

the income bands for the three household types is accounted for by differences in their incomes and expenditure patterns, that is, far more older women are on very low incomes than older men, and far more single older people are on low incomes than older couples.

Households from the corresponding income bands (uprated for inflation) were selected for the discussion groups.

Step Two: *Calculate the adequacy of the diet in terms of Dietary Reference Values (DRVs), taking into account waste, consumption of food by visitors and food purchased and eaten away from home.*

It is important to ensure that an LCA diet satisfies the estimated nutrient requirements of the household members. The energy and nutrient contents of the edible portions of the food purchased were calculated using unpublished MAFF data (MAFF, 1998) on the composition of foods and compared with the estimated requirements of the household members (DoH, 1991), making appropriate allowances for food wastage (10%) (Wenlock et al, 1980); food consumption by visitors (3% for the single-men households, 10% for the single-women households and 7% for the couple households); and allowing for meals purchased and eaten away from home (about 5% in all households).

Estimates of the percentages of meals eaten away from home and the number of visitors were derived from 1992-95 NFS data. Estimates of the costs of food eaten away from home were derived from FES data. The nutrient content of the food purchases was calculated on a desktop PC, using nutrient conversion factors provided by the Ministry of Agriculture, Fisheries and Foods (unpublished). The nutrient content of alcohol was derived from the McCance and Widdowson food composition tables (Holland et al, 1991).

Net balance. In order to be able to estimate the adequacy of a given household's home food purchases, it is first necessary to ascertain the proportion of the diet consumed from the household food supply. Since 1992, the NFS has asked respondents to keep records of all foods purchased and eaten away from home. NFS respondents also keep a menu diary, recording the age and gender of each person present at each meal and the foods served. For the purposes of this report, and to ensure consistency with the Family Budget Unit's (FBU's) Modest-But-Adequate (MBA) diets (Nelson et al, 1993), we have used the NFS 1995 menu diaries to estimate the proportions of the diet eaten by each household type at home. The assumption is that foods eaten away from home are of similar nutritional composition to those eaten at home. For every household member, a *net balance* is calculated, which represents the proportion of total food consumption (excluding alcohol) estimated to have come from the household food supply. Food consumption by visitors is taken into account by using a net balance value which relates to the proportion of that person's meals theoretically derived from the household food supply on the day of the visit.

To calculate the net balance, the NFS assigns the weights to each meal shown below. The last two meals are interchangeable, according to whichever is the larger, or added together if only three meals per day are consumed.

- Breakfast   0.03
- Lunch/dinner   0.04
- Tea   0.02
- Supper   0.05

Over the week of the survey, if all meals are consumed at home, the net balance is equal to 1.0. A record of meals eaten at home by all household members and visitors is kept by the respondent. In 1993 it was estimated that approximately 5% of the diet is obtained from outside the household food supply (Nelson et al, 1993), including food obtained cost-free (for example at a friend's house). The technical details regarding calculation of the adequacy of the diet are also described in the above-mentioned publication.

Step Three: *Make the minimum adjustments to food purchasing profiles to bring them into line with DRV and Health Education Authority guidelines on healthy eating and to meet any nutrient deficiencies identified using the DRVs.*

It is recognised that current food purchasing and consumption patterns are associated with chronic degenerative disease in the population. It cannot be sensible to cost a food budget which is LCA and at the same time unhealthy. Public health goals necessitate adjustments to the food profiles, which address the issues of disease prevention. (This is analogous to ensuring a minimum ambient temperature for the prevention of hypothermia.) Yet it is important not to alter the proposed food profiles so radically as to make them unacceptable to the majority of the population – for example to exclude meat entirely, in the knowledge that vegetarians have lower mortality than omnivores. By prudent substitution of 'healthy' alternatives, which in total shift the diet towards one which is lower in fat and sugar, higher in dietary fibre and more nutrient-dense, it is possible to achieve a balance between the aims of health promotion and consumer acceptability.

The guidelines adopted for the present budgets are as follows:

1 35% or less of dietary energy supplied by fat.

2 Polyunsaturated:saturated fatty acid ratio (P:S ratio) greater than 0.45.

3 Non-milk extrinsic sugar (mainly sucrose) to provide not more than 10% of dietary energy.

4 Dietary fibre, non-starch polysaccharide (NSP), intake at least 17g per day.

5 Energy from carbohydrates approximately 50%.

6 At least five portions (400g in total) of fruit and vegetables (other than potatoes) per person per day.

7 The total diet, including home food purchases, sweets, soft drinks and foods purchased and eaten away from home, to provide 100% of the DRV for energy.

8 At least 100% of the Reference Nutrient Intake for other nutrients.

9 The amount of sodium in the diet to be reduced.

The adjustments accord with the following principles:

1 Skimmed and semi-skimmed milk increased, full fat milk and cream decreased.

2 Chicken and fish increased, substitution of lean for more fatty carcass meat, other meat and meat products decreased.

3 Vegetable oils increased, lard excluded.

4 Polyunsaturated margarine replacing some butter and increased in line with extra bread.

5 Sugar and preserves decreased.

6 Potatoes increased, chips and crisps decreased.

7 Other vegetables increased to provide 200g–250g per person per day.

8 Fruit increased to provide at least 200g per person per day.

9 Fruit and vegetables together to provide 5 servings per day (at lease 400g).

10 Pulses, nuts and cereals increased (including pasta and rice).

11 Wholemeal bread increased, white bread decreased.

12 Cakes, biscuits and puddings decreased.

Step Four: *Adjust the total quantity of food purchased to reflect a diet which provides 100% of the DRV for energy; and reassess the overall adequacy of the diet. Repeat Steps Three and Four until an adequate and healthy food profile is obtained.*

When the food purchases had been adjusted, the totals were assessed to ensure that all of the criteria set out in Step Three were satisfied. Figure A2.1 shows the percentage changes required in 17 food groups, to bring the food baskets into line with healthy eating guidelines for each of the three household types. As expected, the greatest increases required are for fish, potatoes and other vegetables and fruit, while the greatest decreases required are for cereals (including biscuits and cakes), meat products, fats, cheese and sugar.

Figure A2.1: Percent change in consumption (LCA-NFS) in households with people aged 65-74

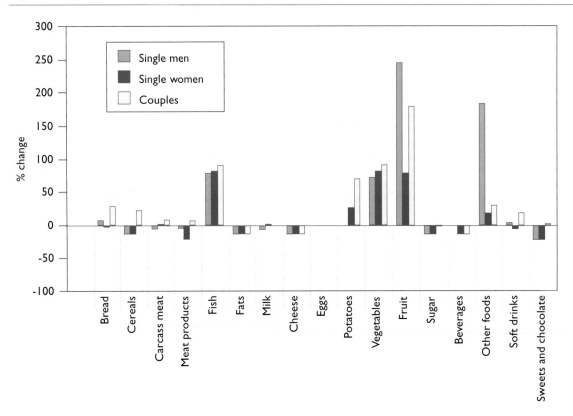

Step Five: *Construct a food basket of items in purchasable quantities, such that the nutrient value is equal to that in Step Four. Specific items identified for pricing were based on 12 discussion groups.*

The FBU aims to provide the estimated costs of actual baskets of goods. The development of the food baskets requires a list of foods which can be purchased in amounts which accord with those available in the shops (for example whole loaves of bread, pints of milk etc) and would be appropriate for feeding people in a given household (for example specific cuts of a particular type of meat and enough of one type of vegetable to provide sufficient servings, etc).

Step Six. *Cost the food basket using Sainsbury's, KwikSave and Co-op food prices in January 1999 and add a component for foods purchased away from home, using Family Expenditure Survey data.*

Food prices are based on data from Sainsbury's, KwikSave and the Co-op (Tables A2.1 to A2.3). The prices are based on actual costs in January 1999. Wherever possible, the 'own label', 'no frills' or economy line foods were selected, but not where a consensus in the low income discussion groups regarded branded goods as the only acceptable ones (eg Weetabix). Two price bases were used from the Co-op. One was based on food prices in a large Co-op supermarket, the other on food prices in a small local Co-op.

Step Seven. *Construct menus which utilise the items in the food basket; allow for meals eaten away from home; and allow for the presence of visitors.*

Because the LCA budgets are more stringent than the MBA budgets and individual choice is much more limited, it was important to ensure that the foods in the baskets could be translated into menus which are acceptable to the households for whom they are intended. Construction of the menus was therefore preceded by consultation with the discussion groups.

Step Eight. *Define a level of alcoholic beverage consumption using HEA guidelines; cost the alcoholic beverages using supermarket prices; and reduce food basket costs (and by implication quantities) to allow for the energy content of the alcoholic drinks.*

Although there is no physiological requirement for alcohol, it is included in the LCA budgets because it

reflects a real expenditure for most households and is 'required' in a social sense. Direct health benefits, in terms of reduced risks of heart disease, hypertension and stroke, may also be associated with moderate alcohol consumption of 1-2 units, or 10-20 grams a day (Friedman et al, 1986).

The NFS does not include information about alcohol consumption. The amounts included in the budgets are based on Health Education Authority guidelines not to exceed 21 units a week for men and 14 units a week for women (HEA, 1996b). In previous budgets we have chosen 14 units a week for men and 10 units a week for women as reasonable levels of consumption. One unit equals half a pint of beer, or a 125ml glass of wine, or a single (25ml) of spirit. In the present budget, we were guided by the estimates of expenditure in the FES (ONS, 1993-96) and feedback from the discussion groups. Whereas single men typically drink at or above the level included in the LCA budgets (as reflected in FES expenditure data), single women and couples typically drink less than two thirds of the HEA safe limits. We have therefore chosen to reflect the average levels of expenditure reported in the FES as the basis for the budget component relating to alcohol in the single-woman and couple households. In the single-man households, two thirds of the Health Education Authority safe limit has been chosen.

Because alcohol contributes energy to the diet, total food expenditure is reduced by corresponding amounts, in order to avoid over-consumption of energy and consequent risk of obesity. Alcohol consumption at the levels proposed for the LCA budgets would contribute between 2.7% and 5.6% of dietary energy, and the food budget has been reduced accordingly. These adjustments are reflected in the summary LCA budgets for food (Table 9, p 23).

Table A2.1:   LCA basket of food for one week: single woman aged 65-74 years
(cf = conversion factor; ep = edible portion)

Description	Purchase quantities and portions	Cost (£)
Yoghurt	2 x 125g pots	0.29
Semi and other skimmed milk	2840ml = 5 pints	1.36
Cheese, natural, hard, Cheddar and Cheddar type	1 x 40g av sandwich portion	0.19
Cheese, processed	1 x 14g cheese triangle	0.07
Beef steak (less expensive)	cf stewing steak = 0.64; 112g cooked medium av portion = 175g raw	0.88
Pork chops	cf pork chops = 0.63; ep rib end chop grilled = 85g = 135g raw	0.62
Bacon and ham, uncooked rashers, not pre-packed	cf bacon back = 0.59, 2 x 25g cooked rashers = 85g raw	0.68
Bacon and ham, cooked, including canned	1 x 23g slices ham	0.16
Broiler chicken, uncooked, including frozen	cf chicken breast roast = 0.67, 1 x medium 130g cooked fillets = 388g raw	1.38
Sausages, uncooked, pork	4 x 20g thin	0.21
Other frozen convenience meats	1 x turkey/chicken in crumb = 100g purchasable qty	0.71
Fish, white, filleted, fresh	cf cod baked fillets = 0.81. 2 x 120g medium fillets = 296g raw	1.67
Salmon, canned	ep canned salmon = 0.81; 1 x 105g tin salmon provides 85g edible (2 x sandwich)	0.74
Eggs	4 eggs	0.43
Butter – Danish	2 x 14g scone spreadings	0.08
Soft margarine	10 x 5g thin spreadings on bread	0.05
Vegetable and salad oils	6 tbsp	0.04
Reduced fat spreads	28 x 5g thin spreadings on bread	0.19
Sugar	5 x 4g level tsp per day + 2 x 20g tbsp per wk	0.11
Marmalade	8 x 15g av spreadings on bread	0.16
Previous year's crop potatoes purchased Jan to Aug	cf = 1; 10 x 170g medium portions	1.10
Cabbages, fresh	cf = 1; ep = 0.77; 3 x 120g large portions = 468g	0.20
Cauliflower, fresh	cf = 1; ep = 0.45; 2 x 120g large portions = 800g	0.50
Leafy salads, fresh	ep = 0.74; 3 x 20g sandwich portions = 81g	0.19
Carrots, fresh	cf = 1; ep = 0.7; 5 x 85g large portions = 607g	0.34
Onions, shallots, leeks, fresh	1 x 150g medium, raw	0.09
Tomatoes, fresh	3 x 85g medium	0.37
Beans, canned	1 x 205g small can	0.29
Frozen peas	2 x 85g portion	0.16
All frozen vegetables and frozen vegetables products not specified elsewhere.	2 x 90g av portion spinach or mixed vegetables	0.26
Other citrus fruit, fresh	ep = 0.75; raw medium without skin 60g = 80g purchase wt (x2)	0.24
Apples, fresh	8 x 112g medium, raw, with core	0.70
Bananas, fresh	ep = 0.66; 3 x 100g medium without skin = 454g purchase wt	0.47
Other canned or bottled fruit	fruit cocktail in juice, 115g av portion	0.12
Dried fruit and dried fruit products	1 x 30g tbsp sultanas	0.04
Fruit juices	7 x 160g av glasses	0.68
Bread, white, sliced standard	1 x 400g small loaf	0.38
Bread, wholemeal, sliced	1 x 800g large loaf	0.42

Table A2.1: Single woman (cont)

Description	Purchase quantities and portions	Cost (£)
Rolls	2 x 48g wholemeal rolls	0.24
Flour	130g/wk	0.06
Buns, scones and teacakes	2 x 50g scones or hot cross buns	0.20
Cakes and pastries	2 x 46g bakewell slices	0.33
Biscuits, other than chocolate	12 x 8g lincoln or marie biscuits (0.5 packet)	0.22
Other high fibre breakfast cereals	14 x 20g Weetabix (2 per day)	0.60
Tea	40 x 2.5g teabags	0.56
Coffee, instant	21 level (10 heaped) tsp	0.20
Soups, canned	2 x 150g small av portions	0.35
Salad dressings	2 x 12g portions mayonnaise	0.06
Pickles and sauces	3 x 20g portion tomato ketchup	0.08
Meat and yeast extracts	3 x 5g tsp gravy browning	0.05
Ice-cream	1 x 75g av serving	0.05
Salt	1 heaped tsp	0.00
Soft drinks, unconcentrated	0.5 litre lemonade	0.18
Boiled sweets and jellies	fruit drops	0.34
Total cost for all foods, home food supply		**20.09**

Table A2.2:   **LCA basket of food for one week: single man aged 65-74 years**
(cf = conversion factor; ep = edible portion)

Description	Purchase quantities and portions	Cost (£)
Yoghurt	1 x 125g pot	0.14
Semi and other skimmed milk	2272ml = 4 pints	1.08
Cheese, natural, hard, Cheddar and Cheddar type	1 x 45g sandwich portion	0.22
Cheese, processed	1 x 14g cheese triangle	0.07
Beef steak (less expensive)	cf. stewing steak = 0.64; ep = 1; 140g cooked medium av portion = 219g raw	1.10
Pork chops	cf pork chops = 0.63; spare rib chop grilled ed portion = 140g cooked = 222g raw	1.01
Bacon and ham, uncooked, rashers, pre-packed	cf bacon back = 0.59, 4 x 25g cooked rashers = 127g raw	0.92
Corned beef	2 x 38g slices	0.50
Broiler chicken, uncooked, including frozen	cf chicken breast roast = 0.67, ep = 1 (no bone); large 150g cooked portion = 224g raw	1.93
Sausages, uncooked, pork	cf thick = 0.72, 4 x 40g thick cooked = 167g raw	0.62
Other frozen convenience meats	shepherd's pie ready meal for one = 300g purchase wt	0.81
Fish, fat, processed, filleted	1 x 170g smoked mackerel	1.24
Other canned or bottled fish	1 x 215g small tin pilchards in tomato sauce (ep assumed = approx 1)	0.40
Frozen convenience fish products	cf fishfingers = 0.93; 100g cod in crumb = 140g raw	0.83
Eggs	4 eggs	0.43
Butter – Danish	2 x 12g scone spreadings	0.08
Soft margarine	10 x 5g thin spreadings on bread	0.05
Vegetable and salad oils	6 tbsp	0.04
Reduced fat spreads	28 x 5g thin spreadings on bread	0.19
Sugar	5 x 4g level tsp/day + 1 x 20 tbsp per wk	0.09
Marmalade	9 x 15g av spreadings on bread	0.18
Previous year's crop potatoes purchased Jan to Aug	cf = 1; 7 x 220g large portions	1.01
Cabbages, fresh	cf = 1; ep = 0.77; 3 x 120g large portions = 468g	0.20
Brussels sprouts, fresh	cf = 1; ep = 0.69; 2 x 90g av 9 sprout portion = 261g	0.36
Carrots, fresh	cf = 1; ep = 0.7; 4 x 85g large portions = 486g	0.27
Onions, shallots, leeks, fresh	1 x 150g medium raw	0.09
Tomatoes, fresh	2 x 85g medium	0.24
Peas, canned	ep = 0.67; 3 x 90g portions = 402g	0.43
Beans, canned	1 x 420g large can (3 x 140g servings)	0.37
Frozen chips and other frozen convenience potato products	1 portion potato crunchies	0.28
All frozen vegetables and frozen vegetables products not specified elsewhere	2 x 85g portions sweetcorn or mixed veg	0.25
Oranges, fresh	ep = 0.7; raw medium without skin 120g = 171g purchase wt	0.23
Apples, fresh	5 x 112g medium raw with core	0.44
Bananas, fresh	ep = 0.66; 5 x 100g medium without skin = 758g purchase wt	0.79
Other canned or bottled fruit	fruit cocktail in juice, 2 x 115g av portion (ep not known, 300g can)	0.28
Fruit juices	7 x 160g av glasses	0.68
Bread, white, sliced standard	1 x 400g small loaf	0.38

Table A2.2: Single man (cont)

Description	Purchase quantities and portions	Cost (£)
Bread, wholemeal, sliced	1 x 800g loaf	0.42
Rolls	3 x 56g granary	0.43
Flour	75g per wk	0.04
Buns, scones and teacakes	2 x 50g scones or hot cross buns	0.20
Cakes and pastries	2 x 46g cherry bakewell slices	0.33
Biscuits, other than chocolate	12 x 8g lincoln or marie biscuits (0.5 packet)	0.22
Other high fibre breakfast cereals	14 x 20g Weetabix (2 per day)	0.60
Canned milk pudding	1 x 150g small can	0.39
Tea	28 x 2.5g teabags	0.39
Coffee, instant	24 level (12 heaped) tsp instant	0.23
Soups, canned	2 x 300g small cans	0.70
Salad dressings	2 x 12g portions mayonnaise	0.06
Pickles and sauces	4 x 20g portions tomato ketchup; 1 x 15g heaped tsp pickle	0.13
Meat and yeast extracts	3 x 5g tsp gravy browning	0.05
Ice-cream	1 x 75g av serving	0.05
Salt	1 x heaped tsp	0.00
Soft drinks, unconcentrated	0.5 litre lemonade	0.18
Boiled sweets and jellies	jellies	0.34
Total cost for all foods, home food supply		**23.00**

Table A2.3: **LCA basket of food for one week: couple (one man and one woman)
aged 65-74 years
(cf = conversion factor; ep = edible portion)**

Description	Purchase quantities and portions	Cost (£)
Yoghurt	2 x 125g pots	0.29
Semi and other skimmed milk	4544ml = 8 pints	2.16
Cheese, natural, hard, Cheddar and Cheddar type	2 x 45g sandwich portions	0.44
Cheese, processed	2 x 14g cheese triangles	0.13
Pork chops	cf pork chops = 0.63; 2 x spare rib chops grilled edible portion = 2 x 140g cooked = 444g raw	2.03
Bacon and ham, uncooked rashers, not pre-packed	cf bacon back = 0.59; 6 x 25g cooked rashers = 254g raw	1.13
Bacon and ham, cooked, including canned	6 x 23g av slices ham	0.96
Broiler chicken, uncooked, including frozen	ep whole roast chicken = 0.65; cf = 0.86; 4 x 140g large portions = 1kg	2.04
Sausages, uncooked, pork	cf grilled pork sausages = 0.72; 6 x 20g thin grilled = 167g raw	0.45
Other frozen convenience meats	2 x turkey/chicken in crumb, purchase wt = 100g each (cf = 0.95)	1.42
Meat pies, pasties and puddings	2 x 140g beef and onion pies	1.13
Fish, white, filleted, fresh	cf cod baked fillets = 0.81.3 x 175g large = 648g raw	3.08
Salmon, canned	ep canned salmon = 0.81; 1 x 110g tin salmon provides 89g edible (2 x sandwich)	0.59
Eggs	6 eggs	0.64
Butter – Danish	5 x 12g scone spreadings	0.20
Soft margarine	20 x 5g thin spreadings on bread	0.09
Vegetable and salad oils	10 tbsp	0.07
Reduced fat spreads	60 x 5g thin spreadings on bread	0.25
Sugar	12 x 4g level tsp/day + 3 x 20g tbsp/wk	0.23
Jams, jellies, fruit curds	19 x 15g av spreadings on bread	0.38
Previous year's crop potatoes purchased Jan to Aug	cf = 1; 15 x 220g large portions	1.46
Cabbages, fresh	cf = 1; ep = 0.77; 6 x 120g large portions = 935g	0.40
Cauliflower, fresh	cf = 1; ep = 0.45; 4 x 120g large portions = 1066g	1.29
Leafy salads, fresh	ep = 0.74; 2 x 30g salad portions, 3 x 20g sandwich portions;	0.29
Carrots, fresh	cf = 1; ep = 0.7; 6 x 85g large portions = 729g	0.38
Turnips and swedes, fresh	ep = 0.73; cf = 1; 4 x 85g large portions = 466g	0.40
Onions, shallots, leeks, fresh	2 x 150g medium raw	0.18
Tomatoes, fresh	4 x 85g medium	0.49
Beans, canned	1 x 420g large can	0.37
Frozen peas	5 x 85g portions	0.33
Frozen chips and other frozen convenience potato products	2 x 90g portions potato crunchies	0.47
All frozen vegetables and frozen vegetables products not specified elsewhere	2 x 90g av portions spinach or mixed veg	0.26
Oranges, fresh	2 x 120g small without skin, ep = 0.7 = 343g purchased	0.45
Other citrus fruit, fresh	6 x 60g raw medium without skin; ep = 0.75; = 480g purchase wt	0.73
Apples, fresh	10 x 112g M raw with core	0.87

Table A2.3: **Couple (cont)**

Description	Purchase quantities and portions	Cost (£)
Bananas, fresh	ep = 0.66; 8 x 100g medium without skin = 1212g purchase wt	1.26
Canned peaches, pears and pineapples	2 x 135g av portion canned pears (ep not known, small tin = 300g)	0.22
Other canned or bottled fruit		0.00
Dried fruit and dried fruit products	2 x 30g tbsp sultanas	0.07
Fruit juices	14 x 160g av glasses	1.12
Bread, white, sliced standard	1 x 800g	0.35
Bread, wholemeal, sliced	1 x 800g, 1 x 400g	0.92
Rolls	7 x 48g wmeal rolls	0.49
Flour	270g/wk	0.04
Buns, scones and teacakes	5 x 50g scones or hot cross buns	0.42
Cakes and pastries	3 x 46g bakewell slices	0.50
Biscuits, other than chocolate	25 x 8g lincoln biscuits (1 packet)	0.46
Other high fibre breakfast cereals	28 x 20g Weetabix (2 each per day)	1.10
Canned milk pudding	1 x 425g large can – 2 portions	0.41
Tea	64 x 2.5g teabags	0.82
Coffee, instant	23 level (11 heaped) tsp	0.22
Soups, canned	1 x 405g large can	0.22
Salad dressings	4 x 12g portions mayonnaise	0.13
Pickles and sauces	6 x 20g portion tomato ketchup; 2 x 15g tsp pickle	0.19
Meat and yeast extracts	6 x 5g tsp gravy granules	0.11
Ice-cream	4 x 75g av servings	0.22
Salt	2 heaped tsp	0.01
Soft drinks, unconcentrated	1 litre lemonade	0.36
Chocolate coated filled bar/sweets	2 x 49g (4 finger Kit-Kat)	0.51
Boiled sweets and jellies	bag of butterscotch sweets	0.68
Total cost for all foods, home food supply		**36.91**

References

Citro, C.C. and Michael, R.T. (eds) (1995) *Measuring poverty: A new approach*, Washington, DC: National Academy Press.

DoH (Department of Health) (1991) *Dietary Reference Values for Food Energy and Nutrients for the United Kingdom*, Report on Health and Social Subjects No 41, London: The Stationery Office.

Friedman, L.A. and Kimball, A.W. (1986) 'Coronary heart disease mortality and alcohol consumption in Framingham', *American Journal Epidemiology*, vol 124, pp 481-9.

HEA (Health Education Authority) (1996) *Think about drink*, London: HEA.

Holland, B., Welch, A.A., Unwin, I.D., Buss, D.H., Paul, A.A. and Southgate, D.A.T. (1991) in McCance and Widdowson, *The composition of foods*, 5th edn, Cambridge: Royal Society of Chemistry.

MAFF (Ministry of Agriculture, Fisheries and Food) (1993-97) *Household food consumption and expenditure 1992-1996*, London: HMSO and The Stationery Office.

MAFF (1998) *Food portion sizes*, 2nd edn, London: The Stationery Office.

Nelson, M., Mayer, A.B. and Manley, P.(1993) 'The food budget', in J. Bradshaw (ed) *Budget standards for the United Kingdom*, Avebury: Aldershot.

ONS (Office for National Statistics) (1993-96) *Family spending 1992-1996*, London: The Stationery Office.

Orshansky, M. (1965) 'Counting the poor, another look at the poverty profile', *Social Security Bulletin*, vol 28-1.

SAS Institute Inc (1998) SAS Campus Drive, Cary, North Carolina 27513.

Wenlock, R.W., Buss, D.H., Derry, B.J. and Dixon, E.J. (1980) 'Household food wastage in Britain', *British Journal of Nutrition*, vol 43, pp 53-70.

Appendix 3

Low-income discussion groups

Shopping patterns

This appendix analyses material indicating the shopping patterns of the FBU's 12 discussion groups. All the groups were composed of older people aged 65-74 years, living independently in single or couple households. Eleven of the groups lived in urban areas; one group lived in a rural area. The discussions focused on key components of expenditure and on issues relating to eating habits, shopping patterns and budget priorities. The criteria for the composition of the groups, their aims and objectives are described in Part Two, Sections 3.5 and 5.2.

1   Shopping methods and frequency

Unlike low-income families with children in the FBU's first LCA budgets (Parker, 1998), most of the older people, or at least those living in urban areas, shopped frequently and at many different outlets. They had time to spare and shopped partly for social reasons. They did most of their shopping in local markets, city supermarkets and traditional high street shops, at intervals which depended on the weight and bulk of the items purchased. In other words the amount of shopping on any one occasion was restricted to what they could carry. Personal shopping trolleys were popular, except for single men. Concessionary bus fares for pensioners encouraged frequent use of public transport, although most bus companies impose restrictions on rush-hour travel at reduced rates. Taxis were seldom used and only 7% of group participants were car owners.

The pattern of rural shopping, as described by the group from Somerset, appears very different from that described by the urban groups. Local village shops were used for everyday shopping, including food, and price was less of an issue. The village store, for example, served as a post office and newsagent. A mobile fish van visited weekly, as did a van selling items such as peat, paraffin and bean sticks. In general the prices charged by village facilities were thought to be reasonable and doorstep delivery of heavy or odd-sized items was particularly appreciated. Shopping in town was irregular, because it meant catching an occasional bus or getting a lift.

2   Shopping for food

Group participants reported shopping for food almost every day and keeping an eye out for 'sell-by date' bargains and special offers. When asked where she bought her food, one person replied, "here, there and everywhere"; and this was found to be the usual pattern of all the groups. The full range of supermarkets was mentioned but often only to pick up bargains at 'reduced' counters. High street butchers were also used, as were doorstep milk deliveries and the local markets. Occasionally someone mentioned freezer shops. All the participants were thrifty; for example they would buy one item to get one free, but not three for the price of two. They preferred loose to packaged goods because this enabled them to select the quality and quantity they needed without waste. In the rural group, but not in the urban groups, many participants grew their own vegetables and used home-produced foods to supplement their diet.

Unlike adults in the FBU's families with children report (Parker, 1998), those in the older people discussion groups usually eat three meals a day: breakfast, one main meal and a lighter meal, plus snacks in between. Breakfast is usually cereal and toast, not a cooked meal, and snacks are of the sweet variety, for example scones, tea-breads, cakes and biscuits especially. Tea is drunk more often than coffee, usually with milk added, and more men than women add sugar. Squash and fizzy drinks are also popular, but very little fresh fruit juice is drunk. Fruit and vegetables are fresh, frozen or tinned: dairy products consist mainly of milk (whole or semi-skimmed), hard cheese and the occasional processed cheese slices or triangles. Meat purchases are usually in the form of chops, mince or cuts suitable for stewing; joints are usually regarded as a luxury. Women are more likely than men to eat reduced-fat spreads.

3   Clothing

Most of the town dwellers frequented charity shops for at least some of their clothing for 'style and quality', 'especially labels', as well as to save money. They also shopped in local markets for 'seconds' or 'firsts' at reduced prices. Mail order catalogues were used, as were discount high street stores. Many participants had at least one pair of 'decent' shoes, bought from a good quality high street shop, often in the sales. Women tended to attach importance to this because of 'foot problems', while the men described their good shoes as 'church shoes', which last for years and are worn with suits.

Relatives and friends are often the source of new or good quality second-hand clothing, as gifts and as 'pass ons' when a family member or close friend dies. The groups of single people were noticeably worse off than couples, often lacking family support and with frugal levels of spending on replacement clothing. All the households, including single men, reported doing their own minor clothing repairs, for example sewing on buttons and repairing seams and hems.

There were some urban/rural differences in preferences for clothing. Country dwellers tended to prefer practical and serviceable rather than fashionable clothing; and could think of few occasions (other than weddings or funerals) when they would require special occasion clothing. They were also more likely to use mail order catalogues, such as Kays, Empire Stores and Littlewoods. Some knit their own accessories, such as hats and gloves.

4 Postage, telephone, travel and services

All the group members had telephones. Single women had the highest telephone bills, which ranged from £50 to £120 a quarter; couples came second, with bills ranging from £15 (special low-user rate) to £65 a quarter; single men had the smallest bills, ranging from £7 (local Ninex telephone system) to £95 each quarter. Communication and services were said to be more expensive in rural than in urban areas. Country dwellers, for example, were said to use postal and telephone services more often, their transport costs were higher and services such as window cleaning were also more expensive for them.

5 Healthcare

Personal care items were generally purchased in high street outlets like Boots, Superdrug or other chemist shops, rather than in supermarkets. Older people reported that they seldom go to the opticians or the dentist, because "they cannot afford

it". When they do require spectacles, however, they buy them at opticians rather than in high street chemist shops, sometimes economising by having their new lenses put in old frames. The most frequently mentioned medications in the first-aid cupboard were paracetamol, indigestion tablets, cold powders, cod liver oil and basic first-aid dressings like Elastoplast.

6 Household services

Only a few household services were purchased. The women in the groups mentioned 'mobile' hairdressers, cutting their own hair and 'pensioner days' at the local hairdresser's. Generally speaking, the women in the groups thought it important to be able to afford (in moderation) things that "made them feel good about their appearance", such as regular hair perms. The men generally went to the barber's every six weeks, but a few of the wives said they cut their husband's hair. Most of the men said they used disposable razors, which lasted on average one week each. Only a few used electric razors. In situations where outside windows had to be cleaned, a window cleaner was employed. On the whole, extended families helped with redecoration; group members did minor tasks themselves or some did not bother. The same applies to heavy cleaning, such as shampooing carpets.

7 Household durables

Furniture was seldom replaced, although some group members reported having had to leave their better furniture behind when moving to smaller accommodation, and refurnish with smaller, less expensive items. Others said they had replaced their furniture through mail order catalogues, shopped around for bargains or high street sales. Some items were inherited from friends or family, and sometimes an item was bought second-hand. High street catalogue shops and local markets were a source of electrical goods.

8 Home entertainment

All the group members had colour TV and most sets were purchased new. A few people rented their TV set. Only one had cable TV. Households including men were more likely to own a video recorder. Single women rarely had videos. Few households had CD players. Couples and single men were more likely than single women to buy newspapers. Women in couple households bought more magazines than single women. Crosswords were commonly mentioned. Some women knit, but the cost of wool these days was said to be expensive. Most households used public libraries, or bought or swapped second-hand books from stalls and clubs. It was common for couples to report that at Christmas they send out about 100 Christmas cards. Single women send out about 60 cards, single men send very few. Many cards were delivered by hand, but this was less common for single men. Giving at Christmas is kept to a minimum (children and grandchildren) and presents tend to be small.

Artificial Christmas trees were in vogue with urban, older people, but the rural group bought fresh trees from their local nursery garden each year. In general, rural people spent more on gardening products than their urban counterparts, of whom only a few mentioned gardening or growing vegetables as an activity. Country dwellers also reported that their hobbies were more expensive than those of city people: for example films and film processing, knitting patterns, knitting wool and needles, especially wooden knitting needles which are 'kinder to arthritic fingers'.

9 Outside activities

In general urban group found trips to the cinema or theatre were too expensive, although some older people, especially single women, said that their local community centre ran coach trips to see a show. There was no clear pattern of leisure activities among these town dwellers, but single women again reported more activities and hobbies than women in couple households, or single men. Activities ranged from line dancing and bowling to reading and walking. Occasionally, an active older person was involved in four or five activities, including swimming, dancing, keep-fit and amateur dramatics. There was little reporting of activities such as bingo or lottery. For the few who did participate, their costs were £1 to £2 a week. Lottery was more often taken to mean a draw at the local hospice than the National Lottery. None of the group members frequented pubs during the evening and only a few said they drank alcohol at all, even in their own

homes. Usually they said they could not afford it. A few said they went to church and contributed £1 to £2 a week to the church collection. Most were not pet owners. When pets were mentioned, a cat, dog or budgie were the most popular.

The rural group participant, on the other hand, reported that they had access to few leisure activities and they appeared less active in local community groups than the city dwellers.

10 Holidays

Few of the group participants could afford an annual holiday, but they do go away from home. Widows and widowers tend to be involved with their adult children, whether house-sitting, visiting family or participating in extended family holidays, sometimes abroad. Others, particularly those with limited family support, join groups on coach trips, usually in the UK and sometimes organised by their local community club. Couples, on the other hand, are more likely to holiday independently. They look for bargains: Blackpool, Cornwall, Turkey, Majorca, and Tenerife, sometimes for a week, sometimes for less. In some cases the holidays are made possible by local community centres, who organise trips and saving schemes. Out of season holidays are acceptable, and even preferred because the accommodation and resorts are less crowded.

11 Budgeting and credit

Only a few of the group members had credit cards, but some had bank accounts and most had Post Office accounts from which they drew their pension. They mainly dealt in cash transactions on a weekly basis. A few, mainly single people reported having either funeral plans or life insurance policies which would pay for their funeral costs. A small number were covered by Home Contents insurance policies. The full range of payment options were used to pay for gas and electricity, that is, standing orders, direct debit, pre-paid, quarterly metered, stamps and cash payments. When asked about their budgeting methods, many said that they budget weekly and save cash in pots for housing bills, birthdays and Christmas. In some areas credit unions were said to be the only place they could get credit. In some instances older people were themselves involved in running a credit union.

When asked what they would do without, should they find themselves short of money, food was the most elastic commodity. A common response was to live out of the store cupboard or freezer and cut down on biscuits. Some said they would cut down on the lottery, or 'hair-dos' at the hairdresser's, or make clothes last longer. Only a few reported drinking alcohol or smoking. Many said they lived so carefully they had few luxuries they could cut down on.

References

Parker, H. (ed) (1998) *Low Cost but Acceptable: A minimum income standard for the UK: Families with young children*, Bristol: The Policy Press.

Budget schedules and prices
Single people and couples aged 65-74 years

Clothing, personal care, household goods,
household services, leisure, transport

Contents

Clothing: Woman aged 65-74 years

Item	Brand	Retailer	Unit Price £	Quantity	Life/Years	Total Price £	Cost/Year £	Cost/Week £
Coats, jackets								
winter coat, with hood, 3/4 length, wool		Bon Marché	39.99	1	5	39.99	8.00	0.154
coat, classic, wool/polyamide		Empire	59.99	1	10	59.99	6.00	0.115
anorak, with hood, water resistant	Original Clothing	Poundstretcher	16.99	1	2	16.99	8.50	0.163
Coats, jackets total						116.97	22.49	**0.433**
Main clothing								
suit, skirt and jacket, polyester		Empire	39.99	1	6	39.99	6.67	0.128
winter dress, velour		Poundstretcher	14.99	2	3	29.98	9.99	0.192
trousers, tailored, comfort, polyester	C&A	C&A	12.00	2	4	24.00	6.00	0.115
skirt, jacquard, stretch	Classic	Poundstretcher	11.99	1	3	11.99	4.00	0.077
trousers, elasticated waist, polyester/elastane		Poundstretcher	7.99	1	1	7.99	7.99	0.154
winter sweater, long sleeves, lambswool rich		Empire	17.99	2	4	35.98	9.00	0.173
winter cardigan, acrylic		Bon Marché	14.99	2	4	29.98	7.50	0.144
sweatshirt, polyester/viscose		Empire	14.99	2	4	29.98	7.50	0.144
ski pants, fleece		Poundstretcher	5.99	2	2	11.98	5.99	0.115
shirt, long sleeve, cotton, pack of 2	Original Clothing	Empire	24.99	1	6	24.99	4.17	0.080
blouse, long sleeves, polyester/elastane		C&A	16.99	1	5	16.99	3.40	0.065
summer jacket, shower resistant	C&A	Index Extra	16.00	1	3	16.00	5.33	0.103
summer dress, short sleeves		JD Williams	12.99	1	4	12.99	3.25	0.062
summer dress, short sleeves		JD Williams	16.99	1	4	16.99	4.25	0.082
summer skirt		JD Williams	10.99	1	4	10.99	2.75	0.053
summer sweater, long sleeves, nylon/acrylic	Accent	Poundstretcher	9.99	1	2	9.99	5.00	0.096
summer cardigan, acrylic		Empire	19.99	1	4	19.99	5.00	0.096
polo T-shirt	Labrada	Empire	9.99	3	4	29.97	7.49	0.144
swim suit, classic leg	Triumph	Index Extra	23.00	1	10	23.00	2.30	0.044
Main clothing total						403.77	107.54	**2.068**
Underwear								
long-line briefs		BHS	2.50	10	2	25.00	12.50	0.240
bra	Playtex	Empire	12.99	4	2	51.96	25.98	0.500
panty girdle		Empire	19.50	1	3	19.50	6.50	0.125
half slip, nylon, pack of 3		Empire	9.99	1	6	9.99	1.67	0.032
vest, thermal		Poundstretcher	3.99	2	2	7.98	3.99	0.077

Family Budget Unit, January 1999 prices

Clothing: Woman aged 65-74 years

Item	Brand	Retailer	Unit Price £	Quantity	Life/Years	Total Price £	Cost/Year £	Cost/Week £
tights, opaque, 40 denier, pack of 3		C&A	2.50	4	1	10.00	10.00	0.192
support tights	Pretty Polly	Co-op	2.60	2	1	5.20	5.20	0.100
winter socks, cotton rich		Poundstretcher	0.99	2	3	1.98	0.66	0.013
pop socks, knee high, pack of 2		Betterware	3.99	1	1	3.99	3.99	0.077
nightdress, polyester		Empire	13.99	2	5	27.98	5.60	0.108
nightshirt, cotton, pack of 2		Empire	12.99	1	3	12.99	4.33	0.083
dressing gown, fleece		Empire	18.99	1	15	18.99	1.27	0.024
Underwear total						**195.56**	**81.68**	**1.571**
Accessories								
hat and gloves set, acrylic		Poundstretcher	1.99	1	2	1.99	1.00	0.019
scarf, acrylic		York Market	1.00	1	1	1.00	1.00	0.019
lightweight scarf, muslin		Daxon	7.99	2	8	15.98	2.00	0.038
sun hat, cotton		Daxon	4.99	1	6	4.99	0.83	0.016
Accessories total						**23.96**	**4.82**	**0.093**
Footwear								
court shoes, leather upper		Shoe City	28.00	1	5	28.00	5.60	0.108
boots, lined, mid-calf		Empire	34.99	1	10	34.99	3.50	0.067
shoes, flat	Brevitt	Empire	34.99	1	3	34.99	11.66	0.224
sandals, leather upper	Hush Puppy Adelaide	Shoe City	30.00	1	6	30.00	5.00	0.096
summer shoes, leather upper	Jouralle	Shoe City	25.00	1	4	25.00	6.25	0.120
wellington boots		Army & Navy	9.99	1	8	9.99	1.25	0.024
slippers		Shoe City	8.00	1	1	8.00	8.00	0.154
Footwear total						**170.97**	**41.26**	**0.793**
Total woman's clothing						**911.23**	**257.80**	**4.958**

Family Budget Unit, January 1999 prices

Clothing: Man aged 65-74 years

Item	Brand	Retailer	Unit Price £	Quantity	Life/Years	Total Price £	Cost/Year £	Cost/Week £
Coats, jackets								
winter jacket, 3/4 length, padded, polyester cotton	C&A	C&A	30.00	1	5	30.00	6.00	**0.115**
jacket, teflon	Westrock	Empire	55.00	1	5	55.00	11.00	**0.212**
cagoule, fleece lined, water resistant	Outdoor Wear	Poundstretcher	16.79	1	5	16.79	3.36	**0.065**
Coats, jackets total						101.79	20.36	**0.392**
Main clothing								
suit, gabardine		Index Extra	85.00	1	7	85.00	12.14	**0.234**
trousers, easycare, polyester	C&A	C&A	16.00	3	3	48.00	16.00	**0.308**
shirt, long sleeves, polyester/cotton		Empire	8.99	2	3	17.98	5.99	**0.115**
shirt, long sleeves, casual, plaid, cotton	C&A	C&A	12.00	2	3	24.00	8.00	**0.154**
pullover, sleeveless, button front, mixed fibres	C&A	C&A	15.00	1	5	15.00	3.00	**0.058**
jumper, long sleeves, acrylic	C&A	C&A	9.00	1	3	9.00	3.00	**0.058**
jumper, chenille	Creed	Poundstretcher	7.99	1	3	7.99	2.66	**0.051**
sweater, knitted acrylic		Empire	17.99	1	3	17.99	6.00	**0.115**
cardigan, knitted acrylic		Empire	19.99	1	3	19.99	6.66	**0.128**
blazer, gabardine		Index Extra	42.00	1	5	42.00	8.40	**0.162**
trousers, summer, polyester/viscose		Index Extra	17.00	2	3	34.00	11.33	**0.218**
shorts, cotton		Index Extra	12.00	1	5	12.00	2.40	**0.046**
shirt, short sleeves, pique, polyester/cotton		Empire	8.99	2	3	17.98	5.99	**0.115**
shirt, polo, cotton		Index Extra	8.00	4	3	32.00	10.67	**0.205**
sweater, summer, acrylic		Empire	11.99	1	3	11.99	4.00	**0.077**
swimming trunks, nylon/polyamide	C&A	C&A	9.00	1	5	9.00	1.80	**0.035**
Main clothing total						403.92	108.05	**2.078**
Underwear								
pants, Y front, cotton		York Market	1.00	8	1	8.00	8.00	**0.154**
vests, thermal, polyester/cotton	Drew Brady	Poundstretcher	3.49	3	3	10.47	3.49	**0.067**
pyjamas, flannelette		Poundstretcher	7.99	3	4	23.97	5.99	**0.115**
dressing gown, fleece		Empire	29.99	1	10	29.99	3.00	**0.058**
winter socks, acrylic/wool, pack of 5		C&A	5.00	1	1	5.00	5.00	**0.096**
summer socks, cotton rich, pack of 3		Poundstretcher	3.99	2	1	7.98	7.98	**0.153**
boot socks		Sainsburys	3.50	1	5	3.50	0.70	**0.013**
Underwear total						88.91	34.16	**0.657**

Family Budget Unit, January 1999 prices

Clothing: Man aged 65-74 years

Item	Brand	Retailer	Unit Price £	Quantity	Life/Years	Total Price £	Cost/Year £	Cost/Week £
Accessories								
hat, knitted		York Market	1.99	1	2	1.99	1.00	0.019
scarf, acrylic		Poundstretcher	1.99	1	1	1.99	1.99	0.038
gloves, acrylic		York Market	1.00	1	1	1.00	1.00	0.019
tie, polyester		C&A	5.00	2	8	10.00	1.25	0.024
belt, leather		C&A	6.00	1	8	6.00	0.75	0.014
hat, baseball		Army & Navy	2.99	1	4	2.99	0.75	0.014
Accessories total						23.97	6.73	0.129
Footwear								
shoes, leather upper	Grosvenor	Shoe City	25.00	2	3	50.00	16.67	0.321
sandals, leather upper	Grosvenor	Shoe City	10.00	1	1	10.00	10.00	0.192
trainers, leather upper	High Tec	Shoe City	25.00	1	3	25.00	8.33	0.160
wellington boots		Army & Navy	9.99	1	8	9.99	1.25	0.024
slippers		Poundstretcher	4.99	1	1	4.99	4.99	0.096
Footwear total						99.98	41.24	0.793
Total man's clothing						718.57	210.54	4.049

Family Budget Unit, January 1999 prices

Sewing materials: Single person aged 65-74 years

Item	Brand	Retailer	Unit Price £	Quantity	Life/Years	Total Price £	Cost/Year £	Cost/Week £
Sewing repair kit								
sewing kit		Co-op	1.89	1	1	1.89	1.89	0.036
scissors	S&S	Co-op	4.99	1	10	4.99	0.50	0.010
buttons, pack of 5		Co-op	0.69	1	1	0.69	0.69	0.013
shoe laces, 2 pairs		Co-op	0.75	1	1	0.75	0.75	0.014
Sewing repair kit total						8.32	3.83	0.074
Total single person's sewing repair kit						8.32	3.83	0.074

Sewing materials: Couple aged 65-74 years

Item	Brand	Retailer	Unit Price £	Quantity	Life/Years	Total Price £	Cost/Year £	Cost/Week £
Sewing repair kit								
sewing kit		Co-op	1.89	1	1	1.89	1.89	0.036
scissors	S&S	Co-op	4.99	1	10	4.99	0.50	0.010
buttons, pack of 5		Co-op	0.69	2	1	1.38	1.38	0.027
shoe laces, 2 pairs		Co-op	0.75	2	1	1.50	1.50	0.029
Sewing repair kit total						9.76	5.27	0.101
Total couple's sewing repair kit						9.76	5.27	0.101

Family Budget Unit, January 1999 prices

Personal care: Woman aged 65-74 years

Item	Brand	Retailer	Unit Price £	Quantity	Life/Years	Total Price £	Cost/Year £	Cost/Week £
Healthcare								
plasters, fabric, pack of 40	No Frills	Kwik Save	0.89	1	1	0.89	0.89	0.017
bandage, crepe, 7.5cm x 4.5m	Superdrug	Superdrug	1.95	1	5	1.95	0.39	0.008
tape, microporous, 5m x 2.5cm	Elastoplast	Superdrug	1.95	1	1	1.95	1.95	0.038
melolin dressing, 5cm x 5cm, pack of 5	Superdrug	Superdrug	1.69	1	2	1.69	0.85	0.016
bandage, cotton, 5cm		Boots	0.99	1	5	0.99	0.20	0.004
bandage, triangular calico, 90cm x 127cm	Superdrug	Superdrug	1.89	1	7	1.89	0.27	0.005
gauze swabs, sterile, 7.5cm x 7.5cm, 5	Boots	Boots	0.75	1	1	0.75	0.75	0.014
scissors, first aid	Superdrug	Superdrug	1.69	1	10	1.69	0.17	0.003
safety pins, pack of 45		Co-op	1.49	1	10	1.49	0.15	0.003
paracetamol, pack of 16	Superdrug	Superdrug	0.32	1	1	0.32	0.32	0.006
thermometer	Boots Easy Read	Boots	2.90	1	10	2.90	0.29	0.006
first aid book		Kwik Save	2.99	1	5	2.99	0.60	0.012
suntan lotion, factor 8, adult, 200ml	Johnson	Co-op	4.41	1	1	4.41	4.41	0.085
indigestion tablets, pack of 96	Superdrug	Superdrug	1.89	1	1	1.89	1.89	0.036
cold powders, pack of 10	Superdrug	Superdrug	1.09	1	1	1.09	1.09	0.021
tissues, pack of 100	No Frills	Kwik Save	0.44	12	1	5.28	5.28	0.102
Healthcare total						32.17	19.49	0.375
Personal hygiene								
toilet soap, 3 x 125gm	Simple	Kwik Save	0.99	4	1	3.96	3.96	0.076
denture cleaning tablets, 30	Superdrug	Superdrug	0.79	12	1	9.48	9.48	0.182
toothpaste, 125gm	No Frills	Kwik Save	0.34	6	1	2.04	2.04	0.039
toothbrush, medium	Kwik Save	Kwik Save	0.85	4	1	3.40	3.40	0.065
hairbrush		Kwik Save	1.49	1	4	1.49	0.37	0.007
comb, pack of 2		Co-op	0.89	1	2	0.89	0.45	0.009
shampoo, 200ml	Elvive Normal	Kwik Save	1.99	4	1	7.96	7.96	0.153
conditioner, 200ml	Elvive Normal	Kwik Save	1.99	2	1	3.98	3.98	0.077
hairspray, 200ml	Sylvikrin	Kwik Save	1.19	1	1	1.19	1.19	0.023
razor, disposable, 10	Bic	Kwik Save	0.79	1	1	0.79	0.79	0.015
nail clippers	Superdrug	Superdrug	0.99	1	10	0.99	0.10	0.002
emery boards, pack of 8	Beauty Essentials	Superdrug	0.79	1	3	0.79	0.26	0.005
deodorant, roll-on, 50ml	Sure	Kwik Save	1.14	2	1	2.28	2.28	0.044

Family Budget Unit, January 1999 prices

Personal care: Woman aged 65-74 years

Item	Brand	Retailer	Unit Price £	Quantity	Life/Years	Total Price £	Cost/Year £	Cost/Week £
talcum powder, 150gm	Imperial Leather	Kwik Save	0.92	1	1	0.92	0.92	**0.018**
hand cream, 100ml	Atrixo	Kwik Save	1.99	1	2	1.99	1.00	**0.019**
hair, permanent wave		local	17.20	2	1	34.40	34.40	**0.662**
haircut, dry trim		local	5.00	3	1	15.00	15.00	**0.288**
Personal hygiene total						91.55	87.57	**1.684**
Personal accessories								
suitcase, trolley	Hawa	Argos	17.99	1	10	17.99	1.80	**0.035**
holdall	Hawa	Argos	12.99	1	10	12.99	1.30	**0.025**
toilet bag		Kwik Save	1.99	1	3	1.99	0.66	**0.013**
shopping trolley	Marketeer	Argos	18.99	1	8	18.99	2.37	**0.046**
handbag, synthetic	C&A	C&A	12.00	1	8	12.00	1.50	**0.029**
purse, leather	Index	Index	5.49	1	8	5.49	0.69	**0.013**
hairdryer	Remington	Argos	14.99	1	4	14.99	3.75	**0.072**
watch, gold plated case	Sekonda Ladies Quartz	Argos	15.99	1	15	15.99	1.07	**0.021**
earring set, 3 pair set		Index	9.99	1	15	9.99	0.67	**0.013**
necklace, 16" simulated pearl		Argos	19.50	1	15	19.50	1.30	**0.025**
umbrella, telescopic		Gulliver	6.00	1	10	6.00	0.60	**0.012**
small mirror	Sainsburys	Sainsburys	2.35	1	10	2.35	0.24	**0.005**
wall mirror		Index	9.99	1	15	9.99	0.67	**0.013**
clock, alarm	Acctim	Index	4.95	1	15	4.95	0.33	**0.006**
clock, quartz, mantel	Acctim	Index	11.99	1	10	11.99	1.20	**0.023**
sun glasses, UVA/UVB protection	Boots	Boots	10.00	1	5	10.00	2.00	**0.038**
Personal accessories total						175.20	20.13	**0.387**
Cosmetics								
lipstick	Collection 2000	Superdrug	1.49	2	1	2.98	2.98	**0.057**
moisturiser, face, 200ml	Nivea	Kwik Save	1.49	1	1	1.49	1.49	**0.029**
spray perfume, 30ml	Anais Anais	Kwik Save	11.99	1	3	11.99	4.00	**0.077**
face powder, loose	Collection 2000	Superdrug	1.99	1	2	1.99	1.00	**0.019**
Cosmetics total						18.45	9.46	**0.182**
Total woman's personal care						317.37	136.66	**2.628**

Family Budget Unit, January 1999 prices

Personal care: Man aged 65-74 years

Item	Brand	Retailer	Unit Price £	Quantity	Life/Years	Total Price £	Cost/Year £	Cost/Week £
Healthcare								
plasters, fabric, pack of 40	No Frills	Kwik Save	0.89	1	1	0.89	0.89	0.017
bandage, crepe, 7.5cm x 4.5m	Superdrug	Superdrug	1.95	1	5	1.95	0.39	0.008
tape, microporous, 5m x 2.5cm	Elastoplast	Superdrug	1.95	1	1	1.95	1.95	0.038
melolin dressing, 5cm x 5cm, pack of 5	Superdrug	Superdrug	1.69	1	2	1.69	0.85	0.016
bandage, cotton, 5cm	Boots	Boots	0.99	1	5	0.99	0.20	0.004
bandage, triangular calico, 90cm x 127cm	Superdrug	Superdrug	1.89	1	7	1.89	0.27	0.005
gauze swabs, sterile, 7.5cm x 7.5cm, 5	Boots	Boots	0.75	1	1	0.75	0.75	0.014
scissors, first aid	Superdrug	Superdrug	1.69	1	10	1.69	0.17	0.003
safety pins, pack of 45		Co-op	1.49	1	10	1.49	0.15	0.003
paracetamol, pack of 16	Superdrug	Superdrug	0.32	1	1	0.32	0.32	0.006
thermometer	Boots Easy Read	Boots	2.90	1	10	2.90	0.29	0.006
first aid book		Kwik Save	2.99	1	5	2.99	0.60	0.012
suntan lotion, factor 8, adult, 200ml	Johnson	Co-op	4.41	1	1	4.41	4.41	0.085
indigestion tablets, pack of 96	Superdrug	Superdrug	1.89	1	1	1.89	1.89	0.036
cold powders, pack of 10	Superdrug	Superdrug	1.09	1	1	1.09	1.09	0.021
tissues, pack of 100	No Frills	Kwik Save	0.44	12	1	5.28	5.28	0.102
Healthcare total						32.17	19.49	0.375
Personal hygiene								
toilet soap, 3 x 125gm	Simple	Kwik Save	0.99	4	1	3.96	3.96	0.076
denture cleaning tablets, 30	Superdrug	Superdrug	0.79	12	1	9.48	9.48	0.182
toothpaste, 125gm	No Frills	Kwik Save	0.34	6	1	2.04	2.04	0.039
toothbrush, medium	Kwik Save	Kwik Save	0.85	4	1	3.40	3.40	0.065
hairbrush		Kwik Save	1.49	1	4	1.49	0.37	0.007
comb, pack of 2		Co-op	0.89	1	2	0.89	0.45	0.009
shampoo, 200ml	Elvive Normal	Kwik Save	1.99	4	1	7.96	7.96	0.153
nail clipper	Superdrug	Superdrug	0.99	1	3	0.99	0.33	0.006
emery boards, pack of 8	Beauty Essentials	Superdrug	0.79	1	5	0.79	0.16	0.003
deodorant, roll-on, 50ml	Sure	Kwik Save	1.14	1	1	1.14	1.14	0.022
razor, disposable, pack of 10	Bic Microglide	Co-op	1.89	6	1	11.34	11.34	0.218
shaving foam 250ml	Co-op	Co-op	1.09	5	1	5.45	5.45	0.105

Family Budget Unit, January 1999 prices

Personal care: Man aged 65-74 years

Item	Brand	Retailer	Unit Price £	Quantity	Life/Years	Total Price £	Cost/Year £	Cost/Week £
talcum powder	Imperial Leather	Kwik Save	0.92	1	2	0.92	0.46	0.009
haircut, dry trim		local	3.50	6	1	21.00	21.00	0.404
Personal hygiene total						70.85	67.54	**1.299**
Personal accessories								
suitcase, trolley	Hawa	Argos	17.99	1	10	17.99	1.80	0.035
holdall	Hawa	Argos	12.99	1	10	12.99	1.30	0.025
toilet bag		Kwik Save	1.99	1	3	1.99	0.66	0.013
wallet, leather	Churchill	Argos	4.99	1	5	4.99	1.00	0.019
watch, gold-plated case	Sekonda Gents Quartz	Argos	19.99	1	15	19.99	1.33	0.026
umbrella, telescopic		Gulliver	6.00	1	10	6.00	0.60	0.012
shaving mirror		Index	5.99	1	10	5.99	0.60	0.012
wall mirror		Index	9.99	1	10	9.99	1.00	0.019
clock, alarm	Acctim	Index	4.95	1	15	4.95	0.33	0.006
clock, quartz, mantel	Acctim	Index	11.99	1	15	11.99	0.80	0.015
sun glasses, UVA/UVB protection	Boots	Boots	10.00	1	5	10.00	2.00	0.038
Personal accessories total						106.87	11.42	**0.220**
Cosmetics								
aftershave lotion, 100ml	Gillette	Sainsburys	4.99	1	1	4.99	4.99	0.096
Cosmetics total						4.99	4.99	**0.096**
Total man's personal care						214.88	103.43	**1.989**

Family Budget Unit, January 1999 prices

Personal care: Couple aged 65-74 years

Item	Brand	Retailer	Unit Price £	Quantity	Life/Years	Total Price £	Cost/Year £	Cost/Week £
Healthcare								
plasters, fabric, pack of 40	No Frills	Kwik Save	0.89	1	1	0.89	0.89	0.017
bandage, crepe, 7.5cm x 4.5m	Superdrug	Superdrug	1.95	2	5	3.90	0.78	0.015
tape, microporous, 5m x 2.5cm	Elastoplast	Superdrug	1.95	1	1	1.95	1.95	0.038
melolin dressing, 5cm x 5cm, pack of 5	Superdrug	Superdrug	1.69	1	1	1.69	1.69	0.033
bandage, cotton, 5cm		Boots	0.99	2	5	1.98	0.40	0.008
bandage, triangular calico, 90cm x 127cm	Superdrug	Superdrug	1.89	1	5	1.89	0.38	0.007
gauze swabs, sterile, 7.5cm x 7.5 cm, 5	Boots	Boots	0.75	1	1	0.75	0.75	0.014
scissors, first aid	Superdrug	Superdrug	1.69	1	10	1.69	0.17	0.003
safety pins, pack of 45	Superdrug	Co-op	1.49	1	10	1.49	0.15	0.003
paracetamol, pack of 16	Superdrug	Superdrug	0.32	2	1	0.64	0.64	0.012
thermometer	Boots Easy Read	Boots	2.90	1	10	2.90	0.29	0.006
first aid book		Kwik Save	2.99	1	5	2.99	0.60	0.012
suntan lotion, factor 8, adult, 200ml	Johnson	Co-op	4.41	2	1	8.82	8.82	0.170
indigestion tablets, pack of 96	Superdrug	Superdrug	1.89	2	1	3.78	3.78	0.073
cold powders, pack of 10	Superdrug	Superdrug	1.09	2	1	2.18	2.18	0.042
tissues, pack of 100	No Frills	Kwik Save	0.44	18	1	7.92	7.92	0.152
Healthcare total						**45.46**	**31.38**	**0.603**
Personal hygiene								
toilet soap, 3 x 125gm	Simple	Kwik Save	0.99	8	1	7.92	7.92	0.152
denture cleaning tablets, 30	Superdrug	Superdrug	0.79	24	1	18.96	18.96	0.365
toothpaste, 125gm	No Frills	Kwik Save	0.34	12	1	4.08	4.08	0.078
toothbrush, medium	Kwik Save	Kwik Save	0.85	8	1	6.80	6.80	0.131
hairbrush		Kwik Save	1.49	1	4	1.49	0.37	0.007
hairbrush		Kwik Save	1.49	1	4	1.49	0.37	0.007
comb, pack of 2		Co-op	0.89	1	2	0.89	0.45	0.009
comb, pack of 2		Co-op	0.89	1	2	0.89	0.45	0.009
shampoo, 200ml	Elvive Normal	Kwik Save	1.99	7	1	13.93	13.93	0.268
conditioner, 200ml	Elvive Normal	Kwik Save	1.99	2	1	3.98	3.98	0.077
hairspray, 200ml	Sylvikrin	Kwik Save	1.19	1	1	1.19	1.19	0.023
razor, disposable, woman, pack of 10	Bic	Kwik Save	0.79	1	1	0.79	0.79	0.015
nail clipper	Superdrug	Superdrug	0.99	1	10	0.99	0.10	0.002
emery boards, pack of 8	Beauty Essentials	Superdrug	0.79	1	3	0.79	0.26	0.005

Family Budget Unit, January 1999 prices

Personal care: Couple aged 65-74 years

Item	Brand	Retailer	Unit Price £	Quantity	Life/Years	Total Price £	Cost/Year £	Cost/Week £
deodorant, roll-on, 50ml	Sure	Kwik Save	1.14	3	1	3.42	3.42	**0.066**
talcum powder, 150gm	Imperial Leather	Kwik Save	0.92	3	2	2.76	1.38	**0.027**
hand cream, 100ml	Atrixo	Kwik Save	1.99	1	2	1.99	1.00	**0.019**
razor, disposable, man, pack of 10	Bic Microglide	Co-op	1.89	6	1	11.34	11.34	**0.218**
shaving foam 250ml	Co-op	Co-op	1.09	5	1	5.45	5.45	**0.105**
hair, permanent wave		local	17.20	2	1	34.40	34.40	**0.662**
haircut, dry trim, woman		local	5.00	3	1	15.00	15.00	**0.288**
haircut, dry trim, man		local	3.50	6	1	21.00	21.00	**0.404**
Personal hygiene total						159.55	152.63	**2.935**
Personal accessories								
suitcase, trolley	Hawa	Argos	17.99	2	10	35.98	3.60	**0.069**
holdall	Hawa	Argos	12.99	1	10	12.99	1.30	**0.025**
toilet bag		Kwik Save	1.99	1	3	1.99	0.66	**0.013**
shopping trolley	Marketeer	Argos	18.99	1	8	18.99	2.37	**0.046**
handbag, synthetic	C&A	C&A	12.00	1	8	12.00	1.50	**0.029**
purse, leather	Index	Index	5.49	1	8	5.49	0.69	**0.013**
wallet, leather	Churchill	Argos	4.99	1	8	4.99	0.62	**0.012**
hairdryer	Remington	Argos	14.99	1	4	14.99	3.75	**0.072**
watch, gold-plated case	Sekonda Ladies Quartz	Argos	15.99	1	15	15.99	1.07	**0.021**
watch, gold-plated case	Sekonda Gents Quartz	Argos	19.99	1	15	19.99	1.33	**0.026**
earring set, 3 pair set		Index	9.99	1	15	9.99	0.67	**0.013**
necklace, 16" simulated pearl		Argos	19.50	1	15	19.50	1.30	**0.025**
umbrella, telescopic		Gulliver	6.00	2	10	12.00	1.20	**0.023**
small mirror	Sainsbury	Sainsburys	2.35	1	10	2.35	0.24	**0.005**
wall mirror		Index	9.99	1	10	9.99	1.00	**0.019**
shaving mirror		Index	5.99	1	10	5.99	0.60	**0.012**
clock, alarm	Acctim	Index	4.95	1	15	4.95	0.33	**0.006**
clock, quartz, mantel	Acctim	Index	11.99	1	15	11.99	0.80	**0.015**
sun glasses, UVA/UVB protection	Boots	Boots	10.00	1	5	10.00	2.00	**0.038**
sun glasses, UVA/UVB protection	Boots	Boots	10.00	1	5	10.00	2.00	**0.038**
Personal accessories total						240.16	27.02	**0.520**

Family Budget Unit, January 1999 prices

Personal care: Couple aged 65-74 years

Item	Brand	Retailer	Unit Price £	Quantity	Life/Years	Total Price £	Cost/Year £	Cost/Week £
Cosmetics								
lipstick	Collection 2000	Superdrug	1.49	2	1	2.98	2.98	0.057
moisturiser, face, 200ml	Nivea	Kwik Save	1.49	1	1	1.49	1.49	0.029
spray perfume, 30ml	Anais Anais	Kwik Save	11.99	1	3	11.99	4.00	0.077
face powder, loose	Collection 2000	Superdrug	1.99	1	2	1.99	1.00	0.019
aftershave lotion, 100ml	Gillette	Sainsburys	4.99	1	1	4.99	4.99	0.096
Cosmetics total						7.97	7.97	0.153
Total couple's personal care						453.14	219.00	4.212

Family Budget Unit, January 1999 prices

Household goods: Furniture, local authority flat

Item	Brand	Retailer	Unit Price £	Quantity	Life/Years	Total Price £	Cost/Year £	Cost/Week £
Lounge/dining furniture								
suite, 3 piece	Christie Tyler	Argos	799.99	1	15	799.99	53.33	1.026
TV stand	Quattro	Argos	28.50	1	25	28.50	1.14	0.022
coffee tables, nest of 3	Westminster	Index	19.99	1	25	19.99	0.80	0.015
table, rectangular, 4 chairs		Index	169.00	1	25	169.00	6.76	0.130
wall unit	Addspace Clifton	Index	97.99	1	25	97.99	3.92	0.075
display cabinet	Addspace Clifton	Index	79.49	1	25	79.49	3.18	0.061
sideboard	Addspace Clifton	Index	59.99	1	25	59.99	2.40	0.046
bookcase		Index	24.99	1	25	24.99	1.00	0.019
Lounge/dining furniture total						1279.94	72.53	1.395
Kitchen furniture		(kitchen units as installed)						
Bedroom furniture								
bed, single divan	Apollo Homeworks	MFI	169.00	1	20	169.00	8.45	0.163
headboard, single, metal	Alamo	MFI	17.00	1	20	17.00	0.85	0.016
mattress, replacement	Silentnight	Index Extra	99.00	1	10	84.00	8.40	0.162
guest bed, folding	De-luxe	Index	69.99	1	25	84.00	3.36	0.065
wardrobe, tall, double	Denver	MFI	58.00	1	25	58.00	2.32	0.045
chest of drawers, bedside, 3-drawer	Denver	MFI	27.00	1	25	27.00	1.08	0.021
chest of drawers, double, 5-drawer	Denver	MFI	49.00	1	25	49.00	1.96	0.038
chest of drawers, single, 3-drawer	Denver	MFI	33.00	1	25	33.00	1.32	0.025
bookshelf, short, wide, 3-shelf	Denver	MFI	29.00	1	25	29.00	1.16	0.022
Bedroom furniture total						550.00	28.90	0.556
Bathroom furniture		(bathroom suite as installed)						
bathroom cabinet	Corinth	Argos	24.99	1	20	24.99	1.25	0.024
Bathroom furniture total						24.99	1.25	0.024
Total furniture, local authority flat						1854.93	102.68	1.975

Family Budget Unit, January 1999 prices

Household goods: Furniture, owner-occupied and local authority houses

Item	Brand	Retailer	Unit Price £	Quantity	Life/Years	Total Price £	Cost/Year £	Cost/Week £
Lounge/dining furniture								
suite, 3 piece	Christie Tyler	Argos	799.99	1	15	799.99	53.33	1.026
TV stand	Quattro	Argos	28.50	1	25	28.50	1.14	0.022
coffee tables, nest of 3	Westminster	Index	19.99	1	25	19.99	0.80	0.015
table, rectangular, 4 chairs		Index	169.00	1	25	169.00	6.76	0.130
wall unit	Addspace Clifton	Index	97.99	1	25	97.99	3.92	0.075
display cabinet	Addspace Clifton	Index	79.49	1	25	79.49	3.18	0.061
sideboard	Addspace Clifton	Index	59.99	1	25	59.99	2.40	0.046
bookcase		Index	24.99	1	25	24.99	1.00	0.019
Lounge/dining furniture total						1279.94	72.53	**1.395**
Kitchen furniture		(kitchen units as installed)						
Bedroom 1 furniture								
bed, double divan	Pegasus Slumber Rest	MFI	269.00	1	20	269.00	13.45	0.259
headboard, velour	Orchestra	MFI	35.00	1	20	35.00	1.75	0.034
mattress, replacement	Silentnight	Index Extra	99.00	1	10	99.00	9.90	0.190
wardrobe, tall, double	Denver	MFI	58.00	1	25	58.00	2.32	0.045
chest of drawers, bedside, 3-drawer	Denver	MFI	27.00	1	25	27.00	1.08	0.021
chest of drawers, double, 5-drawer	Denver	MFI	49.00	1	25	49.00	1.96	0.038
chest of drawers, single, 3-drawer	Denver	MFI	33.00	1	25	33.00	1.32	0.025
Bedroom 1 furniture total						570.00	31.78	**0.611**
Bedroom 2 furniture								
bed, single divan	Apollo Homeworks	MFI	99.00	1	25	99.00	3.96	0.076
headboard, single, metal	Alamo	MFI	17.00	1	25	17.00	0.68	0.013
chest of drawers, bedside, 3-drawer	Denver	MFI	27.00	1	25	27.00	1.08	0.021
chest of drawers, double, 5-drawer	Denver	MFI	49.00	1	25	49.00	1.96	0.038
wardrobe, combination, 3-drawer	Denver	MFI	83.00	1	25	83.00	3.32	0.064
tall boy unit, 1-drawer	Denver	MFI	83.00	1	25	83.00	3.32	0.064
bookshelf, short, wide, 3-shelf	Denver	MFI	29.00	1	25	29.00	1.16	0.022
Bedroom 2 furniture total						387.00	15.48	**0.298**

Family Budget Unit, January 1999 prices

Household goods: Furniture, owner-occupied and local authority houses

Item	Brand	Retailer	Unit Price £	Quantity	Life/Years	Total Price £	Cost/Year £	Cost/Week £
Bathroom furniture			(bathroom suite as installed)					
bathroom cabinet	Corinth	Argos	24.99	1	20	24.99	1.25	**0.024**
Bathroom furniture total						24.99	1.25	**0.024**
Total furniture, owner-occupied and local authority houses						2,261.93	121.04	**2.328**

Family Budget Unit, January 1999 prices

Household goods: Floor coverings etc, owner-occupied house

Item	Brand	Retailer	Unit Price £	Quantity	Life/Years	Total Price £	Cost/Year £	Cost/Week £
Floor covering								
Hall, stairs and landing								
carpet, fitting, underlay, grippers, door plates, 30.8m x 0.9m	Jubilee Twist	Allied Carpets	9.55	1	13	550.90	42.38	**0.815**
Kitchen								
vinyl, fitting, 2.4m x 3.7m	Accent	Allied Carpets	9.55	1	13	157.45	12.11	**0.233**
Dining room								
carpet, fitting, underlay, grippers, door plates, 3.2m x 3.4m	Jubilee Twist	Allied Carpets	9.55	1	13	229.00	17.62	**0.339**
Sitting room								
carpet, fitting, underlay, grippers, door plates, 3.0m x 3.3m	Jubilee Twist	Allied Carpets	9.55	1	13	213.90	16.45	**0.316**
Bathroom								
carpet, fitting, 2.1m x 2.8m	Pacific	Allied Carpets	4.99	1	9	64.30	7.14	**0.137**
Bedroom 1								
carpet, fitting, 3.8m x 3.3m	Albion	Allied Carpets	3.58	1	15	83.02	5.53	**0.106**
Bedroom 2								
carpet, fitting 2.5m x 3.4m	Albion	Allied Carpets	3.58	1	18	64.07	3.56	0.068
Floor coverings total						1362.64	104.80	**2.015**
Curtains								
kitchen, blind, 163cm x 100cm		Argos	14.99	1	10	14.99	1.50	**0.029**
curtain track and fittings		Woolworth	5.99	4	20	23.96	1.20	**0.023**
dining room, thermal backed, pair, 66" x 72"		Index	29.25	1	10	29.25	2.93	**0.056**
sitting room, thermal backed, pair, 90" x 90"		Index	49.99	1	10	49.99	5.00	**0.096**
net curtains		Texstyle World	9.99	1	10	9.99	1.00	**0.019**
bathroom, blind, 117cm x 163cm		Argos	12.99	1	10	12.99	1.30	**0.025**
bedroom 1, thermal backed, pair, 66" x 72"		Argos	29.25	1	10	29.25	2.93	**0.056**
bedroom 2, thermal backed, pair, 66" x 72"		Argos	29.25	1	10	29.25	2.93	**0.056**
Curtains total						199.67	18.77	**0.361**

Family Budget Unit, January 1999 prices

Household goods: Floor coverings etc, owner-occupied house

Item	Brand	Retailer	Unit Price £	Quantity	Life/Years	Total Price £	Cost/Year £	Cost/Week £
Lampshades								
kitchen lampshade		Index	7.99	1	10	7.99	0.80	0.015
living, dining room and hall lampshades		Index	7.99	4	15	31.96	2.13	0.041
bedroom lampshade		Index	4.45	2	15	8.90	0.59	0.011
bathroom light bowl		Argos	3.45	1	15	3.45	0.23	0.004
Lampshades total						52.30	3.75	0.072
Home security								
window locks, pack of 10	Trent Quick Fix	B&Q	10.99	1	15	10.99	0.73	0.014
front door bolt, 4"		B&Q	2.09	1	15	2.09	0.14	0.003
back door bolt, 4"		B&Q	2.09	1	15	2.09	0.14	0.003
smoke detector, pack of 2	Fire Sentry	Argos	6.50	1	15	6.50	0.43	0.008
Home security total						21.67	1.44	0.028
Total floor coverings, curtains, lampshades and home security						273.64	23.97	2.476

Family Budget Unit, January 1999 prices

Household goods: Floor coverings etc, local authority house

Item	Brand	Retailer	Unit Price £	Quantity	Life/Years	Total Price £	Cost/Year £	Cost/Week £
Floor coverings								
Hall, stairs								
carpet, fitting, underlay, grippers, door plates, 8.9m x 0.8m	Jubilee Twist	Allied Carpets	9.55	1	13	225.00	17.31	0.333
Kitchen								
vinyl, fitting, 2.3m x 2.5m	Accent	Allied Carpets	9.55	1	13	99.76	7.67	0.148
Dining room								
carpet, fitting, underlay, grippers, door plates, 2.5m x 3.7m	Jubilee Twist	Allied Carpets	9.55	1	13	185.95	14.30	0.275
carpet, fitting, underlay, grippers, door plates, 4.0m x 3.7m	Jubilee Twist	Allied Carpets	9.55	1	13	287.73	22.13	0.426
Bathroom								
carpet, fitting, 2.3m x 2.1m	Pacific	Allied Carpets	4.99	1	9	53.06	5.90	0.113
Bedroom 1								
carpet, fitting, 3.9m x 2.9m	Albion	Allied Carpets	3.58	1	15	73.53	4.90	0.094
Bedroom 2								
carpet, fitting 2.5m x 2.6m	Albion	Allied Carpets	3.58	1	18	55.92	3.11	0.060
Floor coverings total						**980.95**	**75.32**	**1.449**
Curtains								
kitchen, blind, 125cm x 100cm		Argos	14.99	1	10	14.99	1.50	0.029
curtain track and fittings		Woolworths	5.99	4	20	23.96	1.20	0.023
dining room, thermal backed, pair, 66" x 72"		Argos	29.25	2	10	58.50	5.85	0.113
sitting room, thermal backed, pair, 66" x 72"		Argos	29.25	1	10	29.25	2.93	0.056
net curtains		Texstyle World	9.99	1	10	9.99	1.00	0.019
landing, blind, 90m x 50cm		Argos	14.99	1	10	14.99	1.50	0.029
hall, blind, 75cm x 45cm		Argos	14.99	1	10	14.99	1.50	0.029
bathroom, none								
bedroom 1, thermal backed, pair, 66" x 72"		Argos	29.25	1	10	29.25	2.93	0.056
bedroom 2, thermal backed, pair, 66" x 72"		Argos	29.25	1	10	29.25	2.93	0.050
Curtains total						**225.17**	**21.32**	**0.410**

Family Budget Unit, January 1999 prices

Household goods: Floor coverings etc, local authority house

Item	Brand	Retailer	Unit Price £	Quantity	Life/Years	Total Price £	Cost/Year £	Cost/Week £
Lampshades								
kitchen lampshade		Index	7.99	1	10	7.99	0.80	0.015
living, dining room and hall lampshades		Index	7.99	4	15	31.96	2.13	0.041
bedroom lampshade		Index	4.45	2	15	8.90	0.59	0.011
bathroom light bowl		Argos	3.45	1	15	3.45	0.23	0.004
Lampshades total						52.30	3.75	0.072
Home security								
window locks, pack of 10	Trent Quick Fix	B&Q	10.99	1	15	10.99	0.73	0.014
front door bolt, 4"		B&Q	2.09	1	15	2.09	0.14	0.003
back door bolt, 4"		B&Q	2.09	1	15	2.09	0.14	0.003
smoke detector, pack of 2	Fire Sentry	Argos	6.50	1	15	6.50	0.43	0.008
Home security total						21.67	1.44	0.028
Total floor coverings, curtains, lampshades and home security						299.14	26.52	1.958

Family Budget Unit, January 1999 prices

Household goods: Floor coverings etc, local authority flat

Item	Brand	Retailer	Unit Price £	Quantity	Life/Years	Total Price £	Cost/Year £	Cost/Week £
Floor coverings								
Hall								
carpet, 4.9m x 0.9m	Jubilee Twist	Allied Carpets	9.55	1	13	97.21	7.48	**0.144**
Kitchen								
vinyl, fitting, 2.4m x 2.5m	Accent	Allied Carpets	9.55	1	13	103.88	7.99	**0.154**
Sitting/dining room								
carpet, fitting, underlay, grippers, door plates, 3.5m x3.9 m	Jubilee Twist	Allied Carpets	9.55	1	13	258.93	19.92	**0.383**
Bathroom								
carpet, fitting, 1.8m x 2.2m	Pacific	Allied Carpets	4.99	1	9	46.47	5.16	**0.099**
Bedroom								
carpet, fitting, 3.3m x 3.6m	Albion	Allied Carpets	3.58	1	15	82.97	5.53	**0.106**
Floor coverings total						589.46	46.08	**0.886**
Curtains								
kitchen, blind, 90cm x 110cm		Argos	14.99	1	10	14.99	1.50	**0.029**
curtain track and fittings		Woolworths	5.99	2	20	11.98	0.60	**0.012**
living/dining room, thermal backed, pair, 66" x 54"		Argos	24.99	2	10	49.98	5.00	**0.096**
net curtains		Texstyle World	9.99	1	10	9.99	1.00	**0.019**
bathroom, blind, 100cm x 110cm		Argos	12.99	1	10	12.99	1.30	**0.025**
bedroom, thermal backed, pair, 66" x 54"		Argos	24.99	2	10	49.98	5.00	**0.096**
Curtains total						149.91	14.39	**0.277**
Lampshades								
kitchen lampshade		Index	7.99	1	10	7.99	0.80	**0.015**
living room and hall lampshades		Index	7.99	3	15	23.97	1.60	**0.031**
bedroom lampshade		Index	4.45	1	15	4.45	0.30	**0.006**
bathroom light bowl		Argos	3.45	1	15	3.45	0.23	**0.004**
Lampshades total						39.86	2.92	**0.056**

Family Budget Unit, January 1999 prices

Household goods: Floor coverings etc, local authority flat

Item	Brand	Retailer	Unit Price £	Quantity	Life/Years	Total Price £	Cost/Year £	Cost/Week £
Home security								
window locks, pack of 10	Trent Quick Fix	B&Q	10.99	1	15	10.99	0.73	**0.014**
front door bolt, 4"		B&Q	2.09	1	15	2.09	0.14	**0.003**
back door bolt, 4"		B&Q	2.09	1	15	2.09	0.14	**0.003**
smoke detector, pack of 2	Fire Sentry	Argos	6.50	1	15	6.50	0.43	**0.008**
Home security total						21.67	1.44	**0.028**
Total floor coverings, curtains, lampshades and home security						211.44	18.76	**1.247**

Family Budget Unit, January 1999 prices

Household goods: Household linen, single person aged 65-74 years

Item	Brand	Retailer	Unit Price £	Quantity	Life/Years	Total Price £	Cost/Year £	Cost/Week £
Household linen								
single duvet cover and 1 pillowcase		Index	14.99	2	9	29.98	3.33	0.064
single fitted sheet		Index	5.99	3	9	17.97	2.00	0.038
plain pillowcases		Index	2.99	3	9	8.97	1.00	0.019
single duvet, hollowfibre		Index	24.99	1	10	24.99	2.50	0.048
pillows, polyester fill, pack of 2	Slumberland	Index	7.25	1	6	7.25	1.21	0.023
single duvet cover and 1 pillowcase, guest		Index	14.99	2	15	29.98	2.00	0.038
single fitted sheet, guest		Index	5.99	2	15	11.98	0.80	0.015
plain pillowcases, guest		Index	2.99	2	15	5.98	0.40	0.008
single duvet, hollowfibre, guest		Index	24.99	1	15	24.99	1.67	0.032
pillows, polyester fill, pack of 2, guest	Slumberland	Index	7.25	1	6	7.25	1.21	0.023
face flannel	Accent	Poundstretcher	0.59	2	1	1.18	1.18	0.023
hand towel (kitchen), pack of 2		Index	8.99	1	5	8.99	1.80	0.035
hand towel, pack of 2		Index	8.99	2	5	17.98	3.60	0.069
towel, bath	Accent	Poundstretcher	5.99	3	5	17.97	3.59	0.069
bath sheet	Accent	Poundstretcher	7.99	1	7	7.99	1.14	0.022
bath mat set, 3 piece	Fogarty	Argos	9.99	1	5	9.99	2.00	0.038
tea-towel, terry		Co-op	0.99	6	5	5.94	1.19	0.023
adult apron		Sainsburys	7.45	1	10	7.45	0.75	0.014
oven gloves		Woolworths	2.99	1	5	2.99	0.60	0.012
cushion and cover	World of Cushions	Poundstretcher	3.99	2	8	7.98	1.00	0.019
rectangular tablecloth, 135cm x 175cm		Index	9.99	1	10	9.99	1.00	0.019
Household linen total						**267.79**	**33.94**	**0.653**
Total single person's household linen						267.79	33.94	0.653

Family Budget Unit, January 1999 prices

Household goods: Household linen, couple aged 65-74 years

Item	Brand	Retailer	Unit Price £	Quantity	Life/Years	Total Price £	Cost/Year £	Cost/Week £
Household linen								
single duvet cover and 1 pillowcase, guest		Index	14.99	2	15	29.98	2.00	0.038
double duvet cover and 2 pillowcases		Index	18.99	3	9	56.97	6.33	0.122
single fitted sheet, guest		Index	5.99	2	15	11.98	0.80	0.015
double fitted sheet		Index	6.99	3	9	20.97	2.33	0.045
plain pillowcases		Index	2.99	6	9	17.94	1.99	0.038
double duvet, hollowfibre		Index	32.50	1	10	32.50	3.25	0.063
single duvet, hollowfibre, guest		Index	24.99	1	15	24.99	1.67	0.032
pillows, polyester fill, pack of 2	Slumberland	Index	7.25	3	6	21.75	3.63	0.070
face flannel	Accent	Poundstretcher	0.59	3	1	1.77	1.77	0.034
hand towel (kitchen), pack of 2		Index	8.99	1	5	8.99	1.80	0.035
hand towel, pack of 2		Index	8.99	3	5	26.97	5.39	0.104
towel, bath	Accent	Poundstretcher	5.99	4	5	23.96	4.79	0.092
bath sheet	Accent	Poundstretcher	7.99	2	7	15.98	2.28	0.044
bath mat set, 3 piece	Fogarty	Argos	9.99	1	5	9.99	2.00	0.038
tea-towel, terry		Co-op	0.99	6	5	5.94	1.19	0.023
adult apron		Sainsburys	7.45	1	10	7.45	0.75	0.014
oven gloves		Woolworths	2.99	1	5	2.99	0.60	0.012
cushion and cover	World of Cushions	Poundstretcher	3.99	2	8	7.98	1.00	0.019
rectangular tablecloth, 135cm x 175cm		Index	9.99	1	10	9.99	1.00	0.019
Household linen total						339.09	44.55	0.857
Total couple's household linen						339.09	44.55	0.857

Family Budget Unit, January 1999 prices

Household goods: Gas and electric appliances, single person aged 65-74 years

Item	Brand	Retailer	Unit Price £	Quantity	Life/Years	Total Price £	Cost/Year £	Cost/Week £
Gas and electric appliances								
fridge/freezer	Candy CT140/2 Fridge/Freezer	Northern Electric + Gas	149.99	1	17	149.99	8.82	**0.170**
cooker	Belling G700 Gem	Northern Electric + Gas	299.99	1	17	299.99	17.65	**0.339**
kettle	Morphy Richards	Index	14.50	1	3	14.50	4.83	**0.093**
toaster	Swan	Index	14.50	1	13	14.50	1.12	**0.021**
automatic washing machine	Tricity Bendix AW871	YEB	249.99	1	15	249.99	16.67	**0.321**
electric under-blanket	Dimplex	Index	15.50	1	10	15.50	1.55	**0.030**
iron, steam/dry	Morphy Richards 40450	Argos	13.25	1	13	13.25	1.02	**0.020**
vacuum cleaner (upright)	Hoover 1000w Turbopower	Index	99.00	1	16	99.00	6.19	**0.119**
table lamp, bedroom		Index	8.99	1	15	8.99	0.60	**0.012**
table lamp, sitting room		Index	8.99	1	15	8.99	0.60	**0.012**
Gas and electric appliances total						874.70	59.04	**1.135**
Spares/accessories/repairs								
100w light bulbs, pack of 4		Poundstretcher	0.99	3	1	2.97	2.97	**0.057**
60w light bulbs, pack of 4		Poundstretcher	0.99	2	1	1.98	1.98	**0.038**
3-pin plug, fused, pack of 2	Co-op	Co-op	0.99	5	10	4.95	0.50	**0.010**
vacuum cleaner bags, pack of 5		Sainsburys	2.89	2	3	5.78	1.93	**0.037**
vacuum fan belt, pack of 2	Airflo	Currys	2.69	1	2	2.69	1.35	**0.026**
service cooker		local	56.40	1	17	56.40	3.32	**0.064**
service washing machine		local	70.50	2	15	141.00	9.40	**0.181**
service vacuum cleaner		local	27.03	1	16	27.03	1.69	**0.032**
Spares/accessories/repairs total						242.80	23.12	**0.445**
Total single person's gas/electrical equipment and repairs						1117.50	82.16	**1.580**

Family Budget Unit, January 1999 prices

Household goods: Gas and electric appliances, couple aged 65-74 years

Item	Brand	Retailer	Unit Price £	Quantity	Life/Years	Total Price £	Cost/Year £	Cost/Week £
Gas and electric appliances								
fridge/freezer	Candy CT140/2	Northern Electric + Gas	149.99	1	17	149.99	8.82	0.170
cooker	Belling G700 Gem	Northern Electric + Gas	299.99	1	16	299.99	18.75	0.361
kettle	Morphy Richards	Index	14.50	1	3	14.50	4.83	0.093
toaster	Swan	Index	14.50	1	12	14.50	1.21	0.023
automatic washing machine	Tricity Bendix AW871	YEB	249.99	1	14	249.99	17.86	0.343
electric under-blanket	Dimplex	Index	19.50	1	10	19.50	1.95	0.038
iron, steam/dry	Morphy Richards 40450	Argos	13.25	1	12	13.25	1.10	0.021
vacuum cleaner (upright)	Hoover 1000w Turbopower	Index	99.00	1	15	99.00	6.60	0.127
table lamp, bedroom		Index	8.99	2	15	17.98	1.20	0.023
table lamp, sitting room		Index	8.99	1	15	8.99	0.60	0.012
Gas and electric appliances total						887.69	62.92	1.210
Spares/accessories/repairs								
100w light bulbs, pack of 4		Poundstretcher	0.99	4	1	3.96	3.96	0.076
60w light bulbs, pack of 4		Poundstretcher	0.99	2	1	1.98	1.98	0.038
3-pin plug, fused, pack of 2	Co-op	Co-op	0.99	6	10	5.94	0.59	0.011
vacuum cleaner bags, pack of 5	Airflo	Sainsburys	2.89	2	3	5.78	1.93	0.037
vacuum fan belt, pack of 2		Currys	2.69	1	2	2.69	1.35	0.026
service cooker		local	56.40	1	16	56.40	3.53	0.068
service washing machine		local	70.50	2	14	141.00	10.07	0.194
service vacuum cleaner		local	27.03	1	15	27.03	1.80	0.035
Spares/accessories/repairs total						244.78	25.20	0.485
Total couple's gas/electrical equipment and repairs						1132.47	88.13	1.695

Family Budget Unit, January 1999 prices

Household goods: Crockery, kitchen goods etc

Item	Brand	Retailer	Unit Price £	Quantity	Life/Years	Total Price £	Cost/Year £	Cost/Week £
Crockery/glassware/cutlery								
crockery set, 24 piece	Biltons	Index	22.99	1	10	22.99	2.30	0.044
mug set, 6 piece	Staffordshire	Argos	3.99	1	6	3.99	0.67	0.013
teapot, medium		York Market	1.99	1	10	1.99	0.20	0.004
casserole set, 3 piece	Pyrex	Argos	8.99	1	15	8.99	0.60	0.012
ovenproof dish set, glass, 4 piece	Cooking Crew	Argos	9.99	1	15	9.99	0.67	0.013
salt and pepper mills		Index	4.45	1	10	4.45	0.45	0.009
egg cups, stainless steel, 4	Kitchen Shop	Woolworths	2.49	1	10	2.49	0.25	0.005
glasses set, 18 piece	Luminarc	Argos	3.89	1	10	3.89	0.39	0.007
glass water jug	Co-op	Co-op	1.99	1	4	1.99	0.50	0.010
fruit set, glass, 7 piece	Rayware	Index	3.25	1	15	3.25	0.22	0.004
44 piece cutlery set (stainless steel)	Viners Floret	Index	22.99	1	17	22.99	1.35	0.026
Crockery/glassware/cutlery total						87.01	7.58	0.146
Kitchen equipment/utensils								
glass measuring jug, 0.5 litre	Pyrex	Poundstretcher	2.59	1	10	2.59	0.26	0.005
glass mixing bowl, 0.5 litre	Pyrex	Sainsburys	2.39	1	10	2.39	0.24	0.005
glass mixing bowl, 1.0 litre	Pyrex	Sainsburys	3.19	1	10	3.19	0.32	0.006
non-stick bakeware set, 13 piece	Classic	Argos	8.99	1	12	8.99	0.75	0.014
cake tin, 20cm x 9.5cm	Co-op	Co-op	4.99	1	20	4.99	0.25	0.005
pastry cutters		Co-op	1.99	1	10	1.99	0.20	0.004
cooling rack	Sainsbury	Sainsburys	2.29	1	12	2.29	0.19	0.004
wooden rolling pin	Co-op	Co-op	1.99	1	10	1.99	0.20	0.004
sieve, metal		Poundstretcher	0.49	1	5	0.49	0.10	0.002
piping bag and nozzles set	Co-op	Co-op	2.79	1	10	2.79	0.28	0.005
plastic colander	Microban	Sainsburys	1.99	1	5	1.99	0.40	0.008
kitchen scales	Kenwood	Argos	8.99	1	10	8.99	0.90	0.017
sauce pan set, stainless steel, 4 piece	Imperial	Argos	29.99	1	10	29.99	3.00	0.058
milk pan	Co-op	Co-op	1.99	1	5	1.99	0.40	0.008
knife set and rack, 8 piece	Little Chef	Index	14.99	1	25	14.99	0.60	0.012
utensil set and rack, 6 piece	Poundstretcher	Poundstretcher	2.99	1	5	2.99	0.60	0.012
butterfly tin opener		Poundstretcher	0.59	1	2	0.59	0.30	0.006
potato peeler	Co-op	Co-op	1.25	1	4	1.25	0.31	0.006
lever arm corkscrew	Chef Aid	Poundstretcher	1.49	1	5	1.49	0.30	0.006
kitchen scissors	Index	Index	1.79	1	5	1.79	0.36	0.007
wooden spoon set, 3 piece	Co-op	Co-op	1.75	1	5	1.75	0.35	0.007
plastic/wire tea strainer	Co-op	Co-op	0.99	1	5	0.99	0.20	0.004
nut crackers	Co-op	Co-op	1.69	1	12	1.69	0.14	0.003

Family Budget Unit, January 1999 prices

Household goods: Crockery, kitchen goods etc

Item	Brand	Retailer	Unit Price £	Quantity	Life/Years	Total Price £	Cost/Year £	Cost/Week £
metal food tongs	Co-op	Co-op	1.99	1	17	1.99	0.12	**0.002**
metal balloon whisk	Co-op	Co-op	1.99	1	5	1.99	0.40	**0.008**
lemon squeezer		Kwik Save	0.99	1	12	0.99	0.08	**0.002**
cheese grater, metal	House & Home	Poundstretcher	0.99	1	3	0.99	0.33	**0.006**
worktop saver, glass	Kitchen Devil	Argos	7.49	1	7	7.49	1.07	**0.021**
plastic chopping board, set of 3		Poundstretcher	2.99	1	8	2.99	0.37	**0.007**
minute timer	Salter	Index	4.99	1	10	4.99	0.50	**0.010**
Kitchen equipment/utensils total						123.62	13.50	**0.260**
Storage hardware								
metal bread bin		Argos	8.99	1	6	8.99	1.50	**0.029**
spice rack and 10 spices		Index	9.99	1	15	9.99	0.67	**0.013**
canister set, screw top, 4 piece		Poundstretcher	2.99	1	5	2.99	0.60	**0.012**
plastic vegetable rack		Index	8.49	1	10	8.49	0.85	**0.016**
lunch box	Co-op	Co-op	0.99	1	5	0.99	0.20	**0.004**
plastic food box	Co-op	Co-op	2.75	1	10	2.75	0.28	**0.005**
vacuum flask	Thermos	Argos	6.49	1	10	6.49	0.65	**0.012**
Storage hardware total						40.69	4.73	**0.091**
Cleaning hardware								
mop bucket	Vileda	Sainsburys	5.99	1	12	5.99	0.50	**0.010**
mop		Poundstretcher	1.99	1	1	1.99	1.99	**0.038**
bucket		Co-op	1.19	2	6	2.38	0.40	**0.008**
dust pan and brush	Bently	Poundstretcher	0.99	1	5	0.99	0.20	**0.004**
hand brush		Poundstretcher	0.99	1	10	0.99	0.10	**0.002**
scrubbing brush		Poundstretcher	0.49	1	3	0.49	0.16	**0.003**
shoe brushes, pack of 2		Co-op	2.19	2	7	4.38	0.63	**0.012**
washing-up brush	Vileda	Co-op	0.79	3	1	2.37	2.37	**0.046**
washing-up bowl		Poundstretcher	0.99	1	3	0.99	0.33	**0.006**
cutlery drainer		Poundstretcher	0.99	1	5	0.99	0.20	**0.004**
plate drainer		Poundstretcher	1.99	1	5	1.99	0.40	**0.008**
pedal bin	Fresco	Argos	9.99	1	10	9.99	1.00	**0.019**
waste basket, metal		local	2.99	4	10	11.96	1.20	**0.023**
dustbin, with wheels		local	14.99	1	12	14.99	1.25	**0.024**
broom		Poundstretcher	2.99	1	7	2.99	0.43	**0.008**
Cleaning hardware total						63.48	11.14	**0.214**

Family Budget Unit, January 1999 prices

Household goods: Crockery, kitchen goods etc

Item	Brand	Retailer	Unit Price £	Quantity	Life/Years	Total Price £	Cost/Year £	Cost/Week £
Household consumables								
LR6 batteries, pack of 4	Ever Ready	Co-op	2.45	1	2	2.45	1.23	0.024
LR14 batteries, pack of 2	Ever Ready	Co-op	2.45	1	2	2.45	1.23	0.024
LR20 batteries, pack of 2	Ever Ready	Co-op	2.45	1	2	2.45	1.23	0.024
household candles, box of 6	Kwik Save	Kwik Save	0.89	1	7	0.89	0.13	0.002
freezer bags, pk of 25	No Frills	Kwik Save	0.49	2	2	0.98	0.49	0.009
clingfilm, 30m x 300mm wide	Kwik Save	Kwik Save	0.68	1	1	0.68	0.68	0.013
foil, 5m x 450 mm wide		Kwik Save	0.95	1	1	0.95	0.95	0.018
greaseproof paper, 15m		Kwik Save	1.38	1	1	1.38	1.38	0.027
paper napkins, pack of 25		Co-op	0.99	1	2	0.99	0.50	0.010
Household consumables total						13.22	7.80	**0.150**
Other hardware								
ironing board	Beldry 5 Star	Argos	17.75	1	20	17.75	0.89	0.017
ironing board cover	Besco	Argos	2.39	1	5	2.39	0.48	0.009
indoor clothes airer	Dennison Budget	Argos	9.99	1	20	9.99	0.50	0.010
plastic coated washing line		Poundstretcher	0.99	1	10	0.99	0.10	0.002
clothes pegs, pack of 50		Poundstretcher	0.89	1	3	0.89	0.30	0.006
laundry basket and bin	Imago	Argos	8.99	1	10	8.99	0.90	0.017
bathroom scales	Salter	Argos	9.99	1	12	9.99	0.83	0.016
toilet brush and holder		Index	4.99	1	10	4.99	0.50	0.010
safety bath mat		Index	2.75	1	5	2.75	0.55	0.011
hand/tap shower	Neptune	Index	3.99	1	5	3.99	0.80	0.015
water bottle, hot	Boots	Boots	4.00	1	10	4.00	0.40	0.008
coaster set, 6 piece		Poundstretcher	0.99	1	10	0.99	0.10	0.002
table mats, 12 piece		Poundstretcher	2.99	1	10	2.99	0.30	0.006
tray	House & Home	Poundstretcher	0.99	1	5	0.99	0.20	0.004
vase, glass	Rayware	Argos	10.99	1	10	10.99	1.10	0.021
curtain hooks, pack of 20		local Post Office	0.49	10	20	4.90	0.25	0.005
Other hardware total						87.58	8.179	**0.157**
Total kitchen and hardware						415.60	52.92	**1.018**

Family Budget Unit, January 1999 prices

143

Household goods: Crockery, kitchen goods etc

Item	Brand	Retailer	Unit Price £	Quantity	Life/Years	Total Price £	Cost/Year £	Cost/Week £
Stationery and paper goods								
Birthday card, pack of 10		York Market	0.55	1	1	0.55	0.55	0.011
occasion cards/other cards	Brittania Code 3	Co-op	0.99	1	1	0.99	0.99	0.019
Christmas cards, box of 12		Kwik Save	0.49	4	1	1.96	1.96	0.038
general gift wrap, 3 sheets		Poundstretcher	0.99	2	1	1.98	1.98	0.038
parcel paper, 3 sheets and labels	WH Smith	WH Smith	1.19	1	3	1.19	0.40	0.008
Christmas wrapping paper, 6m		Kwik Save	0.89	2	1	1.78	1.78	0.034
writing paper A5, 40 sheets	Waldorf	Poundstretcher	0.99	1	1	0.99	0.99	0.019
envelopes, pack of 50	Comet	Poundstretcher	0.99	1	2	0.99	0.50	0.010
envelopes, pack of 20, manila		Co-op	0.99	1	2	0.99	0.50	0.010
notelets, box of 10		Co-op	1.25	1	1	1.25	1.25	0.024
writing paper gift pack	Waldorf	WH Smith	4.99	1	2	4.99	2.50	0.048
note book, spiral bound	WH Smith	Kwik Save	0.99	1	1	0.99	0.99	0.019
A4 envelope file	No Frills	WH Smith	0.50	2	5	1.00	0.20	0.004
correcting fluid, 25ml	WH Smith	Co-op	1.55	1	1	1.55	1.55	0.030
erasers, pack of 3	Tipp-Ex	Kwik Save	0.79	1	5	0.79	0.16	0.003
pencil sharpener, pack of 2		Co-op	0.89	1	10	0.89	0.09	0.002
scissors		Kwik Save	0.89	1	10	0.89	0.09	0.002
rule, 30cm		Kwik Save	0.29	1	5	0.29	0.06	0.001
calculator		Co-op	1.89	1	10	1.89	0.19	0.004
string, 40m		Poundstretcher	0.69	1	5	0.69	0.14	0.003
elastic bands, 50gm		Co-op	0.79	1	5	0.79	0.16	0.003
paper clips, box of 125		Co-op	0.95	1	10	0.95	0.10	0.002
glue stick, small size		Kwik Save	0.69	1	2	0.69	0.35	0.007
sellotape		Kwik Save	0.69	2	2	1.38	1.38	0.027
pen, ball point, pack of 10		Co-op	1.89	1	1	1.89	1.89	0.036
fountain and ball point pen set, 15 cartridges	Sheaffer	Index	6.99	1	5	6.99	1.40	0.027
pencil, pack of 5		Co-op	1.25	1	2	1.25	0.63	0.012
Stationery and paper goods total						40.58	22.73	0.437

Total kitchen, hardware and stationery goods   1.455

Family Budget Unit, January 1999 prices

Household goods: Toilet paper, matches, cleaning products, single person aged 65-74 years

Item	Brand	Retailer	Unit Price £	Quantity	Life/Years	Total Price £	Cost/Year £	Cost/Week £
Toilet paper								
toilet paper, 9 rolls		Kwik Save	3.14	6	1	18.84	18.84	0.362
Toilet paper total						18.84	18.84	0.362
Matches								
household matches	Original Cook's matches	Kwik Save	0.53	1	1	0.53	0.53	0.010
Matches total						0.53	0.53	0.010
Cleaning products								
stain remover stick, 75g	Vanish	Co-op	1.99	1	1	1.99	1.99	0.038
washing-up liquid, 500ml	Fairy Liquid	Sainsburys	0.85	6	1	5.10	5.10	0.098
washing powder, 3kg	Persil Auto	Kwik Save	4.59	4	1	18.36	18.36	0.353
fabric conditioner, 1 litre		Kwik Save	0.78	5	1	3.90	3.90	0.075
washing liquid, 250ml	Kwik Save	Kwik Save	0.99	1	1	0.99	0.99	0.019
bleach, 750ml	Kwik Save	Kwik Save	0.78	2	1	1.56	1.56	0.030
lavatory cleaner, 500ml	Frish	Kwik Save	0.59	4	1	2.36	2.36	0.045
air freshener block	Johnson Glade	Kwik Save	0.69	4	1	2.76	2.76	0.053
furniture polish, 300ml	Co-op	Co-op	0.99	2	1	1.98	1.98	0.038
disinfectant, 1 litre	Izal	Kwik Save	0.85	3	1	2.55	2.55	0.049
glass cleaner, 500ml	Co-op	Co-op	1.25	1	1	1.25	1.25	0.024
scouring cleanser, 500ml	Jif	Kwik Save	1.23	3	1	3.69	3.69	0.071
shoe polish, 50ml	Kiwi	Co-op	0.99	1	1	0.99	0.99	0.019
brush cleaner, 500ml	Co-op	Co-op	1.99	1	1	1.99	1.99	0.038
carpet shampoo, 450ml	1001	Kwik Save	1.93	1	1	1.93	0.97	0.019
soap pads, pack of 15	No Frills	Kwik Save	0.43	1	2	0.43	0.22	0.004
dish cloths, pack of 5		York Market	1.00	2	2	2.00	2.00	0.038
floor cloth	Co-op	Co-op	0.69	1	1	0.69	0.69	0.013
sponge wipes, pack of 3	No Frills	Kwik Save	0.23	3	1	0.69	0.69	0.013
household gloves, pack of 2 pairs	Basics	Kwik Save	0.64	1	1	0.64	0.64	0.012
thick sponge		Kwik Save	0.69	1	1	0.69	0.69	0.013
scourers, pack of 2		Kwik Save	0.39	2	1	0.78	0.78	0.015
duster		Kwik Save	0.50	2	1	1.00	1.00	0.019
pedal bin liners, pack of 40	No Frills	Kwik Save	0.45	2	1	0.90	0.90	0.017
Cleaning products total						59.22	58.04	1.116
Total single person's toilet paper, matches, cleaning products						78.59	77.41	1.48

Family Budget Unit, January 1999 prices

Household goods: Toilet paper, matches, cleaning products, couple aged 65-74 years

Item	Brand	Retailer	Unit Price £	Quantity	Life/Years	Total Price £	Cost/Year £	Cost/Week £
Toilet paper								
toilet paper, 9 rolls		Kwik Save	3.14	12	1	37.68	37.68	**0.725**
Toilet paper total						37.68	37.68	**0.725**
Matches								
household matches	Original Cook's matches	Kwik Save	0.53	1	1	0.53	0.53	**0.010**
Matches total						0.53	0.53	**0.010**
Cleaning products								
stain remover stick, 75g	Vanish	Co-op	1.99	1	1	1.99	1.99	0.038
washing-up liquid, 1 litre	Fairy Liquid	Co-op	1.59	6	1	9.54	9.54	0.183
washing powder, 3kg	Persil Auto	Kwik Save	4.59	6	1	27.54	27.54	0.530
fabric conditioner, 1 litre		Kwik Save	0.78	7	1	5.46	5.46	0.105
washing liquid, 250ml	Kwik Save	Kwik Save	0.99	1	1	0.99	0.99	0.019
bleach, 750ml	Kwik Save	Kwik Save	0.78	3	1	2.34	2.34	0.045
lavatory cleaner, 500ml	Frish	Kwik Save	0.59	6	1	3.54	3.54	0.068
air freshener block	Johnson Glade	Kwik Save	0.69	4	1	2.76	2.76	0.053
furniture polish, 300ml	Co-op	Co-op	0.99	2	1	1.98	1.98	0.038
disinfectant, 1 litre	Izal	Kwik Save	0.85	4	1	3.40	3.40	0.065
glass cleaner, 500ml	Co-op	Co-op	1.25	2	1	2.50	2.50	0.048
scouring cleanser, 500ml	Jif	Kwik Save	1.23	4	1	4.92	4.92	0.095
shoe polish, 50ml	Kiwi	Co-op	0.99	2	1	1.98	1.98	0.038
brush cleaner, 500ml	Co-op	Co-op	1.99	1	1	1.99	1.99	0.038
carpet shampoo, 450ml	1001	Kwik Save	1.93	1	2	1.93	0.97	0.019
soap pads, pack of 15	No Frills	Kwik Save	0.43	1	2	0.43	0.22	0.004
dish cloths, pack of 5		York market	1.00	2	1	2.00	2.00	0.038
floor cloth	Co-op	Co-op	0.69	1	1	0.69	0.69	0.013
sponge wipes, pack of 3	No Frills	Kwik Save	0.23	3	1	0.69	0.69	0.013
household gloves, pack of 2 pairs	Basics	Kwik Save	0.64	1	1	0.64	0.64	0.012
thick sponge		Kwik Save	0.69	1	1	0.69	0.69	0.013
scourers, pack of 2		Kwik Save	0.39	2	1	0.78	0.78	0.015
duster		Kwik Save	0.50	2	1	1.00	1.00	0.019
pedal bin liners, pack of 40	No Frills	Kwik Save	0.45	2	1	0.90	0.90	0.017
Cleaning products total						80.68	79.50	**1.529**
Total couple's toilet paper, matches, cleaning products						118.89	117.71	**2.264**

Family Budget Unit, January 1999 prices

Household goods: Gardening, DIY, tools, materials, local authority flat

Item	Brand	Retailer	Unit Price £	Quantity	Life/Years	Total Price £	Cost/Year £	Cost/Week £
Gardening, DIY, tools, materials								
screw-driver set, Phillips	Blueline	Woolworths	1.99	1	15	1.99	0.13	0.003
screw-driver set, straight edge	Blueline	Woolworths	1.49	1	15	1.49	0.10	0.002
claw hammer	Blueline	Woolworths	4.99	1	15	4.99	0.33	0.006
nails, 20		local Post office	0.79	1	10	0.79	0.08	0.002
pliers	Blueline	Woolworths	2.99	1	15	2.99	0.20	0.004
tape measure, steel, 5m	Blueline	Woolworths	1.99	1	15	1.99	0.13	0.003
stanley knife	Blueline	Woolworths	1.99	1	15	1.99	0.13	0.003
hacksaw	Blueline	Woolworths	1.99	1	15	1.99	0.13	0.003
hand torch		Kwik Save	1.79	1	5	1.79	0.36	0.007
watering can and rose		Poundstretcher	1.99	1	5	1.99	0.40	0.008
garden trowel and fork	Wilkinson Sword	Index	14.99	1	15	14.99	1.00	0.019
paint roller and tray set		Woolworths	1.99	1	10	1.99	0.20	0.004
paint brush, set of 5	Acorn	Woolworths	3.99	1	10	3.99	0.40	0.008
paint, emulsion, 2.5 litre	Cover Plus	Woolworths	7.99	2	10	15.98	1.60	0.031
paint, gloss non-drip, 750ml	Cover Plus	Woolworths	3.99	2	10	7.98	0.80	0.015
paint, undercoat, 750ml	Cover Plus	Woolworths	2.99	2	10	5.98	0.60	0.012
tool box, metal	Precision	Argos	3.99	1	10	3.99	0.40	0.008
step-stool	Taurus	Index	14.75	1	15	14.75	0.98	0.019
Gardening, DIY, tools, materials total						91.65	7.97	0.153
Total gardening, DIY, tools, materials, local authority flat						91.65	7.97	0.153

Family Budget Unit, January 1999 prices

Household goods: Gardening, DIY, tools, materials, local authority and owner-occupied houses

Item	Brand	Retailer	Unit Price £	Quantity	Life/Years	Total Price £	Cost/Year £	Cost/Week £
Household goods, gardening, DIY, tools, materials								
garden tool set, coated steel, 6 piece	Hilka	Argos	23.75	1	25	23.75	0.95	0.018
hand shears	Spear and Jackson	Argos	12.99	1	25	12.99	0.52	0.010
by-pass pruner	Hilka	Argos	8.99	1	25	8.99	0.36	0.007
lawn mower (hover)	Flymo	BandQ	36.00	1	20	36.00	1.80	0.035
extension cable reel	Jo-Jo	Argos	11.99	1	17	11.99	0.71	0.014
gardening knee rest/seat	Hozelock	Argos	9.40	1	15	9.40	0.63	0.012
watering can and rose		Poundstretcher	1.99	1	5	1.99	0.40	0.008
garden broom		Kwik Save	1.99	1	5	1.99	0.40	0.008
gardening gloves	Wells Lamont	Poundstretcher	2.99	1	3	2.99	1.00	0.019
screw-driver set, Phillips	Blueline	Woolworths	1.99	1	15	1.99	0.13	0.003
screw-driver set, straight edge	Blueline	Woolworths	1.49	1	15	1.49	0.10	0.002
claw hammer	Blueline	Woolworths	4.99	1	15	4.99	0.33	0.006
pliers	Blueline	Woolworths	2.99	1	15	2.99	0.20	0.004
tape measure, steel, 5m	Blueline	Woolworths	1.99	1	15	1.99	0.13	0.003
stanley knife	Blueline	Woolworths	1.99	1	15	1.99	0.13	0.003
hacksaw	Blueline	Woolworths	1.99	1	15	1.99	0.13	0.003
nails, 20		local Post office	0.79	1	10	0.79	0.08	0.002
hand torch		Kwik Save	1.79	1	5	1.79	0.36	0.007
paint roller and tray set		Woolworths	1.99	1	10	1.99	0.20	0.004
paint brush, set of 5	Acorn	Woolworths	3.99	1	10	3.99	0.40	0.008
paint, emulsion, 2.5 litre	Cover Plus	Woolworths	7.99	2	10	15.98	1.60	0.031
paint, gloss non-drip, 750ml	Cover Plus	Woolworths	3.99	2	10	7.98	0.80	0.015
paint, undercoat, 750ml	Cover Plus	Woolworths	2.99	2	10	5.98	0.60	0.012
tool box, metal	Precision	Argos	3.99	1	10	3.99	0.40	0.008
step-stool	Taurus	Index	14.75	1	15	14.75	0.98	0.019
Gardening, DIY, tools, materials total						184.76	13.33	0.256
Total gardening, DIY, tools, materials, local authority and owner-occupied houses						184.76	13.33	0.256

Family Budget Unit, January 1999 prices

148

Household services: Single woman aged 65-74 years

Item	Service Outlet	Unit Price £	Quantity	Life/Years	Total Price £	Cost/Year £	Cost/Week £
Postage							
first class stamps	Post Office Counters Ltd	0.26	26	1	6.76	6.76	0.130
second class stamps	Post Office Counters Ltd	0.20	35	1	7.00	7.00	0.135
letter postage, 200g	Post Office Counters Ltd	0.60	1	1	0.60	0.60	0.012
parcel postage, 350g	Post Office Counters Ltd	0.92	1	1	0.92	0.92	0.018
airmail letter, zone 1, 20g	Post Office Counters Ltd	0.63	1	1	0.63	0.63	0.012
airmail letter, Europe, 40g	Post Office Counters Ltd	0.44	1	1	0.44	0.44	0.008
Postage total					16.35	16.35	0.314
Telephone expenses (incl VAT)							
exchange line rental	British Telecom	107.12	1	1	107.12	107.12	2.060
telephone, 2 piece	Betacom Vogue, Argos	14.99	1	15	14.99	1.00	0.019
local calls, minimum rate	British Telecom	0.05	468	1	23.10	23.10	0.444
local calls, weekday	British Telecom	0.15	156	1	22.80	22.80	0.438
national calls, weekend	British Telecom	0.18	104	1	18.69	18.69	0.359
calls, fixed to mobile	British Telecom	0.30	26	1	7.67	7.67	0.148
Telephone expenses (incl VAT) total					194.37	180.38	3.469
Window cleaning							
window cleaning service	local	3.00	26	1	78.00	78.00	1.500
Window cleaning total					78.00	78.00	1.500
Shoe repairs							
heel, stick-on, adhesive	Woolworths	2.75	1	2	2.75	1.38	0.026
sole, stick-on, adhesive	Woolworths	3.19	1	2	3.19	1.60	0.031
Shoe repairs total					5.94	2.97	0.057
Dry cleaning							
woman's coat	Sketchley	7.29	1	2	7.29	3.65	0.070
Dry cleaning total					7.29	3.65	0.070
Total single woman's household services					301.95	281.34	5.410

Family Budget Unit, January 1999 prices

Household services: Single man aged 65-74 years

Item	Service Outlet	Unit Price £	Quantity	Life/Years	Total Price £	Cost/Year £	Cost/Week £
Postage							
first class stamps	Post Office Counters Ltd	0.26	26	1	6.76	6.76	0.130
second class stamps	Post Office Counters Ltd	0.20	35	1	7.00	7.00	0.135
letter postage, 200g	Post Office Counters Ltd	0.60	1	1	0.60	0.60	0.012
parcel postage, 350g	Post Office Counters Ltd	0.92	1	1	0.92	0.92	0.018
airmail letter, zone 1, 20g	Post Office Counters Ltd	0.63	1	1	0.63	0.63	0.012
airmail letter, Europe, 40g	Post Office Counters Ltd	0.44	1	1	0.44	0.44	0.008
Postage total					16.35	16.35	0.314
Telephone expenses (incl VAT)							
exchange line rental	British Telecom	107.12	1	1	107.12	107.12	2.060
telephone, 2 piece	Betacom Vogue, Argos	14.99	1	15	14.99	1.00	0.019
local calls, minimum rate	British Telecom	0.05	468	1	23.10	23.10	0.444
local calls, weekday	British Telecom	0.15	156	1	22.80	22.80	0.438
national calls, weekend	British Telecom	0.18	104	1	18.69	18.69	0.359
calls, fixed to mobile	British Telecom	0.30	26	1	7.67	7.67	0.148
Telephone expenses (incl VAT) total					194.37	180.376	3.469
Window cleaning							
window cleaning service	local	3.00	26	1	78.00	78.00	1.500
Window cleaning total					78.00	78.00	1.500
Shoe repairs							
heel, stick-on, adhesive	Woolworths	1.89	1	2	1.89	0.95	0.018
sole, stick-on, adhesive	Woolworths	3.19	1	2	3.19	1.60	0.031
Shoe repairs total					5.08	2.54	0.049
Dry cleaning							
man's suit	Sketchley	7.99	1	2	7.99	4.00	0.077
Dry cleaning total					7.99	4.00	0.077
Total single man's household services					301.79	281.26	5.409

Family Budget Unit, January 1999 prices

Household services: Couple aged 65-74 years

Item	Service Outlet	Unit Price £	Quantity	Life/Years	Total Price £	Cost/Year £	Cost/Week £
Postage							
first class stamps	Post Office Counters Ltd	0.26	51	1	13.26	13.26	0.255
second class stamps	Post Office Counters Ltd	0.20	70	1	14.00	14.00	0.269
letter postage, 200g	Post Office Counters Ltd	0.60	1	1	0.60	0.60	0.012
parcel postage, 350g	Post Office Counters Ltd	0.92	1	1	0.92	0.92	0.018
airmail letter, zone 1, 20g	Post Office Counters Ltd	0.63	2	1	1.26	1.26	0.024
airmail letter, Europe, 40g	Post Office Counters Ltd	0.44	2	1	0.88	0.88	0.017
Postage total					30.92	30.92	**0.595**
Telephone expenses (incl VAT)							
exchange line rental	British Telecom	107.12	1	1	107.12	107.12	2.060
telephone, 2 piece	Betacom Vogue, Argos	14.99	1	15	14.99	1.00	0.019
local calls, minimum rate	British Telecom	0.05	468	1	23.10	23.10	0.444
local calls, weekday	British Telecom	0.15	156	1	22.80	22.80	0.438
national calls, weekend	British Telecom	0.18	104	1	18.69	18.69	0.359
calls, fixed to mobile	British Telecom	0.30	26	1	7.67	7.67	0.148
Telephone expenses (incl VAT) total					194.37	180.38	**3.469**
Window cleaning							
window cleaning service	local	3.00	26	1	78.00	78.00	1.500
Window cleaning total					78.00	78.00	**1.500**
Shoe repairs							
heel, stick-on, adhesive	Woolworths	2.75	1	2	2.75	1.38	0.026
heel, stick-on, adhesive	Woolworths	1.89	1	2	1.89	0.95	0.018
sole, stick-on, adhesive	Woolworths	3.19	2	2	6.38	3.19	0.061
Shoe repairs total					11.02	5.51	**0.106**
Dry cleaning							
woman's coat	Sketchley	7.29	1	2	7.29	3.65	0.070
man's suit	Sketchley	7.99	1	2	7.99	4.00	0.077
Dry cleaning total					15.28	7.65	**0.147**
Total couple's household services					329.59	298.80	**5.816**

Family Budget Unit, January 1999 prices

Leisure goods: Single woman aged 65-74 years, owner-occupied house, garden

Item	Brand	Retailer	Unit Price £	Quantity	Life/Years	Total Price £	Cost/Year £	Cost/Week £
Television, video and audio equipment								
television, colour, 66cm	Beko 28128NX	Northern Electric + Gas	259.99	1	15	259.99	17.33	0.333
mini hi-fi	Sanyo DCF 320	Northern Electric + Gas	149.95	1	12	149.95	12.50	0.240
popular/classical cassettes/cd's	various	WH Smith	9.99	2	1	19.98	19.98	0.384
Television, video and audio equipment total						429.92	49.81	0.958
TV licence								
TV licence, colour		Post Office Counters Ltd	97.50	1	1	97.50	97.50	1.875
TV licence total						97.50	97.50	1.875
Newspapers, magazines, books								
pocket dictionary	Collins New English	WH Smith	10.99	1	20	10.99	0.55	0.011
novel, paperback		ASDA	3.99	1	1	3.99	3.99	0.077
basic gardening book	Hermes House	WH Smith	6.99	1	10	6.99	0.70	0.013
cookery book	Hermes House	WH Smith	10.00	1	15	10.00	0.67	0.013
bible	Oxford Gift	WH Smith	11.99	1	25	11.99	0.48	0.009
People's Friend Album	People's Friend	Co-op	4.55	1	1	4.55	4.55	0.088
daily newspaper	Daily Mirror	Kwik Save	0.30	52	1	15.60	15.60	0.300
local free press		local	0.00	52	1	0.00	0.00	0.000
woman's magazine	Woman's Weekly	Co-op	0.45	12	1	5.40	5.40	0.104
calendar		Kwik Save	0.79	1	1	0.79	0.79	0.015
telephone and address book		Poundstretcher	1.09	1	3	1.09	0.36	0.007
theatre programme		local	1.50	1	1	1.50	1.50	0.029
gift voucher		local	5.00	6	1	30.00	30.00	0.577
Newspapers, magazines, books total						102.89	64.59	1.242
Household games								
pack of cards	Waddington	Woolworths	1.69	1	10	1.69	0.17	0.003
jigsaw, 500 piece	Chad Valley	Woolworths	3.99	1	5	3.99	0.80	0.015
domino set	Chad Valley	Woolworths	2.99	1	20	2.99	0.15	0.003
Household games total						8.67	1.12	0.021

Family Budget Unit, January 1999 prices

Leisure goods: Single woman aged 65-74 years, owner-occupied house, garden

Item	Brand	Retailer	Unit Price £	Quantity	Life/Years	Total Price £	Cost/Year £	Cost/Week £
Knitting, photograhic equipment, processing								
knitting wool, double, 100g × 5	Wendy Peter Pan	Poundstretcher	1.99	3	1	5.97	5.97	0.115
knitting needles	S&S	Co-op	0.89	1	5	0.89	0.18	0.003
knitting pattern		local Post Office	0.95	2	1	1.90	1.90	0.037
buttons, pack of 5	S&S	Co-op	0.65	3	1	1.95	1.95	0.038
35mm compact camera	Olympus Trip XB3	Argos	38.50	1	24	38.50	1.60	0.031
colour print film, 24 × 35mm	Fuji	Co-op	3.99	1	1	3.99	3.99	0.077
film processing, 24 prints	Boots	Boots	3.99	1	1	3.99	3.99	0.077
photo album		Kwik Save	0.99	1	3	0.99	0.33	0.006
Knitting and Photographic equipment, processing total						58.18	19.91	0.383
Seasonal items								
standard tinsel, 9'		Kwik Save	0.44	2	5	0.88	0.18	0.003
Christmas tree, lights and decorations, 91 cm		Argos	9.20	1	5	9.20	1.84	0.035
Seasonal items total						10.08	2.02	0.039
Garden and house plants, flowers and products								
rose bush		Kwik Save	1.99	3	10	5.97	0.60	0.011
bedding plant		Kwik Save	0.50	4	2	2.00	1.00	0.019
spring bulbs, 30		Kwik Save	0.99	1	2	0.99	0.50	0.010
fertilise, general purpose, 40 litre	Growmore	Co-op	1.79	1	2	1.79	0.90	0.017
cut flowers		Kwik Save	1.99	5	1	9.95	9.95	0.191
flowers, mixed spray, local delivery		local	20.00	1	3	20.00	6.67	0.128
flower plant		Co-op	1.49	1	2	1.49	0.75	0.014
houseplant, small		Co-op	1.99	2	5	3.98	0.80	0.015
houseplant, medium		Co-op	2.99	1	5	2.99	0.60	0.012
Garden and house plants, flowers and products totals						49.16	21.74	0.418
Total single woman's leisure goods, owner-occupied house, garden					756.40	256.68	4.936	

Family Budget Unit, January 1999 prices

Leisure goods: Single man aged 65-74 years, owner-occupied house, garden

Item	Brand	Retailer	Unit Price £	Quantity	Life/Years	Total Price £	Cost/Year £	Cost/Week £
Television, video and audio equipment								
television, colour, 66cm	Beko 28128NX	Northern Electric + Gas	259.99	1	15	259.99	17.33	0.333
mini hi-fi	Sanyo DCF 320	Northern Electric + Gas	149.95	1	12	149.95	12.50	0.240
popular/classical cassettes/cd's	various	WH Smith	9.99	2	1	19.98	19.98	0.384
Television, video and audio equipment total						429.92	49.81	0.958
TV licence								
TV licence, colour		Post Office Counters Ltd	97.50	1	1	97.50	97.50	1.875
TV licence total						97.50	97.50	1.875
Newspapers, magazines, books								
pocket dictionary	Collins New English	WH Smith	10.99	1	20	10.99	0.55	0.011
novel, paperback		ASDA	3.99	1	1	3.99	3.99	0.077
basic gardening book	Hermes House	WH Smith	6.99	1	10	6.99	0.70	0.013
cookery book	Hermes House	WH Smith	10.00	1	15	10.00	0.67	0.013
bible	Oxford Gift	WH Smith	11.99	1	25	11.99	0.48	0.009
book, paperback		WH Smith	6.99	1	1	6.99	6.99	0.134
daily newspaper	Daily Mirror	Kwik Save	0.30	52	1	15.60	15.60	0.300
local free press		local	0.00	52	1	0.00	0.00	0.000
magazine	Match	Co-op	0.65	12	1	7.80	7.80	0.150
calendar		Kwik Save	0.79	1	1	0.79	0.79	0.015
telephone and address book		Poundstretcher	1.09	1	3	1.09	0.36	0.007
theatre programme		local	1.50	1	1	1.50	1.50	0.029
gift voucher		local	5.00	6	1	30.00	30.00	0.577
Newspapers, magazines, books total						107.73	69.43	1.335
Household games								
pack of cards	Waddington	Woolworths	1.69	1	10	1.69	0.17	0.003
jigsaw, 500 piece	Chad Valley	Woolworths	3.99	1	5	3.99	0.80	0.015
domino set	Chad Valley	Woolworths	2.99	1	20	2.99	0.15	0.003
Household games total						8.67	1.12	0.021

Family Budget Unit, January 1999 prices

Leisure goods: Single man aged 65-74 years, owner-occupied house, garden

Item	Brand	Retailer	Unit Price £	Quantity	Life/Years	Total Price £	Cost/Year £	Cost/Week £
Photographic equipment and processing								
35mm compact camera	Olympus Trip XB3	Argos	38.50	1	24	38.50	1.60	0.031
colour print film, 24 x 35mm	Fuji	Co-op	3.99	1	1	3.99	3.99	0.077
film processing, 24 prints	Boots	Boots	3.99	1	1	3.99	3.99	0.077
photo album		Kwik Save	0.99	1	3	0.99	0.33	0.006
Photographic equipment and processing total						47.47	9.91	0.191
Seasonal items								
standard tinsel, 9'		Kwik Save	0.44	2	5	0.88	0.18	0.003
Christmas tree, lights and decorations, 91 cm		Argos	9.20	1	5	9.20	1.84	0.035
Seasonal items total						10.08	2.02	0.039
Garden and house plants, flowers and products								
rose bush		Kwik Save	1.99	3	10	5.97	0.60	0.011
bedding plant		Kwik Save	0.50	4	2	2.00	1.00	0.019
spring bulbs, 30		Kwik Save	0.99	1	2	0.99	0.50	0.010
fertilise, general purpose, 40 litres	Growmore	Co-op	1.79	1	2	1.79	0.90	0.017
cut flowers		Kwik Save	1.99	5	1	9.95	9.95	0.191
flowers, mixed spray, local delivery		local	20.00	1	3	20.00	6.67	0.128
flower plant		Co-op	1.49	1	2	1.49	0.75	0.014
houseplant, small		Co-op	1.99	2	5	3.98	0.80	0.015
houseplant, medium		Co-op	2.99	1	5	2.99	0.60	0.012
Garden and house plants, flowers and products total						49.16	21.74	0.418
Total single man's leisure goods, owner-occupied house, garden						750.53	251.53	4.837

Family Budget Unit, January 1999 prices

Leisure goods: Single woman aged 65-74 years, local authority flat, no garden

Item	Brand	Retailer	Unit Price £	Quantity	Life/Years	Total Price £	Cost/Year £	Cost/Week £
Television, video and audio equipment								
television, colour, 66cm	Beko 28128NX	Northern Electric + Gas	259.99	1	15	259.99	17.33	0.333
mini hi-fi	Sanyo DCF 320	Northern Electric + Gas	149.95	1	12	149.95	12.50	0.240
popular/classical cassettes/cd's	various	WH Smith	9.99	2	1	19.98	19.98	0.384
Television, video and audio equipment total						429.92	49.81	0.958
TV licence								
TV licence, colour		Post Office Counters Ltd	97.50	1	1	97.50	97.50	1.875
TV licence total						97.50	97.50	1.875
Newspapers, magazines, books								
pocket dictionary	Collins New English	WH Smith	10.99	1	20	10.99	0.55	0.011
novel, paperback		ASDA	3.99	1	1	3.99	3.99	0.077
cookery book	Hermes House	WH Smith	10.00	1	15	10.00	0.67	0.013
bible	Oxford Gift	WH Smith	11.99	1	25	11.99	0.48	0.009
People's Friend Album	People's Friend	Co-op	4.55	1	1	4.55	4.55	0.088
daily newspaper	Daily Mirror	Kwik Save	0.30	52	1	15.60	15.60	0.300
local free press		local	0.00	52	1	0.00	0.00	0.000
woman's magazine	Woman's Weekly	Co-op	0.45	12	1	5.40	5.40	0.104
calendar		Kwik Save	0.79	1	1	0.79	0.79	0.015
telephone and address book	WH Smith	Poundstretcher	1.09	1	3	1.09	0.36	0.007
theatre programme		local	1.50	1	1	1.50	1.50	0.029
gift voucher		local	5.00	6	1	30.00	30.00	0.577
Newspapers, magazines, books total						95.90	63.89	1.229
Household games								
pack of cards	Waddington	Woolworth	1.69	1	10	1.69	0.17	0.003
jigsaw, 500 piece	Chad Valley	Woolworth	3.99	1	5	3.99	0.80	0.015
domino set	Chad Valley	Woolworth	2.99	1	20	2.99	0.15	0.003
Household games total						8.67	1.12	0.021

Family Budget Unit, January 1999 prices

Leisure goods: Single woman aged 65-74 years, local authority flat, no garden

Item	Brand	Retailer	Unit Price £	Quantity	Life/Years	Total Price £	Cost/Year £	Cost/Week £
Knitting, photographic equipment, processing								
knitting wool, double, 100g x 5		Poundstretcher	1.99	3	1	5.97	5.97	0.115
knitting needles	S&S	Co-op	0.89	1	5	0.89	0.18	0.003
knitting pattern		local Post Office	0.95	2	1	1.90	1.90	0.037
buttons, pack of 5	S&S	Co-op	0.65	3	1	1.95	1.95	0.038
35mm compact camera	Olympus Trip XB3	Argos	38.50	1	24	38.50	1.60	0.031
colour print film, 24 x 35mm	Fuji	Co-op	3.99	1	1	3.99	3.99	0.077
film processing, 24 prints	Boots	Boots	3.99	1	1	3.99	3.99	0.077
photo album		Kwik Save	0.99	1	3	0.99	0.33	0.006
Knitting, photographic equipment, processing total						58.18	19.91	0.383
Seasonal items								
standard tinsel, 9'		Kwik Save	0.44	2	5	0.88	0.18	0.003
Christmas tree with lights and decorations, 91 cm		Argos	9.20	1	5	9.20	1.84	0.035
Seasonal items total						10.08	2.02	0.039
Garden and house plants, flowers and products								
cut flowers		Kwik Save	1.99	10	1	19.90	19.90	0.383
flowers, mixed spray, local delivery		local	20.00	1	3	20.00	6.67	0.128
flower plant		Co-op	1.49	1	2	1.49	0.75	0.014
houseplant, small		Co-op	1.99	2	5	3.98	0.80	0.015
houseplant, medium		Co-op	2.99	1	5	2.99	0.60	0.012
Garden and house plants, flowers and products total						48.36	28.71	0.552
Total single woman's leisure goods, local authority flat, no garden						**748.61**	**262.95**	**5.057**

Family Budget Unit, January 1999 prices

Leisure goods: Single man aged 65-74 years, local authority flat, no garden

Item	Brand	Retailer	Unit Price £	Quantity	Life/Years	Total Price £	Cost/Year £	Cost/Week £
Television, video and audio equipment								
television, colour, 66cm	Beko 28128NX	Northern Electric + Gas	259.99	1	15	259.99	17.33	0.333
mini hi-fi	Sanyo DCF 320	Northern Electric + Gas	149.95	1	12	149.95	12.50	0.240
popular/classical cassettes/cd's	various	WH Smith	9.99	2	1	19.98	19.98	0.384
Television, video and audio equipment total						429.92	49.81	0.958
TV licence								
TV licence, colour		Post Office Counters Ltd	97.50	1	1	97.50	97.50	1.875
TV licence total						97.50	97.50	1.875
Newspapers, magazines, books								
pocket dictionary	Collins New English	WH Smith	10.99	1	20	10.99	0.55	0.011
novel, paperback		ASDA	3.99	1	1	3.99	3.99	0.077
cookery book	Hermes House	WH Smith	10.00	1	15	10.00	0.67	0.013
bible	Oxford Gift	WH Smith	11.99	1	25	11.99	0.48	0.009
book, paperback		WH Smith	6.99	1	1	6.99	6.99	0.134
daily newspaper	Daily Mirror	Kwik Save	0.30	52	1	15.60	15.60	0.300
local free press		local	0.00	52	1	0.00	0.00	0.000
magazine	Match	Co-op	0.65	12	1	7.80	7.80	0.150
calendar		Kwik Save	0.79	1	1	0.79	0.79	0.015
telephone and address book		Poundstretcher	1.09	1	3	1.09	0.36	0.007
theatre programme		local	1.50	1	1	1.50	1.50	0.029
gift voucher		local	5.00	6	1	30.00	30.00	0.577
Newspapers, magazines, books total						100.74	68.73	1.322
Household games								
pack of cards	Waddington	Woolworths	1.69	1	10	1.69	0.17	0.003
jigsaw, 500 piece	Chad Valley	Woolworths	3.99	1	5	3.99	0.80	0.015
domino set	Chad Valley	Woolworths	2.99	1	20	2.99	0.15	0.003
Household games total						8.67	1.12	0.021

Family Budget Unit, January 1999 prices

Leisure goods: Single man aged 65-74 years, local authority flat, no garden

Item	Brand		Unit Price £	Quantity	Life/Years	Total Price £	Cost/Year £	Cost/Week £
Photographic equipment and processing								
35mm compact camera	Olympus Trip XB3	Argos	38.50	1	24	38.50	1.60	0.031
colour print film, 24 x 35mm	Fuji	Co-op	3.99	1	1	3.99	3.99	0.077
film processing, 24 prints	Boots	Boots	3.99	1	1	3.99	3.99	0.077
photo album		Kwik Save	0.99	1	3	0.99	0.33	0.006
Photographic equipment and processing total						47.47	9.91	0.191
Seasonal items								
standard tinsel, 9'		Kwik Save	0.44	2	5	0.88	0.18	0.003
Christmas tree with lights and decorations, 91 cm		Argos	9.20	1	5	9.20	1.84	0.035
Seasonal items total						10.08	2.02	0.039
Garden and house plants, flowers and products								
cut flowers		Kwik Save	1.99	10	1	19.90	19.90	0.383
flowers, mixed spray, local delivery		local	20.00	1	3	20.00	6.67	0.128
flower plant		Co-op	1.49	1	2	1.49	0.75	0.014
houseplant, small		Co-op	1.99	2	5	3.98	0.80	0.015
houseplant, medium		Co-op	2.99	1	5	2.99	0.60	0.012
Garden and house plants, flowers and products total						48.36	28.71	0.552
Total single man's leisure goods, local authority flat, no garden						742.74	257.79	4.957

Family Budget Unit, January 1999 prices

Leisure goods: Couple aged 65-74 years, local authority and owner-occupied houses, garden

Item	Brand	Retailer	Unit Price £	Quantity	Life/Years	Total Price £	Cost/Year £	Cost/Week £
Television, video and audio equipment								
portable radio/cassette player	Matsui RTK 203	Dixons	12.49	1	10	12.49	1.25	**0.024**
television, colour, 66cm	Beko 28128NX	Northern Electric + Gas	259.99	1	15	259.99	17.33	**0.333**
video recorder	Sanyo VHR 778 NICAM	Northern Electric + Gas	199.99	1	10	199.99	20.00	**0.385**
mini hi-fi	Sanyo DCF 320	Northern Electric + Gas	149.95	1	12	149.95	12.50	**0.240**
popular/classical cassettes/cd's	various	WH Smith	9.99	2	1	19.98	19.98	**0.384**
blank video tapes, 180 x 3	Profile	Poundstretcher	2.99	1	1	2.99	2.99	**0.058**
Television, video and audio equipment total						645.39	74.05	**1.424**
TV licence								
TV licence, colour		Post Office Counters Ltd	97.50	1	1	97.50	97.50	**1.875**
TV licence total						97.50	97.50	**1.875**
Newspapers, magazines, books								
pocket dictionary	Collins New English	WH Smith	10.99	1	20	10.99	0.55	**0.011**
novel, paperback		ASDA	3.99	1	1	3.99	3.99	**0.077**
book, paperback		WH Smith	6.99	1	1	6.99	6.99	**0.134**
basic gardening book	Hermes House	WH Smith	6.99	1	10	6.99	0.70	**0.013**
cookery book	Hermes House	WH Smith	10.00	1	15	10.00	0.67	**0.013**
bible	Oxford Gift	WH Smith	11.99	1	25	11.99	0.48	**0.009**
daily newspaper	Daily Mirror	Kwik Save	0.30	52	1	15.60	15.60	**0.300**
local free press		local	0.00	52	1	0.00	0.00	**0.000**
Sunday newspaper	Mail on Sunday	Co-op	0.65	52	1	33.80	33.80	**0.650**
magazine	Match	Co-op	0.65	12	1	7.80	7.80	**0.150**
woman's magazine	Woman's Weekly	Co-op	0.45	12	1	5.40	5.40	**0.104**
calendar		Kwik Save	0.79	1	1	0.79	0.79	**0.015**
telephone and address book		Poundstretcher	1.09	1	3	1.09	0.36	**0.007**
theatre program		local	1.50	1	1	1.50	1.50	**0.029**
gift voucher		local	5.00	6	1	30.00	30.00	**0.577**
Newspapers, magazines, books total						146.93	108.63	**2.089**

Family Budget Unit, January 1999 prices

Leisure goods: Couple aged 65-74 years, local authority and owner-occupied houses, garden

Item	Brand	Retailer	Unit Price £	Quantity	Life/Years	Total Price £	Cost/Year £	Cost/Week £
Household games								
pack of cards	Waddington	Woolworths	1.69	1	10	1.69	0.17	0.003
Scrabble set	Spear's Games	Woolworths	13.50	1	20	13.50	0.68	0.013
jigsaw, 500 piece	Chad Valley	Woolworths	3.99	1	5	3.99	0.80	0.015
chess set	Chad Valley	Woolworths	3.99	1	20	3.99	0.20	0.004
domino set	Chad Valley	Woolworths	2.99	1	20	2.99	0.15	0.003
Household games total						26.16	1.99	0.038
Knitting, photographic equipment, processing								
knitting wool, double, 100g × 5		Poundstretcher	1.99	3	1	5.97	5.97	0.115
knitting needles	S&S	Co-op	0.89	1	5	0.89	0.18	0.003
knitting pattern		local Post Office	0.95	2	1	1.90	1.90	0.037
buttons, pack of 5	S&S	Co-op	0.65	3	1	1.95	1.95	0.038
35mm compact camera	Olympus Trip XB3	Argos	38.50	1	24	38.50	1.60	0.031
colour print film, 24 × 35mm	Fuji	Co-op	3.99	1	1	3.99	3.99	0.077
film processing, 24 prints	Boots	Boots	3.99	1	1	3.99	3.99	0.077
photo album		Kwik Save	0.99	1	3	0.99	0.33	0.006
Knitting, photographic equipment, processing total						58.18	19.91	0.383
Seasonal items								
Christmas tree, lights and decorations, 91 cm		Argos	9.20	1	5	9.20	1.84	0.035
standard tinsel, 9'		Kwik Save	0.44	2	5	0.88	0.18	0.003
Christmas dinner candles		Co-op	1.09	1	1	1.09	1.09	0.021
Seasonal items totals						11.17	3.11	0.060
Garden and house plants, flowers and products								
rose bush		Kwik Save	1.99	3	10	5.97	0.60	0.011
bedding plant		Kwik Save	0.50	4	2	2.00	1.00	0.019
spring bulbs, 30		Kwik Save	0.99	1	2	0.99	0.50	0.010
fertiliser, general purpose, 40 litre	Growmore	Co-op	1.79	1	2	1.79	0.90	0.017
cut flowers		Kwik Save	1.99	6	1	11.94	11.94	0.230
flowers, mixed spray, local delivery		local	20.00	1	3	20.00	6.67	0.128
flower plant		Co-op	1.49	1	2	1.49	0.75	0.014
houseplant, small		Co-op	1.99	2	5	3.98	0.80	0.015
houseplant, medium		Co-op	2.99	1	5	2.99	0.60	0.012
Garden and house plants, flowers and products totals						51.15	23.73	0.456
Total couple's leisure goods, local authority and owner-occupied houses, garden						1036.48	328.92	6.325

Family Budget Unit, January 1999 prices

Leisure activities: Single woman aged 65-74 years

	Service Outlet	Freq/Year	Cost/Unit £	Cost/Year £	Cost/Week £
Sports activities					
swimming	local	6	1.15	6.90	0.133
carpet bowls (social Club)	local	20	2.80	56.00	1.077
dancing, line	local	20	3.00	60.00	1.154
walking (2 miles+)	park/countryside/shops etc	33	0.00	0.00	0.000
Sports activities total			6.95	122.90	2.363
Arts, entertainment, outings					
theatre, amateur	local	1	6.00	6.00	0.115
cinema	local	1	2.20	2.20	0.042
museum	Yorkshire Air	1	3.00	3.00	0.058
museum	Yorvik Viking Centre	1	4.59	4.59	0.088
York Minster		2	0.00	0.00	0.000
day trip, Meadowhall	York Pullman	2	6.00	12.00	0.231
Arts, entertainment, outings total			21.79	27.79	0.534
Holiday expenses					
holiday, Newquay, 7 nights, coach	York Pullman	1	195.00	195.00	3.750
Holiday expenses total			195.00	195.00	3.750
Total single woman's leisure activities			223.74	345.69	6.648

Family Budget Unit, January 1999 prices

Leisure activities: Single man aged 65-74 years

	Service Outlet	Freq/Year	Cost/Unit £	Cost/Year £	Cost/Week £
Sports activities					
swimming	local	6	1.15	6.90	0.133
carpet bowls (Social Club)	local	20	2.80	56.00	1.077
dancing, line	local	20	3.00	60.00	1.154
walking (2 miles+)	park/countryside/shops etc	37	0.00	0.00	0.000
Sports activities total			6.95	122.90	2.363
Arts, entertainment, outings					
theatre, amateur	local	1	6.00	6.00	0.115
cinema	local	1	2.20	2.20	0.042
museum	Yorkshire Air	1	3.00	3.00	0.058
museum	Yorvik Viking Centre	1	4.59	4.59	0.088
York Minster		2	0.00	0.00	0.000
day trip, Meadowhall	York Pullman	2	6.00	12.00	0.231
Arts, entertainment, outings total			21.79	27.79	0.534
Holiday expenses					
holiday, Newquay, 7 nights, coach	York Pullman	1	195.00	195.00	3.750
Holiday expenses total			195.00	195.00	3.750
Total single man's leisure activities			223.74	345.69	6.648

Family Budget Unit, January 1999 prices

Leisure activities: Couple aged 65-74 years

	Service Outlet	Freq/Year	Cost/Unit £	Cost/Year £	Cost/Week £
Sports activities					
walking (2 miles+), man	park/countryside/shops etc	37	0.00	0.00	**0.000**
walking (2 miles+), woman		33	0.00	0.00	**0.000**
dancing, line	local	40	3.00	120.00	**2.308**
carpet bowls (Social Club)	local	40	2.80	112.00	**2.154**
swimming	local	12	1.15	13.80	**0.265**
Sports activities total			6.95	245.80	**4.727**
Arts, entertainment, outings					
theatre, amateur	local	2	6.00	12.00	**0.231**
cinema	local	2	2.20	4.40	**0.085**
museum	Yorkshire Air	2	3.00	6.00	**0.115**
museum	Yorvik Viking Centre	2	4.59	9.18	**0.177**
York Minster		4	0.00	0.00	**0.000**
day trip, Meadowhall	York Pullman	4	6.00	24.00	**0.462**
Arts, entertainment, outings total			21.79	55.58	**1.069**
Holiday expenses					
holiday, Newquay, 7 nights, coach	York Pullman	2	195.00	390.00	**7.500**
Holiday expenses total			195.00	390.00	**7.500**
Total couple's leisure activities			223.74	691.38	**13.296**

Family Budget Unit, January 1999 prices

Transport: no car

Item	Brand	Retailer	Unit Price £	Quantity	Life/Years	Total Price £	Cost/Year £	Cost/Week £
Single person aged 65-74 years								
bus pass		local	6.00	1	1	6.00	6.00	0.115
bus journey		local	0.35	600	1	210.00	210.00	4.038
train journey, York to Leeds return		Northern Spirit	6.80	1	1	6.80	6.80	0.131
taxi journey		local	6.00	2	1	12.00	12.00	0.231
Total single person's transport, no car						234.80	234.80	**4.515**
Couple aged 65-74 years								
bus pass		local	6.00	2	1	12.00	12.00	0.231
bus journey		local	0.35	1200	1	420.00	420.00	8.077
train journey, York to Leeds return		Northern Spirit	6.80	2	1	13.60	13.60	0.262
taxi journey		local	6.00	3	1	18.00	18.00	0.346
Total couple's transport, no car						463.60	463.60	**8.915**

Family Budget Unit, January 1999 prices

Transport: car owners

Item	Brand	Retailer	Unit Price £	Quantity	Life/Years	Total Price £	Cost/Year £	Cost/Week £
Single person aged 65-74 years								
depreciation, Ford Escort		Parker's Guide	407.00	1	1	407.00	407.00	7.827
car parking, 3 hours		local	1.30	13	1	16.90	16.90	0.325
road fund licence, car		DVLA	150.00	1	1	150.00	150.00	2.885
insurance, car, 1 driver		Parker's Guide	69.30	1	1	69.30	69.30	1.333
petrol, unleaded, per gallon	Castrol GTX	local	3.27	125	1	408.75	408.75	7.861
motor oil, litre			3.00	10	3	30.00	10.00	0.192
motor oil, litre			3.00	2	1	6.00	6.00	0.115
tyre, car, including balancing	Datum Mid-Range	ATS	36.92	1	2	36.92	18.46	0.355
service, car, 12,000 miles		ATS	75.00	1	2	75.00	37.50	0.721
test, car, MOT		ATS	30.87	1	1	30.87	30.87	0.594
repairs, general			100.00	1	1	100.00	100.00	1.923
train journey, York to Leeds return		Northern Spirit	6.80	1	1	6.80	6.80	0.131
bus pass		local	6.00	1	1	6.00	6.00	0.115
bus journey		local	0.35	24	1	8.40	8.40	0.162
Total single person's transport, car owner						1351.94	1275.98	24.538
Couple aged 65-74 years								
depreciation, Ford Escort		Parker's Guide	407.00	1	1	407.00	407.00	7.827
car parking, 3 hours		local	1.30	13	1	16.90	16.90	0.325
road fund licence, car		DVLA	150.00	1	1	150.00	150.00	2.885
insurance, car, 2 drivers		Parker's Guide	76.23	1	1	76.23	76.23	1.466
petrol, unleaded, per gallon	Castrol GTX	local	3.27	125	1	408.75	408.75	7.861
motor oil, litre			3.00	10	3	30.00	10.00	0.192
motor oil, litre			3.00	2	1	6.00	6.00	0.115
tyre, car, including balancing	Datum Mid-Range	ATS	36.92	1	2	36.92	18.46	0.355
service, car, 12,000 miles		ATS	75.00	1	2	75.00	37.50	0.721
test, car, MOT		ATS	30.87	1	1	30.87	30.87	0.594
repairs, general			100.00	1	1	100.00	100.00	1.923
train journey, York to Leeds return		Northern Spirit	6.80	2	1	13.60	13.60	0.262
bus pass		local	6.00	2	1	12.00	12.00	0.231
bus journey		local	0.35	48	1	16.80	16.80	0.323
Total couple's transport, car owner						1380.07	1304.11	25.079

Family Budget Unit, January 1999 prices